THE CAMBRIDGE COMPANION TO
GANDHI

Even today, six decades after his assassination in January 1948, Mahatma Gandhi is still revered as the father of the Indian nation. His intellectual and moral legacy – encapsulated in works such as *Hind Swaraj* – as well as the example of his life and politics serve as an inspiration to human rights and peace movements, political activists, and students in classroom discussions throughout the world. This book, comprising essays by renowned experts in the fields of Indian history and philosophy, traces Gandhi's extraordinary story. The first part of the book, the biography, explores his transformation from a small-town lawyer during his early life in South Africa into a skilled political activist and leader of civil resistance in India. The second part is devoted to Gandhi's key writings and his thinking on a broad range of topics, including religion, conflict, politics, and social relations. The final part reflects on Gandhi's image – how he has been portrayed in literature and film – and on his legacy in India, the West, and beyond.

Judith M. Brown is Beit Professor of Commonwealth History at the University of Oxford. Her many publications include *Gandhi's Rise to Power: Indian Politics 1915–1922* (1972), *Gandhi and Civil Disobedience: The Mahatma in Indian Politics 1928–1934* (1977), *Gandhi. Prisoner of Hope* (1989), *Modern India: The Origins of an Asian Democracy* (1984), *Global South Asians: Introducing the Modern Diaspora* (2006), *Nehru: A Political Life* (2005), and *The Oxford History of the British Empire: The Twentieth Century*, co-edited with William Roger Louis (2001).

Anthony Parel is Professor Emeritus of Political Science at the University of Calgary. His published works include *Gandhi: Hind Swaraj and Other Writings Centenary Edition* (2009) and *Gandhi's Philosophy and the Quest for Harmony* (2007).

THE CAMBRIDGE COMPANION TO

GANDHI

Edited by Judith M. Brown
University of Oxford

Anthony Parel
University of Calgary

CAMBRIDGE
UNIVERSITY PRESS

CAMBRIDGE UNIVERSITY PRESS
Cambridge, New York, Melbourne, Madrid, Cape Town, Singapore,
São Paulo, Delhi, Dubai, Tokyo, Mexico City

Cambridge University Press
32 Avenue of the Americas, New York, NY 10013-2473, USA

www.cambridge.org
Information on this title: www.cambridge.org/9780521133456

First published 2011

Printed in the United States of America

A catalogue record for this publication is available from the British Library.

Library of Congress Cataloguing in Publication data

The Cambridge companion to Gandhi / [edited by] Judith Brown, Anthony Parel.
  p. cm. – (Cambridge companions to religion)
Includes bibliographical references and index.
ISBN 978-0-521-11670-1 (hardback) – ISBN 978-0-521-13345-6 (pbk.)
 1. Gandhi, Mahatma, 1869–1948.   2. Gandhi, Mahatma, 1869–1948 – Political
and social views.   3. Gandhi, Mahatma, 1869–1948 – Influence.   4. Statesmen –
India – Biography.   5. Nationalists – India – Biography.   6. Political activists –
India – Biography.   7. Civil rights workers – India – Biography.   8. Pacifists –
India – Biography.   9. India – Politics and government – 1919–1947.   I. Brown,
Judith M. (Judith Margaret), 1944–   II. Parel, Anthony.   III. Title.   IV. Series.
DS481.G3C36   2011
954.03′5092–dc22   2010027387

ISBN 978-0-521-11670-1 Hardback
ISBN 978-0-521-13345-6 Paperback

Contents

Part III.   *The contemporary Gandhi*

Notes on contributors

Akeel Bilgrami holds the Johnsonian Chair of Philosophy at Columbia University and is a member of Columbia's Committee on Global Thought. After a first degree in English from Elphinstone College at Bombay University, he went to Oxford as a Rhodes Scholar where he read Philosophy, Politics, and Economics. He has a Ph.D. from the University of Chicago. He is the author of *Belief and Meaning* (1992), *Self-Knowledge and Resentment* (2006), and *Politics and the Moral Psychology of Identity* (forthcoming). He is currently working on a short book on Gandhi's philosophy.

Judith M. Brown is Beit Professor of Commonwealth History at the University of Oxford and Professorial Fellow of Balliol College. She has written widely on Indian history and politics and has published major studies of Gandhi and Nehru. She recently edited a new edition of the volume of Gandhi's writings in the Oxford World's Classics series, *Mahatma Gandhi. The Essential Writings* (2008), and her latest book is a series of methodological essays, *Windows into the Past: Life Histories and the Historian of South Asia* (2009).

David Hardiman lived and worked in Gujarat for many years, and is now Professor of History at the University of Warwick, UK. He is the author of *Peasant Nationalists of Gujarat: Kheda District 1917–1934* (1981), *The Coming of the Devi: Adivasi Assertion in Western India* (1987), *Feeding the Baniya: Peasants and Usurers in Western India* (1996), *Gandhi: In His Time and Ours* (2003), and *Missionaries and Their Medicine: A Christian Modernity for Tribal India* (2008).

Jonathan Hyslop is Professor in the Department of Sociology at the University of Pretoria. He is a long-standing member of the Johannesburg History Workshop and has published widely in the field of late-nineteenth-century and twentieth-century southern African social history. His current research focuses on the impact of militarism on modern South African politics and society and on the world of maritime labour in the British Empire from 1880 to 1950.

Yasmin Khan was educated at the University of Oxford and is a Lecturer at Royal Holloway, University of London. Her principal research interests are the twentieth-century history and contemporary politics of India and Pakistan, particularly decolonization, ethnic conflict, and nationalism. Her first book, *The Great Partition: The Making of India and Pakistan* (2007), won the Gladstone Prize from the Royal Historical Society.

Anthony Parel is Professor Emeritus of Political Science at the University of Calgary. His research interests include Western political thought and Indian political thought, with a focus on Gandhi. He is the author of *The Machiavellian Cosmos* (1982) and *Gandhi's Philosophy and the Quest for Harmony* (2006), and the editor of *Gandhi: Hind Swaraj and Other Writings* (1997, 2009).

Tanika Sarkar is Professor of Modern History at the Centre for Historical Studies, Jawaharlal Nehru University, Delhi. Her recent publications include *Rebels, Wives and Saints: Designing Selves and Nations in Colonial Times* (2009); and she co-edited with Sumit Sarkar, *Women and Middle Class Social Reform*, Vols. 1 and 2 (2008).

Tridip Suhrud is a political scientist and a cultural historian, working on the Gandhian intellectual tradition and the social history of Gujarat of the nineteenth and twentieth centuries. He is a Professor at Dhirubhai Ambani Institute of Information and Communication Technology, Gandhinagar. He translated from Gujarati and edited C. B. Dalal's *Harilal Gandhi: A Life* (2007) and Narayan Desai's four-volume biography of Gandhi, *My Life Is My Message* (2009). His other books include *Writing Life: Three Gujarati Thinkers* (2008) and *Hind Swaraj Vishe* (2008) and *An Autobiography or The Story of My Experiments with Truth: A Table of Concordance* (2009), and, with Suresh Sharma, a bilingual critical edition of *Hind Swaraj*. At present, he is working on the English translation of Govardhanram Tripathi's four-part novel *Saraswatichandra*.

Ronald J. Terchek is Professor Emeritus of Government and Politics at the University of Maryland, College Park, and the author of *Gandhi: Struggling for Autonomy* (2000) and numerous articles on Gandhi. He is also the author of *Republican Paradoxes and Liberal Anxieties* (1997), as well as co-editor of *Theories of Democracy* (2001). He is currently writing on the connection of ethics and economics in Gandhi's thought.

Harish Trivedi is Professor of English at the University of Delhi, and has been Visiting Professor at the Universities of Chicago and London. He is the author of *Colonial Transactions: English Literature and India* (1993: rpt. 1995), and has co-edited *The Nation across the World* (2007), *Literature and Nation: Britain and India 1800–1990* (2000), and *Interrogating Post-Colonialism: Theory, Text and Context* (1996; rpt. 2000, 2006).

Thomas Weber is a Reader in the Politics and International Relations Program and head of Peace Studies at Melbourne's La Trobe University. He has been researching and writing on Gandhi's life and legacy for more than thirty years. His most recent publications include *The Shanti Sena: Philosophy, History and Action* (2009); *Gandhi, Gandhism and the Gandhians* (2006); and *Gandhi as Disciple and Mentor* (2004). He is currently working on Gandhi's relationship with Western women.

Glossary

Adhikar: authority, qualification

Adivasis: aboriginal inhabitants of India

Advaita: branch of Vedanta philosophy emphasizing the unity of the individual and God

Ahimsa: nonviolence

Anasakta: one who acts without attachment to the fruits of action

Aparigraha: non-possession

Artha: pursuit of wealth and power

Ashram: religious community in the Indian tradition

Ashramite: member of an ashram

Atmakatha: autobiography

Atman: highest principle of life affecting everything in the world; a person's soul

Bania: merchant caste

Bhangi: sweeper caste

Bhoodan: gift of land (movement started by Vinoba Bhave)

Brahmachari: one who practises brahmacharya, celibate

Brahmacharya: celibacy

Charkha: spinning wheel

Dadagiri: bullying, loutish behaviour

Dalits: lit. 'the oppressed', name preferred by Untouchables for themselves

Dharma: duty, ethics, religion

Diwan: senior minister of Indian princely state

Dvaita: the part of Hindu philosophy that states that the individual and God have separate existences

Ek-praja: one nation

Gandhigiri: a Hindi neologism, indicating opportunist or hypocritical practice of Gandhian teachings and methods

Gandhivad: Gandhi's philosophy

Gandhivadi: a follower of Gandhi's philosophy

Gramdan: gift of a village (movement started by Vinoba Bhave)

Harijan: lit. 'child of God', name chosen by Gandhi for Untouchables

Himsa: violence

Hindutva: an aggressive sense of Hindu identity, which presupposes a Hindu state

Holi: Hindu spring festival

Itihas: 'history'

Jati: 'caste', popular name for local caste groups

Kala pani: lit. 'black water', the sea

Kama: pleasure

Khadi: hand-spun cloth

Khalifah: Caliph, spiritual head of worldwide Muslim community

Kshatriyas: warriors, one of the four varnas

Kudhar: bad civilization

Langoti: loincloth

Mahatma: 'great soul', honourific title

Mohurram: Muslim festival

Moksha: spiritual liberation, salvation

Panchayat: village council

Praja: nation

Purna swaraj: full independence

Purusharthas: the aims of life

Raj: rule (hence British raj)

Ramanam(a): recitation of the name of Ram

Ramarajya: kingdom/rule of Ram

Rishi: Hindu wise man, hermit

Sadhana: ascetic discipline, spiritual path

Sadhu: Hindu holy man

Sanatani: orthodox Hindu

Sant: saint

Sarvodaya: welfare of all

Sati: self-immolation of a widow on her husband's funeral pyre

Satya: Truth

Satyagraha: truth force, nonviolent resistance to wrong

Satyagrahi: practitioner of satyagraha

Savarnas: upper castes

Sena: army

Shudra: one of the four varnas

Smriti: tradition that is remembered, as distinct from divine revelation

Sthitpragnya: person of stable wisdom

Sudhar: good civilization

Surajya: the good state

Swadharma: one's own duty

Swadeshi: use of things made in one's own country

Swaraj: self-rule, independence

Vaishnavism: Hindu sect

Varna: 'caste', scriptural name for caste

Varnashrama dharma: the caste system

Yajna: sacrifice

A chronology of Gandhi's life

1869   2 October, Mohandas Karamchand Gandhi born, Porbandar, Kathiawar, Gujarat. Son of Karamchand and Putlibai.
1876   Moves to Rajkot with family; attends primary school there.
1882   Marries Kasturba Makanji.
1885   Death of father.
1888   Goes to England to study law. Enrols in the Inner Temple, London.
1891   June, called to the Bar and returns to India.
1893   April, leaves India for South Africa on a one-year contract with the firm of Dad Abdullah & Co., after failing to establish legal practice in India. June, thrown off a train at Pietermaritzburg Station, Natal: a critical experience of discrimination.
1894   Helps found the Natal Indian Congress, and enrols as barrister in the High Courts of Natal and Transvaal.
1895   Begins major publicity for Indian rights, including a pamphlet, *The Indian Franchise: An Appeal to Every Briton in South Africa*.
1896   June–November, visits India and brings his family to South Africa.
1899   Boer War; organizes Indian Ambulance Corps.
1901   October, returns to India with his family, intending to stay. Meets Indian politicians.
1902   November, returns with family to South Africa to fight for Indian rights in the Transvaal.
1903   Sets up legal practice in Johannesburg. Launches *Indian Opinion*.
1904   Reads J. Ruskin, *Unto This Last*: establishes Phoenix Settlement near Durban.
1906   June–July, Zulu Rebellion, does ambulance work. Takes vow of celibacy. September, addresses mass meeting at Empire Theatre in Johannesburg when a large number of Indians agreed to resist the proposed Asiatic Registration Bill. October–December, visits London to campaign for Indian rights in South Africa.
1907   Start of Passive Resistance, later called satyagraha from 1908.
1908   January and October–December, imprisoned.
1909   February–May, imprisoned. June–November, visits England; writes *Hind Swaraj* on return voyage.
1910   Establishes second community at Tolstoy Farm, near Johannesburg.
1911   Agreement with J. C. Smuts leads to suspension of satyagraha.

1913   Renews satyagraha. Women joined the struggle, including Kasturba, who is imprisoned. November–December, Gandhi imprisoned for fourth time.

1914   January, reaches agreement with Smuts and suspends satyagraha. July, leaves South Africa finally and sails to London. Outbreak of World War I. In London, clearly ill after his work and periods in prison in South Africa. Helps to organize Field Ambulance Training Corps for Indian students in London to help empire at war, and particularly Indian soldiers wounded in Europe. December, sails for India.

1915   January, arrives in India. May, founds ashram at Ahmedabad. Awarded the Kaiser-i-Hind gold medal for services to Indians in South Africa.

1917   April, begins working on problems of farmers growing indigo in Champaran, Bihar; leads to individual satyagraha.

1918   February–March, leads satyagraha on behalf of millworkers, Ahmedabad. March–June, leads satyagraha in Kaira district, Gujarat, on the issue of land revenue. November, end of World War I.

1919   6–18 April, leads all-India satyagraha against the Rowlatt legislation and suspends it after outbreaks of violence; admits to a 'Himalayan miscalculation'. 13 April, massacre at Jallianwalla Bagh, Amritsar. Becomes editor of *Navajivan* and *Young India*. Becomes involved in the issue of the Khilafat (the post-war future of the Sultan of Turkey). December, advises Congress to respond to the Royal Proclamation and cooperate with the reforms provided for by the 1919 Government of India Act; thinks this marks his real entry into Congress politics.

1920   September, advises non-cooperation with the government on the issues of the Punjab and the Khilafat. September, special session of Congress at Calcutta accepts the programme of non-cooperation, and this is confirmed by the December session at Nagpur. November, Congressmen in significant numbers boycott elections to the new legislatures.

1920–2 Non-cooperation movement (withdrawal of lawyers from courts, students from government schools, return of titles, swadeshi, etc.).

1921   August, rebellion in Malabar, southwest India. October, vows to spin daily. December, preparations for civil disobedience under strict conditions.

1922   4 February, massacre of policemen in Chauri Chaura, UP. Gandhi fasts in protest against violence and calls off civil disobedience. March, arrested, pleaded guilty to inciting disaffection towards the government, and jailed until February 1924.

1923   Begins writing *Satyagraha In South Africa*.

1924   January, operated on for appendicitis and released in February. Supports satyagraha in Vaikom, Travancore, to allow Untouchables to use roads around temples. September, three-week fast for Hindu–Muslim unity.

1925   Congress President for the year. Founds All-India Spinners' Association.

1926   Year spent in the Ahmedabad ashram.

1927   Extensive tours publicizing khadi. Serious ill health from overwork. Publishes *Autobiography* initially in a series of newspaper articles.

1928   February–August, satyagraha in Bardoli district, Gujarat, on issue of land revenue, led by Vallabhbhai Patel under Gandhi's direction. Publishes

Satyagraha In South Africa. Moves resolution at Calcutta Congress in favour of independence if dominion status is not granted by the end of 1929.

1929   Declines Congress Presidentship and suggests Jawaharlal Nehru instead. Tours rural India to publicize khadi. Declaration of Viceroy, Lord Irwin, announcing dominion status as goal for India, offering Round Table Conference in London as first step; but negotiations between Gandhi, Congressmen, and Moderates to accept this proved abortive. Frames main resolution passed at Congress session in Lahore, calling for independence, and also boycott of the legislatures and civil disobedience.

1930   26 January, declaration of independence prepared by Gandhi proclaimed. Gandhi plans forthcoming civil disobedience movement, which begins with his march (12 March–6 April) from the Sabarmati ashram to Dandi on the coast to make salt illegally, thus launching civil disobedience on 6 April, imprisoned May 1930–January 1931. Round Table Conference in London leads to hope of a major political advance and British government wishes to include Congress in subsequent discussions if possible.

1931   26 January, Gandhi and other Congress leaders released. Gandhi negotiates a settlement with the Viceroy, Lord Irwin, to end civil disobedience; their 'Pact' signed on 4 March. September–December, Gandhi is in England for the second session of the Round Table Conference. Stays at Kingsley Hall in Bow, in the East End. Apart from attending the conference and its committee work, he visits several important places where there are groups of people he wishes to influence, including Lancashire, Oxford and Cambridge, and Eton. He also meets a wide range of Christian leaders.

1932   Civil disobedience resumes; and Gandhi arrested and imprisoned in Yeravda jail, Poona, from January 1932 to May 1933. September, Gandhi begins fast to death on the issue of separate electorates for Untouchables given by the British 'Communal Award' after Congress and the minorities fail to reach agreement at the second Round Table Conference. Gives up his fast after a compromise worked out with Untouchable leaders, the so-called Poona Pact.

1933   Founds Harijan Sevak Sangh and new paper, *Harijan*. May, three-week fast; released from prison. Announces disbanding of Ahmedabad ashram. August, rearrested and released after less than a month. Begins extensive tour on the Harijan cause, which lasts from November 1933 to June 1934.

1934   April–May, Gandhi suggests suspension of civil disobedience and revival of work in the legislatures by those Congressmen who wished to. June, escapes bomb attempt on his life. September, announces decision to retire from politics and engage in rural development, work for Harijans and new forms of education. Inaugurates All-India Village Industries Association and resigns from Congress.

1935   Government of India Act provides for provincial autonomy and plans for India's future as a dominion, bringing together British India and the princely states. (The latter part of the plan never achieved because of the outbreak of war in 1939; the first part came into force after elections to the new legislatures in 1937.)

1936   April, settles at Sevagram, near Wardha, Central Provinces, making his ashram there his home and headquarters.

1937   October, presides over Educational Conference in October at Wardha and sets out a scheme of Basic Education. Congress becomes government in seven provinces in British India following elections.

1939   Fasts in early March in protest at ruler of Rajkot's refusal to reform his administration. September, outbreak of World War II. October, Congress withdraws from cooperation in provincial government, reflecting Gandhi's wishes. Gandhi becomes central again in Congress politics.

1940   March, Congress at Ramgarh demands independence and a constituent assembly to frame new constitution. Announces that it plans to embark again on civil disobedience. Muslim League at Lahore demands 'Pakistan' for Muslims at independence. October, Gandhi launches individual satyagraha by handpicked volunteers to protest against cooperation in the war effort.

1941   December, Japanese attack Pearl Harbour and begin drive through Burma. United States enters the war. Gandhi writes *Constructive Programme: Its Meaning and Place.*

1942   February, fall of Singapore. March–April, mission of Sir Stafford Cripps to India on behalf of British government, offering elected body after war to frame new constitution for India, and during war Indian participation in government. Envisages India as dominion after war but with the implication that secession from the Empire-Commonwealth would also be possible. Also assumes that no part of India could be forced to join dominion, thus opening path to some form of partition. Congress and League reject Cripps's offer. August, Congress launches 'Quit India' movement of civil disobedience. It is declared unlawful organization, leaders imprisoned and violence firmly controlled. Gandhi imprisoned from August 1942 to May 1944. During this prison term, Mahadev Desai dies (1942) as does Kasturba (1944).

1944   May, released from prison because of ill health. September, abortive talks with Jinnah on future of Indian Muslims.

1945   May, surrender of Germany and end of war in Europe. June–July, Gandhi attends conference at Simla as Viceroy Wavell attempts to restart the political process by reconstituting his Executive council from among Indian politicians. Conference fails. August, surrender of Japan and end of war in Asia.

1946   March–June, Cabinet Mission visits India, sent by new Labour government, in attempt to achieve political settlement. Gandhi meets members of Mission. Congress and League both reject Cabinet Mission Plan. Severe communal violence in Bengal and Bihar, and Gandhi tours area on foot for four months from November.

1947   Communal situation deteriorates as there is no political agreement and British authority wanes. February, Prime Minister Attlee announces that British will leave India by June 1948 and send Mountbatten to India as Viceroy to replace Wavell. June, Mountbatten announces plan of partition of India at independence and British intention to withdraw in August 1947. Gandhi deeply distressed at plan for partition but does not block it. His political influence is clearly waning. 15 August, subcontinent attains independence and is partitioned into India and Pakistan. Violence breaks out, particularly in Punjab, and mass migrations of people occur as they attempt to move to the side of the border where they think they will be safe, Muslims to Pakistan and Hindus and Sikhs to India. Congress becomes the party of government in India and Jawaharlal Nehru becomes India's first Prime Minister. September, Gandhi fasts in Calcutta for communal peace.

1948   13–18 January, Gandhi fasts in Delhi for communal unity. Gandhi writes document advising Congress to disband as a political organization and devote itself to social service. 30 January, Gandhi assassinated by Hindu man who confronts him as he is walking to prayer meeting in grounds of Birla House, New Delhi.

THE CAMBRIDGE COMPANION TO
GANDHI

Introduction

JUDITH M. BROWN

Mohandas Karamchand Gandhi was born in Western India in 1869, a child of the Victorian age at the heyday of British imperial rule in India. He was assassinated by one of his own countrymen nearly eighty years later, in January 1948, just months after the subcontinent had gained political independence. During his long life, he had become known as Mahatma or 'great soul', and had risen from obscurity as a failed lawyer to become one of the most outstanding Indians active in the public life of his country and of the British Empire in the first half of the twentieth century. He is often spoken of as the 'father' of the new nation-state of India, but more seriously is recognized as a major practitioner of and thinker about nonviolence as a form of managing conflict and resisting injustice. Public interest in his career and thought has continued to develop into the next century, particularly as numerous groups have drawn on his example and attempted throughout the world to use non-violence to resist multiple forms of political violence and control. There are therefore numerous reasons why it is timely to gather a collection of serious but accessible essays on his life and thought in a *Cambridge Companion*, designed to reach a wide readership, both inside and outside the world of education, who may know little about India but wish to know more about such a significant and intriguing figure.

The most utilitarian justification for this *Companion* is the growth of interest in Gandhi and his times, at university level and even among school students. In part, this is because history and politics courses often now spread their range well beyond older national histories and political analyses, and invite students to study global themes and subjects. The spread of a large diaspora from South Asia means that there are also many students of South Asian ethnic descent in schools and colleges in the English-speaking world, outside the country of their ancestors' origin, who wish to know more about that country and its emergence as a subcontinent of global significance in so many ways at the start of the twenty-first century.

Gandhi is also worth serious attention because of his intrinsic importance as a major thinker and publicist on the meaning of Indian nationalism and the nature of the Indian nation, as well as being the single most important organizer of the numerous movements that cohered loosely as a nationalist movement against imperial rule in India. Moreover, as we have noted, he was the chief ideologue and exponent in practice of non-violence as a form of resistance to British rule and other perceived social and political wrongs. He was not a trained philosopher or professional writer, yet he thought deeply about a whole series of key moral, religious, and public issues that were crucial in his day and are still of significance long after his death; and he wrote copiously about them in ephemeral and more permanent formats, which still have the power to challenge, irritate, and inspire. Gandhi also lives on: and one might say there are many 'contemporary Gandhis' as people consider his thought and his example, and are motivated to follow, use, and adapt much of what he suggested, as they seek to resist injustice in the contemporary world. This *Companion* therefore seeks first to provide readers with what they need to know to understand Gandhi in his own lifetime – this being the subject matter of Part 1, 'Gandhi: The historical life'. It then proceeds to examine his key writings and his considered thinking about major contemporary problems in India, while emphasizing that Gandhi was both thinker and activist, and that his thinking was profoundly influenced by the problems he was forced to face, as well as vice versa. Part 2, 'Gandhi: Thinker and activist', deals with these issues. Part 3 offers some clues to the reality of 'The contemporary Gandhi', the image and memory that still has power long after his death in his homeland and far beyond its shores.

A brief reminder here of the shape and nature of Gandhi's life provides the background for the interpretive essays that make up the substance of this book. Gandhi was born in what is now the state of Gujarat, in Western India, in Porbandar, a port city looking out on the Indian Ocean. The area was then made up of a number of small princely states under British suzerainty, and his father was employed in state administration. It was a backwater compared with parts of India under direct British imperial rule, particularly in terms of its political organization and connections, and Gandhi grew up in a very traditional Hindu family of middling caste rank, where his mother at least paid considerable attention to religious ritual and observance. In keeping with Hindu practice, the parents arranged the marriage of their son while he was only thirteen years old – much to his later embarrassment when he had to explain to Europeans that he was married at such an early age. The young Gandhi was sent to school and then to an English-speaking college but was undistinguished in his performance and apparent potential. However, his life changed dramatically when his father died in 1885, when he was himself still a teenager. His family decided to send him to England to study law in the hope that he would return to India and make a success of his professional life and so be able to support his extended family. In 1888, he set sail from Bombay, travelling into the unknown, afraid even to stir from his cabin for much of the voyage.

London was Gandhi's home until 1891. Having enrolled at the Inner Temple, he studied law and was eventually called to the Bar. But this professional status, important though it would be for a considerable part of his life, was not the only legacy of his time in London. He honed his knowledge of the English language – a key to his future professional and political career in South Africa and in India, where command of the imperial language was of crucial importance, and where it was the one common language for educated people on the subcontinent. He joined the Vegetarian Society and, despite his natural shyness and nerves, began to acquire experience of public speaking. He began to mix with different sorts of English people and to gain some knowledge of the Christian tradition, of which he knew virtually nothing before. Largely out of necessity because he had little money, he also refined habits of very simple living and regular physical exercise, which were to be important aspects of his later life.

The status of a barrister was insufficient to guarantee the young man professional success on his return home, and he failed to make a living as a lawyer in Bombay and to fulfil his family's hopes of their investment in his future. Rescue from this situation came in the form of an invitation to go on a year's contract to South Africa to work for a Gujarati trading firm that needed a lawyer who knew English and Gujarati. What should have been a year's visit in 1893–4, enabling him to send money home to his family, turned into half a life's sojourn. He returned several times to India briefly, but only returned permanently early in 1915. By this time, he was a genuinely imperial figure, known in South Africa, Britain, and India as the champion of the rights of Indians in South Africa in the face of growing white discrimination. He had initially set himself up as a Westernized lawyer, but increasingly was drawn into politics in defence of Indians who were subjected to controls on entry, places of work, and residence, and were denied political freedoms and rights due to them as British subjects. They were also subjected to social harassment – as he was himself when he was thrown out of a first-class railway carriage at Pietermaritzburg soon after arriving in the country because a white passenger objected to travelling with him. Drawn into political activism in South Africa by the needs of Indians, he developed skills that would eventually be vital to his work in India. He became a newspaper editor and journalist, using a journal, *Indian Opinion*, as his mouthpiece. He learnt the arts of political organization, of creating and presenting petitions to authority in Africa and Britain, and of negotiation with local and imperial political authorities. But above all, he began to experiment with a new mode of resistance to wrong – nonviolent resistance, which he called satyagraha, truth force. The pursuit of this idea and strategy was to land him in prison, but was eventually to mark him out on his return to India as a public activist with both a message of moral politics and a method to sustain it.

Perhaps more important than the external transformation of the failed lawyer into a successful lawyer, publicist, and political activist was the inner change in Gandhi, as his new environment and its challenges forced him to consider his ultimate values and goals. By the first decade of the new century, he was divesting himself of the trappings of a Western lifestyle and had gathered round him an international group of like-minded men and women dedicated to the simple life and to a search for Truth or God in two communities like Hindu ashrams, groups of devotees clustered round a spiritual teacher. Increasingly, he was drawn to value the many insights in the religious traditions of Christianity and Islam to which he was now exposed, to question and evaluate his own Hindu upbringing and traditions, and to speak of religion as beyond all specific religious traditions, and as, at its root, a search for Truth. This confirmed him in his simple lifestyle, and led him ultimately to take a vow of celibacy in 1906 as a way of affirming his search for Truth and his life as one of service to humanity at large, particularly the poor. By this time, he was the father of four sons, as well as the long-standing husband of Kasturba, his childhood bride. Although at least one of his sons rebelled against the life his father now chose to lead, his wife remained steadfastly at his side until her death with him in prison in 1944. As Gandhi matured into middle age, it was clear he had become a singular type of 'politician', one prompted by ideals and beliefs more than the pursuit of power, and that he had moulded his life to match his message.

Although Gandhi's campaigns in South Africa were becoming known in India and he was honoured for them by his compatriots and indeed by the British rulers of India, there was no natural home for him among the highly Westernized political leaders in India itself. Indeed, when he did return, many of them found his demeanour and social practices disquieting for they did not share his values. Moreover, when he returned to the homeland from which he had been absent for two decades, he did not seem to have in mind a political career for himself, but rather intended to pursue his own spiritual journey. He had, however, already made one intervention in the politics of his homeland, through the publication in 1909 of a pamphlet entitled *Hind Swaraj* (Indian Home Rule). In this, he had made it plain that, for him, India's swaraj was not political independence from the British, but a radical return to her moral roots and what he saw as the values of her traditional civilization. His main concern was not with British rule but with the divisions among Indians that had made this possible from the eighteenth century and with what he interpreted as India's moral crisis, as so many of its leaders in politics and the modern professions seemed to be enslaved to the values of Western civilization and to be intent on creating an Indian version of a Western state. This extraordinary document – intriguing and thought-provoking even today – indicated that the newcomer on the Indian scene was likely to be a disruptive force to Indians and the British alike, just as his commitment to satyagraha presaged new styles of political action if Indians were to follow him.

Gandhi's first years back in India during World War I saw him concentrate on establishing his family, kin, and small group of followers from South Africa in his first Indian ashram in Ahmedabad, the premier city of his home region. This was the place where he 'experimented with Truth' (to use the phrase with which he subtitled his partial autobiography), where he practised simplicity, prayer, and nonviolence, and aimed to create new Indian men and women who would spearhead his broad work for swaraj. It was to become the powerhouse of his personal and political life until he moved to found another community in central India in the mid-1930s, which was to be his home and his base of operations until his death. Despite appearances, he believed that these two communities were his best work, the heart of what he was trying to do for India.

Gandhi's Indian career is assessed in detail in Chapter 3. Here, it is necessary to recognize that, despite his great reputation as a nationalist leader, he was always an ambiguous figure in Indian politics, and few ever shared his core values and goals. It was for this reason that so much of what he hoped and worked for never materialized in independent India, and why at the end of his life he felt that most of his countrymen had never understood or shared the ideal of satyagraha but had merely used nonviolent resistance as a temporary and disposable strategy. Gandhi first introduced his idea of satyagraha in India in the context of local issues where he felt it would be of use in righting specific 'wrongs'. It was not until 1919–20 that he suggested it might be used on a national scale in response to British policies, which many came to feel demeaned Indians and undermined the prospect of serious political reform that many had hoped would be the outcome of World War I. In 1920, the premier Indian political organization, the Indian National Congress, adopted a form of satyagraha, Non-cooperation with many aspects of British rule, and this was the start of Gandhi's meteoric rise to all-India leadership. However, leadership may be the wrong word to use. Although he remained a figure of major significance right up to his death in 1948, the number of those who were truly Gandhian in ideology and lifestyle remained very few. Many political activists were deeply moved by his political creativity and his fearless resistance to the British. But most remained unconvinced by his core ideology or by his insistence that satyagraha was the only moral mode of political action, and that cooperation in the politics of British institutions such as legislatures and local councils was a snare and deviation from the work of radical reconstruction of Indian society and the body politic. Consequently, the Congress never permanently committed itself to satyagraha, but only reverted to it when it seemed that more regular modes of politics were failing to pressurize the British into more constitutional reform, more devolution of power into Indian hands through expanding legislatures, and a widening franchise. The major campaigns of satyagraha occurred in 1920–2, 1930–4, and 1940–2. The first two ended when Gandhi recognized that they were degenerating into violence or that his contemporaries in politics felt that they were a drag on their legitimate political aspirations and activities. The final one petered out as the British struck hard to control the resistance seen as a major danger in war time, and imprisoned the whole Congress leadership.

When India achieved its independence in August 1947, Gandhi did not join the celebrations. His deepest sadness was that the subcontinent had been divided on religious grounds into India and Pakistan after Indian politicians failed to find a formula for a united India incorporating those of all religious affiliations. This was totally contrary to Gandhi's belief that Hindus and Muslims were brothers, or like two eyes in one Indian face, and indicated that his tireless work for religious unity had failed. Moreover, the partition was accompanied by large-scale violence, hundreds of thousands of murders in the name of religion, and the terrible displacements of more than a million people who fled across the new international borders to escape violence but at the cost of losing virtually everything they owned. Ironically and tragically, Gandhi was himself murdered by a Hindu who believed him to be responsible for agreeing to the partition. In Gandhi's eyes, the failure of many of his hopes for India also lay in the persistence of many of the socio-economic problems whose resolution he saw as fundamental to the creation of true swaraj – the many ways in which women were treated as second-class citizens and of less value than men, the multiple burdens of exclusion laid on those at the base of Hindu society who were known as Untouchable, the issues of poverty, dirt, illiteracy, and ill health for many rural people, and the determination of the new government under Jawaharlal Nehru to build a strong industrial India on the pattern of modern Western economies. He was also deeply suspicious of the modern nation-state with its potential for control bordering on violence, and the fact that it took from citizens the moral requirement to order their personal and public lives and interactions.

Gandhi's assassination led to widespread national mourning, and indeed a global recognition that one of the greatest men of his generation had passed away in tragic and undeserved violence. The way in which the new nation state appropriated Gandhi as national founder, hero, and martyr masked the fact that, in his lifetime and since, people have understood his life and role in many different ways. As we have noted, for many in Congress, he was strange, even unworldly, but nonetheless very important because of the way he inspired so many people to support the nationalist movement, and his capacity to cohere so many loose movements of resistance to imperial rule. But to many Muslims, he was a Hindu Mahatma who stood for majoritarian Hindu rule. Similarly, to many Untouchables, he seemed to represent a patronizing caste Hindu stance, which offered them no real change in their deprived situation in the future. To some Hindus, like his assassin, he spoke of unity with Muslims in a new India, whereas they felt that Indian national identity should be built entirely on Hindu bonds of race, birth, and belief. To the left wing in politics (and to later left-wing historians), he was a man who tied Congress and nationalism to the propertied and business classes, and shied away from radical politics to redistribute wealth and address poverty. To the British, he was an enigma, for though he had the appearance of a holy man, he often seemed to be a consummate politician and a committed enemy. It is hardly surprising that historical interpretations of his life have followed as many trajectories as these critiques while he was living. What is clear is that no one interested in modern India can ignore Gandhi's life and contribution to the making of the new nation state. While anyone who considers many of the fundamental issues of human life, its goals, its capacities, and the nature of men and women in public communities, issues of violence and cooperation, and of ends and means, will find that Gandhi has been there before, and struggled with them. This volume is offered without a particular agenda or single interpretation of Gandhi shared among the authors, but with the hope of providing an entry point into a deeper understanding of Gandhi's life and the multiple issues it raised and continues to raise.

Part I

Gandhi: The historical life

1 Gandhi's world

YASMIN KHAN

Mohandas Karamchand Gandhi was born in the Victorian era. He was thus as much a person of the nineteenth as the twentieth century. Born in 1869, only twelve years after the uprising of 1857 that reconfigured British rule in South Asia, he witnessed the acceleration of imperial rule in India as a child and as a young man. His life was lived against the backdrop of the monumental changes that brought the British Empire to the peak of its extent across the globe and then its retraction and demise. During these years, the British harnessed the Indian economy for metropolitan benefit and presided over an increasingly interventionist state. Gandhi was, in many ways, a product of the Victorian age, and made as much use of ships, telegrams, railways, and print as anyone of his generation. Conversely, he quickly perceived the coercive and exploitative nature of British assumptions of supremacy, and the ways in which the fusion of the Indian and British economies was at the cost of the well-being of many Indians. He was an onlooker, seeing through the Victorian world of pomp and ritual splendour to the calculated imperial brutality that it sustained. His was a world of agrarian extraction from the countryside alongside growing urban poverty and sprawl. Gandhi was thirty before his first major political triumphs in South Africa, and nearly fifty before he emerged as a national figure of unrivalled stature on the Indian stage. His ideas were honed during a religious Indian childhood and by his early encounters with the British Empire in its numerous incarnations and guises: from the subtle and indirect influence of culture and language to the face-to-face confrontations with imperial administrators and British officials. His ideas and philosophy were also sharpened in a number of imperial settings; living in a princely state, in African colonies, in the margins of the British Empire in Gujarat, and also in its imperial centre, London. This chapter does not pretend to be comprehensive given the scope of this geography and the rich variety of Gandhi's global encounters. However, it does try to set out what some of this Victorian world may have looked like through the eyes of a young

man coming of age in the 1880s in Western India in a moderately prosperous family, and aims to trace Gandhi's world from his birth until the
writing of *Hind Swaraj* in 1909, which marks the maturation of many
of his ideas.[1]

I. BETWEEN PORBANDAR AND A WIDER WORLD

Through the eyes of Gandhi's childhood town, both the great reach
and the severe limits of British imperial power in South Asia are tangi-
ble. Gandhi's early childhood was spent in Porbandar, a coastal town in
the western Kathiawar peninsula, in today's Gujarat; his family moved
to the nearby town of Rajkot for his education at the time of his father's
appointment as a leading adviser to the Rajasthanik court in 1876, when
he was eight. The princely states, like the state in which Gandhi was
born, still made up two-fifths of India, and were only indirectly controlled by the British. After the shock of 1857, when violent rebellion
had been widespread and, at points, well coordinated, British policies of
annexation had shifted to accommodation with existing Indian maharajas. The form of indirect rule in the Kathiawar peninsula relied on the
manipulation of kinship and patronage networks by two hundred and
twenty nominal princes and upon close ties to British residents and
representatives who had the final power to arbitrate. There were only
ever fewer than two thousand British colonial officials in the whole of
India, although there were also missionaries, soldiers, and businessmen.
Nonetheless, the princely states were under British control in a system of
informal imperialism; Diwans (senior ministers of princely states) were
often handpicked by British residents, and princely heirs were denied
their right to rule at the whim of British officials. The social composition of India was overwhelmingly agrarian and rural; more than ninety
per cent of Indians lived in rural areas in 1901, with many others living
in smaller towns of fewer than five thousand inhabitants. As an urban
child, Gandhi was not well connected to the hinterlands of his home
town: what today are quite short journeys then took many days by bul-
lock cart. Yet even at this local level, the politics of British rule were
decisively demonstrated and felt. Rajkot was a divided town, with one
half acting as a small British cantonment town and civil station, while
the other, much poorer half was the capital of Kathiawar state.[2]

Quashing the uprising of 1857 had come at a considerable financial
and psychological cost; the British killed many thousands of Indians in
retaliation and spent £36 million in the process. First-hand accounts
of the rebellion and folk songs about the uprising were in circulation

during Gandhi's childhood, although Gujarat was not at the epicentre of the events that had dominated Delhi and the United Provinces in 1857. Indian royal families, such as those of the Kathiawar princes whom Gandhi's family had served as advisers for six generations, were being disempowered or carefully armlocked by the power of the state. By the time Gandhi was eight years old, the first Delhi Durbar was being celebrated to mark the coronation and proclamation of Queen Victoria as Empress of India. The introduction of monarchical concepts of feudal loyalty and fealty, from Indian landowners and princes to the sovereign, were being institutionalized with theatrical flair. While he attended primary school in the late 1870s, the British were trying to secure the frontiers of the Raj against Russian threats in Afghanistan, and by the time Gandhi was attending high school in Rajkot, British imperial ascendancy was being consolidated across the globe. The race to annex sub-Saharan Africa sped up after the Berlin conference of 1885. Protectorates were being continually established and consolidated in Africa through Gandhi's youth; rebels in the Sudanese Mahdi rebellion suppressed and Egypt formally occupied. As an avid reader, he would have been exposed to, and felt himself to be part of, this global perspective on world affairs, even from the small and poorly connected rural town of his youth.

Looking around the rural cotton-growing districts near his town, he would have been aware of the cash croppers, day labourers, and landless peasants living in the countryside, poorly dressed and living from hand to mouth. Cotton from Maharashtra and Gujarat would be shipped to Britain from Bombay. Elsewhere, eastern Bengal was supplying the world with jute, and white-owned tea plantations were established in Assam and Darjeeling. It was on an indigo plantation at Champaran, in Bihar, that Gandhi would later launch one of his first campaigns on Indian soil. Mines in Eastern India provided coal and coke for export, and fuelled the work of Indian factories.

Gandhi would have been far less aware that peasant cultivators were being settled on the land in India, armed brigades and local armies were being disarmed by imperial forces, the extensive forest lands of India shrinking, and nomadic peoples pushed into settled agriculture. The 1871 Criminal Tribes Act restricted wandering nomadic groups, and there would have been far less sign of these groups in Kathiawar than a generation earlier. Some actions by the imperial state rarely impinged directly on urban service elites like those in Gandhi's own milieu, although he would have certainly seen soldiers passing through Rajkot. By 1880, there were sixty-six thousand British and one hundred and thirty thousand Indian troops in the Indian army. Some of these

troops were being sent into the rural hinterlands to crush further uprisings against British incursions. In the 1880s and 1890s, tribal revolts in
Bihar and the North East were suppressed, Moplah uprisings continued
on the Southern Coast. Growing urban areas were not immune from
unrest. Early labour consciousness was apparent in Calcutta jute-mill
riots, and there were no-revenue movements against agricultural taxa-
tion at times of famine in Maharashtra.[3]

The Raj and the changing patterns of power in the Indian subcontinent impinged directly on Gandhi's childhood education. Gandhi viscer-
ally felt the British presence in India at school: from the fourth standard,
English had become the medium of education for him for most subjects;
textbooks were carefully controlled and vetted by the British administration. Macaulay's 1835 minute on education, and his aim to create "a class
of persons Indian in blood and colour, but English in tastes, in opinions,
in morals" had long been superseded by perspectives on empire, which
stressed the maintenance of a firm line of difference between Indians
and British rulers based on spurious racial or civilizational rationales.[4]
Nevertheless, English was the medium of education, and an English
school inspector whom Gandhi's teacher wished to impress is the first
European to feature in Gandhi's memories of boyhood.[5] In British India,
the state had acknowledged its duty to expand primary education since
1854, albeit a duty that remained more honoured in the breach than in
the observance: male literacy rates were a little over 11% for British
India in 1911 and just over 1% for women.[6] Gandhi's failed attempts to
teach his child bride to read and write haunted his memories. Education remained an elite privilege with a bias towards higher education in
the presidency cities, which skewed education towards those who could
directly profit from engagement with the Raj. Missionaries were one
important presence on the edge of Gandhi's childhood. "In those days
Christian missionaries used to stand in a corner near the high school
and hold forth, pouring abuse on Hindus and their Gods", he recalls in
the *Autobiography*, and certainly, the zeal of missions in South Asia
has increased considerably in the latter part of the nineteenth century.[7]
British evangelical groups were joined by missionaries from the United
States and Europe, who usually lived apart and were somewhat excluded
from the polite society of the Raj.

One thread that ran through much of this experience, and which
pushed a young man like Gandhi towards eating meat, wearing Western suits, learning English, and studying the law, was the invocation
of racial superiority and British greatness inherent in many different
facets of imperial rule. As Britain's relative position in the world was

steadily threatened, the defensive reactionary responses of an empire grounded in a hierarchical conservatism and scientific racism came to the fore. This was justified by a perception of Indians that emphasized their separateness, difference, and backwardness, whether in scientific experiments, photography, or paintings. In Britain itself, class distinctions were being challenged, and the franchise was extended in 1866. Yet in India, the utilitarian vision of an empire based on a commonwealth of equals (only ever popular among a limited section of the British elite) had been superseded.[8] Liberal pressures for increasing Indian participation in the consultative spheres of the Raj had to be squared with the assumption of Indian difference and repeated assertion that Indians were not capable or ready for self-rule. Undermining this, and clearly apparent to a man of Gandhi's intelligence from a young age, was the contradictory logic of an imperial system that also suggested that Indians could become 'gentlemen' and could be admitted into the system. This was a confusing and contradictory world for a young man. British imperial greatness, and metropolitan imperatives, were routinely invoked – but from the perspective of Porbandar and Rajkot, much of this was viewed through the lens of an imaginary world created in newspapers, textbooks, and pamphlets.

Gandhi was reading printed pamphlets 'from cover to cover' during his youth. This would have been impossible for someone of an older generation. "About the time of my marriage, little pamphlets costing a pice or a pie (I now forget how much), used to be issued, in which conjugal love, thrift, child marriages and other such subjects were discussed".[9] It is difficult to underestimate the impact that printing and the distribution of reformist literature by Indian publishers was having on late nineteenth-century India. Gandhi's youth coincided with the commercialization of vernacular print literature. Low-priced pamphlets and a range of books were more freely and cheaply available than ever before. For the first time, these became affordable commodities that the literate classes could own. In Urdu, for instance, there was a fourfold increase in the production of books from 1868 to 1895.[10] The advantages of lithography over moveable type had become apparent in the early nineteenth century, but the increasing availability of paper produced in local mills and the adoption of the steam press meant that books and pamphlets could be produced much more cheaply than in the past. Furthermore, rather than relying on imported texts or European ownership, more Indians, such as Naval Kishore in Lucknow, were moving into publishing, establishing presses and newspapers. The mushrooming of public libraries, the creation of dictionaries, and translation between English and Indian languages added to the democratization of print. The development of a Gujarati print culture was well underway – the Gujarat Vernacular Society, for example, was founded in 1844 – and Gandhi himself would play no minor part in developing this through his own writings such as *Hind Swaraj*. Many books and pamphlets presented the escapist pleasures of romantic poetry or historical stories, but there was a strong tendency towards the discussion of pressing questions of social reform in pamphlets. Pamphlet wars had long been part of the encounter between Christian missionaries (some of the first people to own and use printing presses in India) and spokespeople for Islam and Hindusim. By the late nineteenth century, popular subjects included child marriage and family relations, sex, diet, and women's education; all topics that would be greatly significant to the development of Gandhi's thought. Similarly, vernacular newspapers that had been in circulation since the early nineteenth century took on new significance, reaching larger numbers of readers and using more colloquial language. It was a good moment for a gifted writer and journalist like Gandhi to emerge in the public sphere.

Modern government stretched out its tentacles, as the Company Raj was transformed into a modern bureaucratic system manned by officers who taxed, policed, codified, and punished. In 1885, before Gandhi had finished school, local self-government was expanded, significantly in the same year that the urban-based Indian National Congress met in Bombay for the first time, with the blessings of the Viceroy. In 1892, legislative councils were created, and in 1909, a new but restricted franchise meant that Indians could form majorities in (non-binding) legislative assemblies. The Indian colonial system was based on the Indian Civil Service (ICS), whose officers, the so-called heaven born, were almost invariably white at the highest levels until the interwar years. Satyendanath Tagore was the first Indian to pass the Indian Civil Service examination in 1863, but the system was stacked against Indians, as the competitive entry examination had to be sat in London, and the questions and age limit all favoured British gentlemen. Approximately four thousand Indians worked for less remuneration and lower prestige in the 'uncovenanted' civil service. The racial differentiation between the different branches of the Raj, and between Europeans and Indians in general, was becoming more pronounced, as British men (and increasingly more women) in India secluded themselves by developing hill stations as holiday retreats, and residential quarters in most towns, which set them apart from the Indian 'masses', as did their preferred leisure activities. Beneath this apparently ordered surface, Europeans experienced tensions: anxieties about Christian doctrine and the place of missionaries; fears of racial miscegenation; the difficulties of the remaining small communities of Anglo-Indians and poor whites; the tensions of progressive Indianization of the services; and, by the turn of the century, the problems of recruiting enough suitable British candidates to join the ICS and to officer the Indian army. Anxiety about the protection of racial superiority fuelled the reaction to the Ilbert Bill in 1883–4; a vocal European outcry against the extension of Indian magistrate's power to try Europeans prosecuted in criminal cases. Gandhi was growing up in a world where the solidity of British power in India was not as secure as it seemed at first glance and where the extension of power to Indians within the civil service, military, and policing arms of the state was the only way to underpin the continued structures of the Raj. Gandhi was well attuned to the vulnerabilities in this system: even before leaving for South Africa in 1893, he had been ejected from the office of a Political Agent in Kathiawar when making a request on behalf of his brother, on the British Political Agent's orders, but at the hands of an Indian peon, who "placed his hands on my shoulders and put me out of the room".[11] The erosion of these coercive bonds between Indian subordinates and British colonial superiors was part of Gandhi's psychological and political achievement.

Much of Kathiawar was peripheral to the central foci of the British Empire. Western Gujarat was a seafaring place in an empire that was increasingly land oriented; Gandhi's world was a princely state, rather than a directly administered area of British India, and far from the imperial presidency cities of Calcutta, Madras, and Bombay where the rapid pace of imperial intrusions was most obviously visible. Gandhi's first visit to Bombay was as an adult en route to England, and he had only travelled to the textile town of Ahmedabad, the closest major city to his childhood home, for the first time in the previous year to take his matriculation exam. Therefore Gandhi's early life was far more directly shaped by the customs and local traditions of Porbandar and Rajkot, growing up in a parochial fisherman's and sea trader's world, which was "renowned for its toughness and shrewdness" far more than by direct encounters with the Raj.[12] Gandhi's boyhood was shaped by the politics of the Kathiawar peninsula and by the domestic politics of living in a three-storey ancestral house shared by his father and his five brothers and their families. This gave him a unique vantage point from which to view the British Empire and also meant that his world was not simply shaped by dichotomies between metropolis and periphery in London and Delhi. As Gandhi is at pains to indicate in the *Autobiography*, the "imperial geographies" of his imaginative, boyhood landscape were not dictated simply by the power of the Raj.[13]

Sea routes and trading links connected what is now Gujarat to many parts of the empire. Gandhi was also closely connected to this maritime world. Across the Bay of Bengal and the Arabian Sea, complex webs linked together ports from Durban, Zanzibar, and Aden to Rangoon, Penang, and Colombo. The post-dated projection of nationalism and national borders may have been far less important to labourers, merchants, and traders using these routes than later accounts suggest.[14] Indentured labour recruited from the north Indian regions of UP and Bihar was shipped to work on white-owned sugar plantations in Natal and Mauritius until the early twentieth century (the indenture system was banned in 1917); in the mid-1880s, there were still ten thousand Indians resident in Natal as indentured labourers, working for a nominal pittance and locked into labour agreements of five years or more.[15] The elite Gujarati diaspora, of which Gandhi would become such a distinguished member during his two decades in South Africa, stretched from Bombay and Karachi to Mombassa, Aden, Durban, and the Indian Ocean ports. This group of traders, businessmen, and professionals made their living from trading goods like cloves and pearls, warehouse storage, money lending, currency exchange, and supplying goods and services. "In the hundred years from the 1830s to the 1930s nearly thirty million Indians travelled overseas and some twenty-four million returned".[16] Indian-ness and a shared sense of national community could be imagined and constructed with more saliency by those living away from home than on Indian soil. Gandhi's aspiration to travel and live abroad was far from unique, and these patterns of remittances, investment, and labour migration paved the way for the great worldwide diaspora of South Asians in the twentieth century and its contradictory impulses of cosmopolitanism and national pride. Imperial trade and business networks meant that Gandhi and his colleagues moved seamlessly between South Africa and India. A job offer to work for a law firm in South Africa reached him in Gujarat, and he made several return visits to India during the two decades he lived in South Africa. While in South Africa, he maintained contact with leaders in India and built relationships with reformers like Gokhale by sending letters and exchanging articles. Naturally, this also meant he could construct political methods in South Africa that would also have resonance in India.

England loomed large in Gandhi's thinking as a young man and as the symbolic destination for achievement and advancement in life. The idea of London as the centre of the world had percolated into the thinking of colonized subjects. "Time hung heavily on my hands in Bombay", he later remembered. "I dreamt continually of going to England".[17] After his matriculation, Gandhi was determined to study law in London. Rajkot's population of thirty-six thousand was a tiny fraction of Bombay's, which had more than half a million inhabitants and paled in comparison to London's three and half million. Urbanization and industrialization were driving connections between the imperial metropolitan centre and the rapidly booming Indian cities. Communications and technologies meant that people and goods could travel more rapidly than ever before: between 1873 and 1890, the rail freight carried on Indian railways grew more than fivefold, and there were eight and a half thousand miles of track and twenty thousand miles of telegraph wire by 1880. Rajkot's inclusion in the rail system was important enough to warrant a mention in the *Autobiography* and delivered some of the greatest changes to his hometown that Gandhi saw in his lifetime. Gandhi's later campaigns would make much of the railways, as he spent countless days and nights covering vast distances. He also denigrated railways in *Hind Swaraj* for 'impoverishing' the country, bringing speed, greed, and divisiveness.[18] The real beneficiaries of the railways were investors and military commanders who could move troops at great speed, but a by-product was the opportunity for travel and political connection for Gandhi and his contemporaries. Sea routes similarly opened up connections between cities, ports, and metropole. The Suez Canal was opened in 1869, the year of Gandhi's birth, and it was not only elite Indians who could consider long-distance journeys for Haj, pilgrimage, family visits, or trade. According to the London City Mission, there were between ten and twelve thousand seamen or *lascars*, the majority of Indian origin, in London by the late nineteenth century.[19]

Gandhi left for England in 1888 and stayed there until 1891: the journey by ship took a little over six weeks. Shipping would come to have a double function in the nationalist imaginary: it was both a real and pressing issue of industry and opportunity, linked to trade and supply routes, the possibilities for investment and revenue but also an emotive and symbolic issue. As Javed Majeed wrote, "One of the ways in which travel disempowered Indian travellers in the nineteenth century was the increasing awareness they had of the extent of British power as they journeyed from India to Britain, usually on British ships".[20]

During his travels, Gandhi also saw the shipping of raw materials from India with his own eyes. Much of Britain's growth was being driven by Indian goods. Industrialization and the expansion of cotton mills favoured the mechanization of production and the growth of the satanic mills of the Midlands. 'De-industrialized' India was turned into a supplier of unprocessed raw materials. Textile imports into India were peaking during Gandhi's childhood, making up nearly half of all imports in 1870–1. The Indian landscape was being transformed by the growth of cities too; Indian factories also began to boom, jute was processed in Calcutta and cotton in Ahmedabad and Bombay, although usually to the benefit of European financiers, managing agents, and entrepreneurs who created monopolies for themselves. Upcountry migrant labour drafted in from the rural hinterlands or pushed off agricultural land by famine or unemployment was locked into seasonal production or worked for day wages. "The workers in the mills of Bombay have become slaves", Gandhi commented in *Hind Swaraj*.[21] The development of these mega-cities – Bombay, for instance, tripled in size in Gandhi's lifetime – marked a sharp departure from the power of the regional bazaar and administrative towns, such as Allahabad, which had been typical of the earlier nineteenth century.

In these presidency cities, the solid, European buildings of the presidency capitals such as Madras Fort, "extensions of Europe in Asia", gave way to Indo-Saracenic building projects, clearly intended to impress upon Indians the supremacy of British power, while legitimizing such claims by styling them in an Indian idiom.[22] Bombay's Victoria Terminus embodied the Gothic revival and was opened to celebrate Queen Victoria's Golden Jubilee in 1887. This rail terminus linked up the cotton grown in the Western Indian villages of India with the British Empire. Gandhi must have seen the new, famed rail terminus, completed one year earlier, when he made his first visit to Bombay en route to Britain the following year; it was an echo of St. Pancras station, which was twenty years older and in the heart of Gandhi's Bloomsbury. These new architectural projects were closely linked to the force of imperial ideas. Thomas Metcalf notes, for instance, the sudden proliferation of municipal clock towers in Indian cities after 1857, albeit framed in elaborate Indo-Saracenic towers; a reminder of the Victorian virtues of punctuality and industry perceived to be missing in Indians.[23] Calcutta, which remained the capital of British India until 1911 when it was replaced by New Delhi, must have seemed a very distant Eastern place – and the domination of Indian politics by Bengali *bhadralok* elites educated in the Presidency town was alien and remote from Gandhi's experience before the twentieth century. It was his good fortune that the gravitational centre of Indian politics was shifting westwards across the country, as the economic boom of Bombay and the westward orientation of the empire brought Calcutta into eclipse. Later, through dialogue with the Bengali poet, Rabindranath Tagore, and through his support of the swadeshi movement against the Partition of Bengal in 1905, Gandhi would also find inspiration in the east of India, and close the circle in his geographical imagination of India as a territorial entity.

The all-encompassing nature of the Victorian empire, the power of the imperial myth, and the difficulties of subverting the imperial system are reflected in Gandhi's continuing loyalty to the empire, when, even as a frustrated citizen in South Africa where he battled racial prejudice, unfair legislation, and pioneered his campaigns while developing his spiritual practice, he continued to view his world through the inevitable framework of British imperial rule. He lived in South Africa from 1893 until leaving Durban for the last time in 1914. During the Boer War of 1899–1902, Gandhi famously organized an ambulance corps in support of the British. Indian troops were again being used against the Boer rebels, and his own participation in this war tested Gandhi spiritually and morally:

> Suffice it to say that my loyalty to the British rule drove me
> to participation with the British in that war. I felt that, if I
> demanded rights as a British citizen, it was also my duty, as
> such, to participate in the defence of the British Empire. I held
> then that India could achieve her complete emancipation only
> within and through the British Empire.[24]

The *Autobiography* cannot be taken as merely a historical document, and this statement also works at a metaphorical level; Gandhi's relationship with the idea of the Raj was clearly highly nuanced by this stage. Perhaps the point to note here, however, is the imperial pressures and strands of loyalty were so intricately interwoven, and connected so many different aspects of life, that it took many years for Gandhi to think in terms of an Indian nation-state or independence from British rule. The paradigm shift from an imperial world, in which European empires ruled, fought wars, and carved up territory, to one of nation-states was a revolutionary change from Victorian to twentieth-century thought.

2. THE CHANGING SOCIAL WORLD

For all its internationalism, Gandhi's world was also rooted in a quintessentially Indian home. The ancestral house of the Gandhis was built around two temples, and it was questions of religious propriety, women's duties in the household, diet, and marriage that set the rhythms of everyday life. His mother is idealized in Gandhi's writings as a loyal Indian woman: chaste, devout, and dutiful, fasting and eating after others, rising early and dealing with all the children of the extended household. A sharp demarcation of domestic and public space, however, seems to have been less clear in Gandhi's Porbandar than in other contemporaneous parts of Raj; the courtyard and public spaces of the house were constantly open to his father's visitors who would come to eat in the family home. Gandhi's father would even carry out domestic chores while discussing business matters. Local people remembered Gandhi's father "sitting in the Shrinathji temple day after day, peeling and paring the vegetables for his wife's kitchen, while he discussed politics".[25] The house was therefore not a sealed domestic middle-class space but was closely connected to the politics of the Kathiawar peninsula. This reflects Gandhi's own fusion of private and public politics. This part of Gandhi's world, seeped in caste, religion, gender politics, and Indian tradition, was equally important to his later career; his knowledge and experience of religion and caste in the late nineteenth century would help him to pull together the threads of Indian nationalism in the twentieth century, and to construct his powerful reformist vision of Indian-ness.

Gandhi's Vaishnavite family was steeped in religious practice and custom. His mother visited the Vaisnava temple daily, fasted, and prayed, and his father listened to recitations of the Ramayana, which left a deep impression on the young Gandhi. As with all the major religions in the subcontinent processes of classification, social reform and regularization were formalizing Indian experiences of religion in the nineteenth century, and increasingly questions were raised about the orthodoxy or appropriateness of particular religious expressions. The Arya Samaj was founded in 1875 in Bombay and in 1877 in Lahore, and influentially campaigned for a reformist Hinduism, heavily influenced by Christianity, which rejected Brahmanism and pilgrimage and emphasized a textual basis for Hinduism. The leader of the movement, Dayanand Saraswati – an older Gujarati from Kathiawar – visited Rajkot in the 1870s and started a branch in Gandhi's childhood town.

This was also an era of the 'traditionalization' of Indian society as society became more stratified, static, and settled; the rapid expansion of cash cropping, boosted by the arrival of the railways, increased the mercantile power of Hindus engaged in supplying agricultural credit and merchants entered district councils and caste associations. Respectability and caste hierarchies helped to prove credit worthiness and to cement political leadership, and the expansion of cow protection leagues, social reform movements, and the patronage of festivals and temples was central to this. Hindu expressions of piety therefore were closely imbricated with politics. Merchants took a leading role in religious reform and in political mobilization. On his return from London, Gandhi had a profound spiritual encounter with Raychandbhai in Bombay, a family friend and jeweller, "Raychandbhai's commercial transactions covered hundreds of thousands. He was a connoisseur of pearls and diamonds. No knotty business problem was too difficult for him. But all these things were not the centre around which his life revolved. That centre was the passion to see God face to face".[26] Trade, business, and piety were entirely complementary in Gandhi's experience.

Caste, perhaps the central organizing principle of Hindu society, was being institutionalized as caste associations, and literacy made it possible for fellow caste members to link up across longer distances in new ways. Jatis and caste subdivisions predated colonial rule in India. This was the primary kinship group one looked to for marriage partners, economic ties, and benefits. Now, new processes of modernity and imperial codification meant that caste was being expressed in more vocal and obvious ways. Texts became the foundation for caste and piety, purity, and status were more regularly scrutinized. This is vividly shown in Gandhi's own youth. When he chose to cross the 'kala pani' or black water to go to London to study law – thereby, according to the beliefs of some Hindus, 'breaking' caste – he was disowned by one section of his caste's association. This decision was communicated from a caste meeting in Bombay back to the community leaders of his home.

> Meanwhile my caste people were agitated over my going abroad. No Modh Bania had been to England up to now and if I dared to do so I ought to be brought to book! A general meeting of the caste was called and I was summoned to appear before it.[27]

The headman, incensed by Gandhi's intransigence, swore at him and promised to fine anyone who assisted his passage. Gandhi's experience also shows though how, paradoxically, transport connections and new wealth were also making it harder for caste leaders to dictate to their fellow kin. Gandhi left for London despite the admonition of his caste headman. Caste associations and groups looked for uplift and higher status, claimed status based on genealogies and real and invented family lineages, and policed who was in and out of the caste. The Aryan claims of Brahmins were reinforced by new ethnologies and the emerging arts of Western scientists who used physiological characteristics and the new technologies of photography to classify and label their subjects of study. Lower-caste groups seeking uplift through 'sanskritization' were rarely successful, although some moved from unclean occupations such as toddy-tapping to raise their collective position over the course of the century: many Untouchables would later contest caste by rejecting their place in the Hindu tradition entirely, seeking status as 'dalits' and by claiming pre-Hindu indigeneity within India – an idea that would bring them into direct conflict with Gandhi whose own position on caste remained reformist but conservative.

This was a heterodox and reformist world then, but also one that was far more influenced by Jainism and Hinduism than by Islam. Gandhi's hometown was far from the remaining Mughal courtly cultures and large urban concentrations of Muslims, which shaped the political dynamics of Delhi and North India. India's Muslim population was more than twenty-five per cent. During the process of colonial encounter, the Muslim community was asking many of the same questions about propriety and rightful action as the other religious groups. The educational centres for Muslims in the United Provinces at Deoband, Lahore, and Aligarh were founded during Gandhi's youth. Deoband would play a vital role in directing orthodoxy and formalizing an Islamic curriculum for Indian Muslim students, while Aligarh was a space for modernizing Muslim elites to square piety, reform, and Western scientific ideas. It was a Muslim firm that employed Gandhi and attracted him from Gujarat to South Africa. But Gandhi's early life was lived far from these North Indian Persian–Islamicate centres (in comparison to Nehru's early life, which was much more influenced by the old Persianate elite) and his knowledge of Islam was circumscribed and mediated through Gujarati trading Muslim castes and, later, through close interaction with Muslims in South Africa and, later still, during the Khilafat movement.

Pre-colonial histories of community conflict and regional warfare had undoubtedly been exacerbated by colonial processes that simplistically divided communities against each other through administrative interventions and decisions. Older histories and myths of conquest and domination created regional heroes such as Shivaji and lineages, which relied on the demonization of the Mughal other. Gandhi was astutely aware of this; in *Hind Swaraj* he poses the question, "Has the introduction of Mohammedanism not unmade the nation?" to rebut this with a firm assertion of British divide and rule policies and a strong call to unity-in-diversity.[28] Indians lived with a community consciousness by the late nineteenth century: an awareness of religious community, of purity-pollution and of community difference but this had not yet hardened into frequent violence. Muslim political separatism and political self-definition in Delhi, Punjab, and the United Provinces became more salient in later years alongside the growth of Hindu fundamentalism expressed in militia groups like the RSS, founded in 1925. In the twentieth century, conflict between nationalist and exclusionary visions of Hinduism and Islam would evolve into their most destructive forms. Separate electorates were created in the Morley-Minto reforms of 1909, and violent clashes in the name of religion became routine in some urban areas around issues such as cow protection, music being played in front of mosques at prayer time, and the observance of religious festivals of Holi and Mohurram.

Gandhi's life was also shaped by his interaction with women – in particular, his wife and mother, Gandhian followers, social workers, and teachers. As he remarked, "I have worshipped woman as the living embodiment of the spirit of service and sacrifice", and he frequently invoked the ideal of Sita as a model to which women should aspire. By the late nineteenth century, reform groups had mushroomed in many urban areas of India; "they focused on sati, female infanticide, polygyny, child marriage, purdah, prohibitions on female education, devadasis (temple dancers wedded to the gods) and the patrilocal joint family".[29] The leading reformers were men. Reforming the worst excesses of violence against women and protecting children may have been inspired by male patriarchal control more than humanitarian concern for woman as a general category. The symbolic category of woman and the political sensitivity of 'the woman question' may have mattered more than the actual daily experience of women themselves. Certainly, it was a hotly contested ground between colonial reformers and Indian nationalists who wished to demonstrate their own cultural superiority or claims to progress and enlightenment.

Child marriage was a feature of Indian life in the nineteenth century that particularly concerned Gandhi because of his own boyhood marriage at the age of thirteen, something he denounced as a 'cruel custom' in his writings.[30] This was a fraught subject between reformers and the colonial officials – some British officials used salacious details to slur Indian morality and 'backwardness', while Indians defended, explained, or campaigned against the custom. In 1891, the criminal code amended the law to raise the age of consent to twelve years, but it was an issue that would repeatedly become a political battleground in the twentieth century, especially when Katherine Mayo's infamous book, *Mother India*, denouncing Indian treatment of women, appeared in the interwar years. As with sati for the earlier generation, so now child marriage was a locus for much broader debates about modernity and authority.[31]

It is evident that educated mothers were seen as the desirable guardians of new nationalist citizens, and that the control of family diet, cleanliness, and purchases was an important space for articulating a will to political autonomy. This was a space where the Indian householder could try to control the intrusions and assaults on the Indian moral economy by the colonial regime; this applied to Muslim women, as well as Hindu women, and magazines and books urging Muslim women's education and reform and urging against superstition were published from Lahore and Aligarh. Gradual improvements in women's education and literacy rates enabled many more women to have an important stake in their families' budgeting, nutrition, and housekeeping, and to consume new products as they came onto the market: hair oil, lipstick, machine-made saris, and soap. Nevertheless, literacy was still an elite skill for women. Even at independence in 1947, female literacy was estimated at ten per cent.

The 'new patriarchy', as Partha Chatterjee terms it, may have created an illusory effect of new freedoms, while middle-class Bengali women became the repositories of all that was respectable, proper, and spiritual in the Indian home, and their respectability had to be more carefully policed than ever before.[32] Gandhi's leadership was well attuned to political methods such as fasting, spinning, and salt making, which chimed with the everyday duties and responsibilities of 'decent' women, drawing heavily on middle-class respectability and pride in women's thrift, cleanliness, and chastity. Gandhi cleverly negotiated the boundaries of colonial masculinity and femininity set by the Raj and drew many women into political activism in the twentieth century.

CONCLUSION

Gandhi's youth coincided with 'the great acceleration' of European imperialisms, the invasive modernity and boom in laissez-faire trade which reoriented the world system around the European metropoles. Goods and people could be moved around the globe at a new pace, and profits could be accumulated quickly. Gandhi's early life was set against the background of a growing imperial reach and systematic expansion of imperial control in India, much of which was implemented by Indians themselves. Much took place imperceptibly over the *longue durée* and was invisible to the naked eye. There was a shift from capital vested in land to business and banking interests. Moneterization, cash cropping, and the interconnectedness of markets developed. Hunter-gatherers and nomadic peoples were being pushed to the margins or eliminated altogether. Growing uniformity in the bureaucratic ambitions of nation states meant the erosion of older forms of sovereignty, ongoing shifts in religious and local forms of authority, and encroachments on the moral economy of peasant livelihoods. In turn, radical resistance intensified, national attachments arose, and racial awareness was exacerbated.[33] Part of Gandhi's genius was his vivid and palpable awareness of these changes and their coercive force. The strength of feeling in Gandhi's *Hind Swaraj* against 'civilization' and the 'progress' presupposedly brought by new technologies and transport systems can be properly understood only in this light.[34] Gandhi railed against the invasive and immoral aspects of modernity in *Hind Swaraj*. This was a deep and complex outcry against the long and steady incursions into a premodern society that could no longer be revived or even properly remembered. This was not an isolated reaction but one shared by some intellectuals across the globe – hence Gandhi's sympathy with Ruskin and Tolstoy.

Victorian imperialism had a pompous and theatrical Victorian façade, which emphasized the rights of an 'invented' traditional ruling order in India and loyalty to the Queen Empress. Gandhi experienced some of these grandiose imperial visions directly. Beneath it also lurked the uncertainties and inner contradictions of the British in India, which began surfacing with increasing regularity. Gandhi's life bridged the peak of this imperial hubris, and its decline and demise; he perceived the weakness of the imperial system and was able to invert orientalist stereotypes of Indian spirituality and rural stasis against the imperial regime in his unique political philosophy.[35]

Gandhi's own position was peculiarly marginal to the great contemporary debates in British imperial policy in India, compared to, say, Jawaharlal Nehru who was born in Allahabad – a classical colonial corporate town – and who grew up in the thick of colonial debates about legal reform, religious conflict, land ownership, and provincial self-government. Gandhi's world was quite different and was both parochial and international. This peripheral role, looking outwards to the broader oceanic networks and inwards to local pre-colonial 'traditions' meant that Gandhi inhabited a very particular space in Indian nationalism. It gave him simultaneously the detailed insight of a local boy matched with the global insight of an international observer. It enabled him to conceive Indian independence in a reworked and unique fashion, drawing on local idioms but refashioned for the twentieth century.

Notes

1 For good general overviews and accounts of the late nineteenth century in India, see Judith M. Brown, *Modern India: The Origins of an Asian Democracy*, 2nd edn. (Oxford, England: Oxford University Press, 1994); Crispin Bates, *Subalterns and the Raj: South Asia Since 1600* (London: Routledge, 2007); Sumit Sarkar, *Modern India: 1985–1947* (Basingstoke, England: Macmillan, 1983); Peter Robb, *A History of India* (London and New York: Palgrave, 2002); Sugata Bose and Ayesha Jalal, *Modern South Asia: History, Culture, Political Economy*, 2nd edn. (London: Routledge, 2004); Barbara Metcalf and Thomas Metcalf, *A Concise History of Modern India* (Cambridge and New York: Cambridge University Press, 2006); M. K. Gandhi, *Hind Swaraj and Other Writings*, ed. A. J. Parel (Cambridge, England: Cambridge University Press, 1997).

2 For an interesting insight into Gandhi's childhood, see Erik Erikson, *Gandhi's Truth: On the Origins of Militant Non-Violence* (New York: W. W. Norton, 1969).

3 Sarkar, *Modern India*, pp. 43–65.

4 For a discussion of the various ideologies driving British rule in India, see Thomas Metcalf, *Ideologies of the Raj* (Cambridge, England: Cambridge University Press, 1995).

5 M. K. Gandhi, *An Autobiography or The Story of My Experiments with Truth*, trans. Mahadev Desai, first pub. in serial form in 1927, part I, chapter II.

6 Brown, *Modern India*, pp. 96–148.

7 Gandhi, *An Autobiography*, part I, chapter IV.

8 Metcalf, *Ideologies of the Raj*.

9 Gandhi, *An Autobiography*, part I, chapter IV.

10 On the development of print literature in modern India, see Ulrike Stark, *An Empire of Books: The Naval Kishore Press and the Diffusion of the Printed Word in Colonial India* (New Delhi, India: Permanent Black, 2007); Francis Robinson, *Islam and Muslim History in South Asia* (Oxford, England: Oxford University Press, 2001); Francesca Orsini, *The Hindi Public Sphere 1920–1940: Language and Literature in the Age of Nationalism* (Oxford, England: Oxford University Press, 2002).

11 Gandhi, *An Autobiography*, part II, chapter IV.

12 Erikson, *Gandhi's Truth*, p. 103.

13 For an excellent reading of Gandhi's *Autobiography*, see Javed Majeed, *Autobiography, Travel and Postnational Identity: Gandhi, Nehru and Iqbal* (London: Palgrave Macmillan, 2007).

14 On the Indian Ocean as a social and political arena in the late nineteenth and early twentieth centuries, see Sugata Bose, *A Hundred Horizons: The Indian Ocean in the Age of Global Empire* (Cambridge, MA: Harvard University Press, 2006).

15 Thomas Metcalf, *Forging the Raj: Essays on British India in the Heyday of Empire* (Oxford and New York: Oxford University Press, 2005), p. 208.

16 Bose, *A Hundred Horizons*, p. 73.

17 Gandhi, *An Autobiography*, part I, chapter XII.

18 Gandhi, *Hind Swaraj*, chapter IX.

19 On South Asians in Britain and the wider Diaspora, see Michael H. Fisher, Shompa Lahiri, and Shinder Thandi, *A South-Asian History of Britain: Four Centuries of Peoples from the Indian Sub-Continent* (Westport, CT: Greenwood, 2007); Siddiq Sayyid, N. Ali, and V. S. Kalra, *A Postcolonial People: South Asians in Britain* (London: Hurst, 2006); Judith M. Brown, *Global South Asians: Introducing the Modern Diaspora* (Cambridge, England: Cambridge University Press, 2006); Humayun Ansari, *The Infidel Within: The History of Muslims in Britain, 1800 to the Present* (London: Hurst, 2004).

20 Majeed, *Autobiography, Travel and Postnational Identity*, p. 76.

21 Gandhi, *Hind Swaraj*, chapter XIX.

22 Metcalf, *Forging the Raj*, pp. 106–35.

23 *Ibid.*, p. 127.

24 Gandhi, *An Autobiography*, part III, chapter X.

25 Pyarelal, *Mahatma Gandhi, The Early Phase* (Ahmedabad, India: Navajivan, 1965), pp. 192–3.

26 Gandhi, *An Autobiography*, part II, chapter I.

27 *Ibid.*, part I, chapter XII.

28 Gandhi, *Hind Swaraj*, chapter X.

29 Geraldine Forbes, *Women in Modern India* (Cambridge, England: Cambridge University Press, 1999), pp. 1–10, 92–121.

30 Gandhi, *An Autobiography*, part I, chapter III.

31 On reform and debates about women in India, see Mrinalini Sinha, *Colonial Masculinity: The 'Manly Englishman' and the 'Effeminate Bengali' in the Late Nineteenth Century* (Manchester, England: Manchester University Press, 1995), and *Specters of Mother India: The Global Restructuring of an Empire* (Durham, England: Duke University Press, 2006).

32 Partha Chatterjee, 'Colonialism, Nationalism, and Colonialized Women: The Contest in India', *American Ethnologist*, 16.4 (Nov., 1989), pp. 622–33.

33 C. A. Bayly, *The Birth of the Modern World 1780–1914. Global Connections and Comparisons* (Oxford, England: Blackwell, 2004).

34 Gandhi, *Hind Swaraj*. See also Parel's introduction in *Gandhi: Hind Swaraj and Other Writings*.

35 Richard G. Fox makes important arguments about Gandhi's 'affirmative orientalism'. See Richard G. Fox, *Gandhian Utopia: Experiments with Culture* (Boston: Beacon Press, 1989).

2 Gandhi 1869–1915: The transnational emergence of a public figure

JONATHAN HYSLOP

On 9 January 1915, M. K. Gandhi disembarked in Bombay to a hero's welcome. His ideas and personal leadership exercised a powerful pull on India's nationalist elite, and were seen by many to hold the political key to the country's future. For a young Calcutta student of the time: "[a]lready . . . the man who was to bring in the masses and conduct the passive resistance campaign had become identified to us as Mr. (not yet Mahatma) Gandhi. Although all the old leaders . . . were still living and active, our eyes were fixed on Gandhi as the coming man".[1]

Yet Gandhi had spent little of his adult life in India. He had been a student in England, and had subsequently made several extended visits there; and for more than two decades, his home had been in southern Africa. How, then, was Gandhi able to achieve a position as a major Indian public figure from outside the country? This was all the more remarkable because, in his early years, he had shown little trace of personal or intellectual distinction. The Gandhi who went to the colony of Natal in 1893 had not been an outstanding student and had failed in his attempt to make a legal career in India because of his intense shyness. So another puzzle arises: what sort of personal transformation could have underpinned his rise?

It is only recently that historians have come to recognize the centrality of his time abroad in Gandhi's life, and in particular, the significance of his southern African years.[2] Earlier writers on Gandhi tended to treat his youth and middle years as a mere prelude to the really important part of his career.[3] Yet it was in southern Africa that he developed the entire spiritual, philosophical, and political programme that he would implement in India. Moreover, it was in Africa that he became a master of reading the political moment and of the political use of the print media. Gandhi's political and intellectual projects, as they evolved in these years, operated across political boundaries, linking India, South Africa, and Britain itself, as well as points beyond. Gandhi was a man formed by transnational processes and who acted across borders, and made himself known internationally before he ever returned to India. The crucial context for Gandhi's personal development was provided by the cosmopolitanism of Johannesburg, the brutal yet culturally and politically dynamic city of gold mining. This chapter traces the conditions and circumstances that enabled Gandhi to accumulate the skills and cultural resources to become a national leader. It examines the way in which, through a long and slowly developing 'presentation of self',[4] performing the roles of political leader and holy man, Gandhi fashioned himself into the figure who Rabindranath Tagore would hail after his return to India as a Mahatma (great soul).

In tackling this enterprise, the biographer should note that Gandhi's *Autobiography* is both a wonderful resource and a source of danger.[5] This extraordinary work of introspection and self-revelation, written in the mid-1920s, provides a level of access to his interiority that most biographers can only dream of attaining in their investigations of their subjects. But its literary brilliance can lure the researcher into an excessively credulous acceptance of Gandhi's account of his personal life, which by its nature is difficult or impossible to check against other sources. As Claude Markovits has remarked, Gandhi managed to establish the book as the main source for all later treatments of his early life: "Astonishingly even Gandhi's most improbable claims have been accepted uncritically... "[6]. There is no alternative to using the *Autobiography* as a source, but it does need to be treated with the same degree of scepticism that a biographer would accord to any other historical document.

The previous chapter introduced us to Gandhi's early childhood in Porbandar, Western India, where his father, Karamchand (or Kaba) was the long-serving senior minister to the ruler. Gandhi's mother was Putlibai. They belonged to the Modh bania caste of traders (in Gujarati, *gandhi* means grocer). Kaba was a follower of the Pushtimagri Vaishnavite sect of Hinduism, but was noted for his openness to other religions and his willingness to debate theology with their adherents. Putlibai was particularly devout and belonged to the Pranami sect, which was distinguished by its integration of elements of Islamic practice into the Hindu tradition and its asceticism. Gandhi was deeply devoted to both parents.[7]

In 1876, the family moved to the nearby principality of Rajkot, where Kaba again assumed the position of senior minister. As was a normal Hindu practice, Gandhi entered into an arranged marriage at the age of thirteen. His wife, Kasturba, became a devoted spouse. But Gandhi's relationship with her evolved in a complex way, marked by guilt. Many have tried to explain it psychoanalytically, focusing on Gandhi's own account of the death of his father. In this narrative, during his father's last illness, Gandhi had faithfully nursed him. But one night, he left his duties to make love with Kasturba. While they were together, his father died and Gandhi felt intense responsibility.[8] This story lends itself to explanations of Gandhi's personal formation as based on a single traumatic event. But one could equally speculate that Gandhi loaded a much longer-term and diffusely originated sense of sexual guilt into the story.

After an only moderately successful schooling in Rajkot and a brief period at Samaldas College, Gandhi's family decided on the advice of a friend to send the young man to London to study law at the Inner Temple. Gandhi's determination to go to London, in the face of considerable social pressure not to do so, was the first sign of a strong will in the young man. His mother feared that in England he would not be able to observe Hindu rituals. As a condition of her agreement for him to go, Gandhi took an oath to abstain from women, meat, and alcohol. He then faced considerable opposition from his caste to his journey. Many Hindus believed that by crossing the kala pani (black water), one's caste was broken. As Gandhi was waiting for his ship in Bombay, a caste leader got up opposition to his plans. When Gandhi persisted, he was expelled from the caste.

Gandhi's time in London, from 1888 to 1891, was the modest beginning of his transformation. Experiences in the imperial metropolis were crucial to the personal and political development of a small but significant section of young, elite Indians, a number of whom were to play important political or professional roles in later life.[9] By 1890, there were about 200 Indian students in London. Their common marginal position pushed them together, in a crossing of regional, ethnic, and religious boundaries that would have been uncommon in India itself. What Antoinette Burton calls the 'voyage in' to the imperial centre allowed these young intellectuals to imagine their common identity as imperial subjects. In this social world, 'Indian' was not a fixed identity, but a work in progress; its possible definitions were constructed in conversations and social practices. The reticent Gandhi made little mark in this London milieu – but he was initiated into a conversation about the nation in which he would eventually become the most powerful voice. Particularly important were the meetings that Gandhi attended of the National Indian Association. Here, Gandhi, despite his chronic shyness, struck up a close friendship with a Bengali writer, Narayan Hemchandra, a type of personal and intellectual relationship he would have been unlikely to make at home.

To be in London raised issues of self-identity and a relation to modernity at the level of bodily practice. Gandhi embarrassed himself by arriving in the city in a white suit of the kind worn by British officials in India but never seen in London. He initially invested considerable time and money on trying to dress like a modern English gentleman. Gandhi quickly became more sartorially restrained, but he was not to abandon a besuited, starched collared style of dress for the next two decades.[10] And at this time, there was no question in Gandhi's mind of the benefits to India of imperial citizenship. He was deeply impressed by the words of Queen Victoria's 1858 declaration in the wake of the Indian uprising, pledging fair treatment and non-discrimination to her Indian subjects. That document appeared to him to give Indians a special and protected status within the Empire. The Indian intellectuals of London, around 1890, thought in terms of gradual political reform and democratization, based on Indian claims to Britishness. This imperial loyalist viewpoint was to be almost unquestioned by Gandhi until 1906; and even then, he moved to a demand for home rule within the Empire rather than full independence, a perspective he still advocated at the time of his return to India in 1915. In a world where the British Empire seemed invulnerable, and Indian elite reformers sought many of the same goals as British liberals, this seemed an eminently pragmatic outlook.

At a personal and political level, though, an important experience in the metropolis for the young Gandhi was his encounter with the British vegetarian movement. On the voyage from India and in his first weeks in London, Gandhi suffered from his inability to get adequate vegetarian food when confronted with the offerings of the ship's kitchens and of London boarding houses. It was thus with a sense of revelation that he encountered the vegetarian Central Restaurant in Farringdon Street and spotted in the window Henry Salt's book, *A Plea for Vegetarianism*. Entering the restaurant, he enjoyed a hearty meal, bought the book, and subsequently read it, becoming a convert to the vegetarian cause. This was the start of an active involvement in vegetarianism, which was Gandhi's main political activity until he left London. Vegetarianism was a highly organized movement, and Gandhi found the members of the vegetarian societies very hospitable. Through attending conferences, organizing meetings, sitting on committees, and writing newspaper articles, Gandhi learned the techniques of procedure, organization, and propaganda that would serve him well in the future. Vegetarianism also gave Gandhi cultural and political orientations that would be important in future. At home in Rajkot, Gandhi had been influenced by the common

Indian nationalist trope of a connection between meat and modernity. It was widely believed that the superior political strength of the British was based in a superior physical strength, rooted in their consumption of meat. Thus, some ideologues argued, Hindus should overcome their prohibition on meat in order to strengthen their bodies, and thus their capacity for self-assertion. In pursuit of this doctrine, Gandhi and his friends in Rajkot had engaged in experiments in meat eating, although stricken with conscience as a result. In the London vegetarians, Gandhi found a group whose practice allowed him to reconcile his loyalty to his mother, and his oath to her, with his aspirations to modernity. They claimed the sanction of Western science for the same practices to which Gandhi was committed. At the same time, the vegetarians had a critical stance towards the civilization in which they lived. Radical vegetarians were hostile to industrialism and the modern city; they accepted the anti-urbanism common amongst Victorian intellectuals. The vegetarians were also sympathetic towards Hinduism because of its dietary practices, thus allowing for a revaluation of Indian civilization and creating an inclination to be critical of British rule in India. Salt, whose vegetarian tract had a lasting impact on Gandhi, was influenced by the anarchist thought of Kropotkin, and in his work sought to link vegetarianism to critiques of colonial policy, factory conditions, the legal system, prisons, and cruelty to animals.[11] Contemporary readers are often puzzled by the apparent obsession with food in Gandhi's writings; but the centrality of vegetarianism to his process of self-definition helps to explain this.

The young man who returned to India in 1891 was not outwardly impressive. He had completed his studies in London but had not done especially well. He attempted to make a career as a barrister in Bombay, but suffered a humiliating failure because his stage fright made him unable to speak in public. He retreated to Rajkot, where he made a meagre living from drafting legal documents. Then, a way out of this dead end opened up. Gandhi was offered a relatively lucrative job in southern Africa. Dada Abdulla, a firm of Muslim merchants based in Porbandar, but which also operated in the British colony of Natal and the Boer Republic of the Transvaal, needed a trustworthy lawyer to act for them in an internecine family legal dispute. Gandhi decided to take the opportunity. Leaving his family behind, he set off for Africa.

No such political entity as 'South Africa' existed at the time that Gandhi arrived in the Natal port of Durban in 1893. Natal was a settler colony, dominated by a rather incompetent plantocracy based on sugar estates. Because of the difficulty of obtaining adequate numbers of African workers for these farms, the British had, since 1860, been importing indentured labourers from India, the majority of them Tamil and Telugu, but some from North India as well. In their wake had come so-called passenger Indians, largely Muslim Gujaratis, who had established themselves as storekeepers and come to play a crucial role in the retail economy of the region. The African population of the colony had been politically subordinated since the British military defeat of the Zulu kingdom in 1879, and the fragmentation of the Zulu state through civil war that had followed on it. The adjoining Transvaal had been, until 1886, an oligarchic white Afrikaner republic, a weak state with a huge African subject population, predominantly living within a subsistence economy. This social order was dramatically changed by the discovery of gold. The city of Johannesburg mushroomed as a centre of this industry, with an international population. This situation generated a crisis for the Boer regime. On the one hand, the government now had adequate revenues for the administrative and military strengthening of their state; but on the other, they were threatened by the huge concentration of British immigrants on the Rand (the area around Johannesburg), who were demanding the franchise, and thus threatening to take over power. Because the British government claimed a vague 'suzerainty', the Boers feared British intervention. In a world where renewed economic growth was being constrained by the shortage of gold, control of the Transvaal was an important stake in global politics. A number of Indians had moved into the Transvaal, particularly Muslim traders, but also some time-expired indentured labourers.

Gandhi's first weeks in southern Africa subjected him to a whole range of racial humiliations. In Durban, a magistrate had him removed from a court session for wearing a turban. He set off by train for the Transvaal, but at Pietermaritzburg, the Natal capital, he was thrown off the train by a policeman and spent the night on a freezing station platform. Proceeding the next day by train, he had to change to the stagecoach at Charlestown, where there was a break in the line. During this trip, he was forced to sit on the outside of the coach and assaulted by a company official. On arrival at Johannesburg, he was refused accommodation in the Grand National Hotel.[12] In the Gandhi legend as recounted in the *Autobiography* and elaborated by Gandhi's followers, these episodes, and particularly the night on the station at Pietermaritzburg, are portrayed as the turning point, in which he decides to stay in southern Africa and fight. But it is difficult to tell whether this was indeed the case or whether it is a retrospective construction put on events. Certainly though, Gandhi, who does not seem to have previously experienced racial violence or extreme humiliation in India or Britain, was deeply traumatized by these events.

Gandhi spent much of the next year in the Transvaal capital of Pretoria. It was here that he seems to have undergone the growth in personal confidence that would be necessary to his role as a leader. Perhaps his resentment of racism provided the energy. But his legal skills, literary ability, and command of English made him highly unusual in the small Pretoria Indian community, which was dominated by astute but poorly educated merchants. Gandhi was, in a short time, able to establish himself as the leader of the local community. He instituted regular community meetings, trained people in procedure and speaking techniques, urged better sanitary practices and a higher level of business on his followers, and taught English language classes. He successfully resolved the Dada Abdulla case through an out-of-court settlement, a technique that was to become the basis of his extensive and lucrative southern African legal career. By the time he returned to Durban, Gandhi had started to become an effective young leader.[13]

Gandhi was about to return to India, but at a Durban farewell party given for him by his merchant patrons, he saw a newspaper report that the Natal colonists' assembly was considering a measure to deprive those few Indians who had the vote on a qualified franchise basis of their right to it. Gandhi began a discussion of this issue with his hosts, characterizing the bill as striking at the root of Indians' self-respect. The assembled Muslim businessmen responded by calling on him to stay and fight the bill.[14] Gandhi portrays this decision in purely ethical and spiritual terms, and most biographers have taken him at his word. But as someone who was now a respected figure amongst the Indians in southern African, the return to poor prospects in India must surely have been unattractive. The state's move was certainly racist, but it affected only a tiny handful of rich merchants. What Gandhi had done was to create a rationale for himself to stay in southern Africa and to build on his local reputation.

The campaign on the franchise saw Gandhi make a first successful use of a whole gamut of techniques of which he was to become the master. A petition was organized and presented to the assembly, but nevertheless, the bill was passed. Gandhi then created a much more extensive petition campaign, with a structure of volunteers who fanned out across the countryside. The appeal was directed over the heads of the Natal colonists, to the Secretary for Colonies in London. Gandhi sent information to newspapers in Britain and India and received support from important publications in both countries. He went on to consolidate the gains of his campaign, founding the Natal Indian Congress as a permanent organization representing the interests of 'British Indians'. He established an education group and produced pamphlets. In the aftermath of the campaign, he also began to develop a practice of giving free legal advice to indentured workers, whose appalling social conditions he also began to publicize in India. Gandhi became a local and international lobbyist against the many forms of discrimination that Indians faced in Natal and the Transvaal.[15]

Gandhi was yet to elaborate a distinctive philosophy and political strategy. He was still working essentially in the interests of the merchant elite.[16] But he had already started to use his accumulated skills and his prominence in his part of the Indian diaspora to project globally himself and his campaign. There were important historical reasons why he was able to do this, and to progress to far more effective southern African-based campaigns.

First, Gandhi's years in southern Africa coincided almost exactly with what C. A. Bayly has called the period of the 'Great Acceleration'.[17] Bayly points out how, from 1890 to 1914, the global advance of rapid transport (steamships and railways), instantaneous global communication through the undersea telegraph network, and the international spread of newspapers interacted with the creation of new political movements. These circumstances generated unprecedented opportunities for astute political activists to publicize their cause internationally through the print media; and news from one country could be received in time to generate an immediate political response in another. Gandhi was to become a superb practitioner of this world media politics. He was particularly well placed to do so because of the uniquely complicated administrative position of India within the British Empire. There was an awkward, structurally conflictual relationship between the Viceroy's government in Calcutta and the India Office in London. By the 1890s, and even more in the subsequent decade, the Government of India was becoming concerned with managing the political demands of the Indian elite, and thus was alert to an emerging public opinion. The Viceroy claimed responsibility for disapora Indians, such as those in Natal, but in doing so came against the problem that other colonies – such as Natal – were subordinated to the Colonial Office in London. The Colonial Office was often concerned to conciliate settler opinion. But it also needed to moderate the worst racist excesses of the colonials to placate paternalist opinion in the UK. Thus it was to be possible for Gandhi to appeal to public opinion in India about the position of Indians in southern Africa with some prospect that the Viceroy's government would take an interest. He could then play on the tensions between the local interests of settler colonials and the broader interests of the imperial centre.

Second, the period was one of the rise of white racial states in the Anglophone world. Marilyn Lake and Henry Reynolds[18] have identified the turn of the century as a moment in which settler populations in Australia, New Zealand, southern Africa, British Columbia, and the western United States sought to create polities that were based in a populist protection of racially defined interests. These 'White Men's Countries' would supposedly guard white workers and small business people against the competition of people of colour. Frequently, the crucial impetus to these projects was given by attempts to prevent or stop Asian immigration. By the 1890s, white Natalians, now outnumbered by the Indians and regarding them as competitors in commerce and in the labour market, were pursuing measures aimed at making life in Natal less attractive to immigrants of colour. In 1895, Natal imposed a £3 annual tax on former indentured labourers, with the explicit intention of driving them to return to India. But, as Lake and Reynolds point out, it was precisely the international wave of racist mobilization that stimulated Asian nationalists to a new level of self-assertion. Gandhi was able to devise an innovative response to this changed racial politics.

In 1896, Gandhi returned to India. There, he made a deep and lasting friendship with the leader of the moderates in the Indian National Congress, G. K. Gokhale. He also spoke at public meetings about the sufferings of the Indians in southern Africa. Reported through the Reuters telegraph service, the news of his speeches caused outrage amongst the Natal colonists. When, towards the end of the year, he set off for Natal with his family on the *S.S. Courland*, he became the focus of a rabidly xenophobic campaign by the white workers and traders of Durban. The *Courland* sailed at the same time as another ship, the *S.S. Naderi*, and these two vessels came, in the minds of the Natal colonists, to embody the Asian threat. Not only was Gandhi, their detractor, arriving, the ships brought hundreds of new Indian workers. Moreover, the vessels had voyaged out during an international panic caused by an epidemic of bubonic plague, thought to have originated in India. A toxic mix of racial, political, and sanitary discourses mobilized the white Natalians. When the ships arrived off Durban, the authorities dealt with the situation by imposing a lengthy period of quarantine on the grounds of the danger of plague. But on 16 January 1897, Gandhi and his companions were allowed to disembark. They were met by a rampaging mob of more than three thousand men. Some demonstrators managed to isolate

Gandhi and beat him severely. He was saved from possible death by the intervention of Mrs. Alexander, the wife of the Durban police superintendent, who interposed herself between Gandhi and his assailants.[19] The demonstration against Gandhi was part of the lead up to the passage of what became known as the Natal Act, which enacted a literacy test for immigrants designed to exclude indentured labourers and traders. The Act pleased the Colonial Office, as it allowed the colonists to engage in racial exclusion in practice, while not embarrassing Whitehall by using explicitly racial labels. The Natal literacy test as a model of discriminatory immigration legislation was to be widely copied across the world.

The outbreak of war between the British Empire and the Boer republics of Transvaal and the Orange Free State in 1899 gave Gandhi an opportunity to press the claims of the Natal Indians as loyalists to the Empire. He offered to muster and lead an Indian ambulance corps. Gandhi was not without sympathy for the Boers; an understandable position, for the war had been blatantly engineered by the British proconsul, Sir Alfred Milner, and was surely not unconnected with British interest in the Rand's gold mines. However, Gandhi took the view that, in a war, subjects had a moral obligation to demonstrate their loyalty to the Crown if they were to enjoy the benefits of its protection. There was also a complex politics of masculinity at stake. Given the rampant British tendency to stereotype Hindus as weak and cowardly, it was important to demonstrate courage and fortitude, important in the Victorian discourse of manliness in which Gandhi was steeped. After much official resistance, the authorities, threatened by defeat with the advance of the Boers into Natal, gave permission for the unit to be raised. Gandhi organized it with conspicuous efficiency and success. The corps distinguished itself under fire, receiving some acclaim from the British authorities and even the colonists for their efforts.[20]

In 1901, Gandhi, his reputation at home further strengthened by his role in the war, returned to India. He may well have considered a political career there. Yet he still had apparently little to offer that any number of smart, British-educated, articulate Indian professional men did not. For all the respect he had earned in Natal, the role he could play was not apparent. The war in southern Africa came to an end after two-and-a-half years of bloody fighting. Thus at the end of 1902, when he was asked to return to southern Africa to represent the Indian communities in a meeting with visiting colonial secretary, Joseph Chamberlain, Gandhi accepted.

Once back in southern Africa, Gandhi began to develop an extensive legal practice in Johannesburg. While he retained footholds in Durban, the Transvaal, now under British occupation, became the main scene of Gandhi's activities. He became one of Johannesburg's more prominent and successful lawyers and took an elegant two-storey house in the suburb of Troyeville, from which he made the long walk to the city centre every morning.

Johannesburg was to be the most important city for Gandhi's personal, intellectual, and political growth. It was from here that he produced himself as a leader of unique qualities. On the face of it, the city was an unpromising venue for such an evolution. Presided over by mining magnates of legendary rapaciousness, the gold industry was run with an efficiency that took little account of the needs of the workforce and the wider community. It employed cheap African labour from all over southern Africa, as well as tens of thousands of Chinese indentured workers, in harrowing, dangerous, and disease-ridden conditions. Immigrant British workers provided mining and artisanal skills; but they found their supposedly high wages offset by the high cost of living, and were decimated by industrial lung disease, which killed many of them before the age of forty. The city was dominated by the yellow mine dumps, off which blew a continuous dust containing particles of cyanide used in the processing of the ore, and by scores of industrial chimneys belching smoke. The new British authorities did attempt to improve the planning and urban amenities of the town, with some effect. But they did so within a framework of intense colour discrimination and administrative brutalism. For example, when plague broke out in the inner Johannesburg slum occupied by Indian immigrants in 1904, Gandhi heroically tended the sick. The city administration responded by 'solving' the problem by using the fire brigade to burn down the whole area and move the people to a site on the far periphery of the city.[21]

Yet, in two respects, the city had an important creative impact on Gandhi. First, it was an exemplar of all the negative features of industrial capitalism, providing a context in which anyone of Gandhi's sensitivities would certainly have been inclined to question further the claims of modernity. Second, the city was extraordinarily cosmopolitan, with its African, Chinese, and Cornish miners, Scottish and English artisans and civil servants, Indian and Lithuanian traders, American mining engineers, and urbanizing Afrikaners impoverished by war. This cosmopolitanism produced a real intellectual and cultural ferment, in a way that was quite untypical of a philistine settler colonial town. Johannesburg could, then, have a strange appeal to those like Gandhi, open to the possibilities of reshaping themselves and the world they lived in. Gandhi's close friend, Rev. J. J. Doke, wrote of it in 1909 in the first published

Gandhi biography, that "the cosmopolitan character of the population forms at once the attractiveness and perplexity of the place. There is no cohesion, there is no monotony ... Surely of all places this is the most perplexing and perhaps the most fascinating. Few live here long without loving it".[22]

Although Gandhi was, throughout the 1890s, interested in spiritual questions, his time in Johannesburg provided the context not only of an intensification of this pursuit, but also of the elaboration of a connection between theology and political practice. A crucial role in this development was played by the presence in Johannesburg of a group of young, predominantly Jewish intellectuals who were influenced by the esoteric cult known as Theosophy. This somewhat bogus synthesis of Buddhist and Hindu themes had a considerable appeal to Western intellectuals of the time, feeding into their sense of disillusionment with science and rationality. Gandhi had met Theosophy's leaders in London, but he did not join the movement or become particularly attracted to it. The openness of the Theosophists to Indian religious thought had then stimulated Gandhi to begin studying the Bhagavad Gita. But Johannesburg was where Theosophy had its major intersection with Gandhi's life. There was an active Theosophy group in the city, and a number of its members became friends or supporters of Gandhi. These included Hermann Kallenbach from Germany and H. S. L. Polak from England, who were to play crucial parts in Gandhi's struggles. It was out of his discussions with the Johannesburg Theosophists that Gandhi began a much more intensive devotion to the study of the Hindu sacred texts. Thus there is a paradoxical way in which Gandhi's self-invention as an Indian spiritual figure came out of a connection with Western mystics.[23]

Gandhi's emerging spiritual thought was extremely eclectic. He had in his youth an extremely negative view of Christianity, but in London, he had read the Bible at the urging of a friend and had become enraptured with the Sermon on the Mount. In Pretoria, he had had a number of Christian acquaintances, and was drawn into theological discussion with them. He even attended an evangelical rally in the Cape Colony. Gandhi resisted all calls to convert to Christianity, arguing that different faiths represented varying paths to God, and that it was best to develop one's own faith. He had a respectful interest in Islam; he recalled being impressed by Carlyle's remarkably favourable account of the Prophet in *Heroes and Hero Worship*. He subsequently read the Koran. And of course, his long and warm collaboration with Muslim merchants meant that he had a good understanding of the faith.[24]

Another element of Gandhi's thought derived from Leo Tolstoy. The great novelist's quasi-anarchist, quasi-Christian ethical writing, with its advocacy of the simple life and its extreme hostility towards the state, attracted his attention in the 1890s, and would loom steadily larger in its influence as time went on. Gandhi was in a sense developing his own religion, largely Hindu in form, but infused with Christian, Islamic, Jewish, Jain, secular-philosophical, and Theosophist ideas and texts.

Gandhi acquired control of the newspaper *Indian Opinion*, which he used to propagate his views. In 1904, while taking a train trip from Johannesburg to Durban, he read a copy of John Ruskin's *Unto this Last*, which Polak had given him. Ruskin's text, with its denunciation of industrial society and its advocacy of the simple life, enraptured Gandhi. On arrival in Natal, he went to visit a relative who had a plot of ground some distance outside Durban. He at once conceived of the idea of establishing an experiment in communal living there. At this site, named Phoenix, he established a group of his followers who conducted agricultural activity and ran workshops, and he had the press and editorial office of *Indian Opinion* transferred there.[25] Six years later, Gandhi was to establish another commune in the Transvaal, at Tolstoy Farm, about twenty miles outside Johannesburg, a property bought for him by Kallenbach.[26] These projects embodied the anti-industrial ideals that Gandhi had absorbed from his reading of Tolstoy, Ruskin, and (later) Thoreau.

The demands of Gandhi's version of communal living were extremely rigorous and austere, involving much manual work, prayer, and moral earnestness. He made particularly harsh demands on his family. Kasturba resented some of the austerities to which she was subjected. Gandhi acted with considerable, if well-intentioned harshness towards his children, and denied them formal schooling because of its supposedly corrupting effects. The most troubled of the children, Harilal, in later life became an alcoholic dropout. The more dutiful Manilal remained in South Africa for most of his life, continuing to produce *Indian Opinion*, and playing an admirable role in South African politics: but he was not left with psychological scars.[27]

Another major step in Gandhi's redefinition of himself came with the Bambatha Rebellion in Natal in 1906. Several Zulu-speaking groups revolted against tax impositions, and a few outbursts of violence took place. Natal Colony mobilized its settler militia, and Gandhi once more, and for similar reasons as in 1899, offered the services of an Indian ambulance unit. The implausibly titled Sergeant Major Gandhi was horrified by what he saw. The colonial troops carried out a one-sided massacre. The ambulance corps tended to the Zulu wounded, but also had to look after the enormous number of Zulu systematically flogged by the colonials. This moment seems to have turned Gandhi towards the adoption of a more systematic (although not always consistent) pacifism. His feelings had a particular expression when, during the campaign, he decided that he would give up sex.[28] It is important here to recognize that such a renunciation was an established practice of Hindu devotion, known as brahmacharya. Gandhi's adoption of it was also part of his self-presentation as a holy man in the eyes to his followers, and certainly added to his prestige amongst devout Hindus. Nevertheless, Gandhi seems to have had a guilt and fear-ridden attitude to sexuality; in this respect, he was perhaps more a Victorian than a Hindu traditionalist. Gandhi seems to have seen sex as an inherently violent act and thus to have made a connection between the abandonment of war and chastity. Despite his determination to regard his female followers as sisters, there was a hint of misogyny in his relations to them.[29]

The paradox in Gandhi's theological expositions, celibacy, and communal living was that he was apparently withdrawing from the world, but at the same time, by making this asceticism an increasingly central part of his self-image, he was able to present himself as a figure of unique political authority. The contrast is perhaps best captured by the presence of a modern newspaper, with an extensive international network of contacts, at the heart of the Phoenix Settlement. Gandhi's nominally anti-modernist project was propagated through a classically modern set of technologies. And although his work was informed by a genuine sense of spiritual quest, his saintliness became important political capital.

The year 1906 was a turning point for southern Africa. In that year, a new Liberal government came to power in Britain. Ridden with guilt over the British role in the Boer War, the Liberals decided to confer representative government on the whites of the Transvaal and the Orange Free State. While the British had done little for people of colour in the former Boer republics over the last few years, this was a direct betrayal of the hopes of African and Indian elites for racial reform. In the Transvaal, General Louis Botha formed a government, with his lieutenant Jan Smuts as the driving force of the administration. Smuts, with British support, worked towards the union of the two former Boer republics, the Cape Colony and Natal. This was achieved in 1910, with Botha as the Prime Minister of the South African state and Smuts as his right-hand man. The constitution, based on a white franchise, represented the total surrender of Whitehall of the rights of people of colour to the interests of the Boers and the British settlers.

Thus, from 1906, there were few external constraints on settler policy. Driven by hostility to Indian immigration, Smuts was determined to pass what became known as the Black Act, under which all Asians in the Transvaal would be forced to register and give their fingerprints. Gandhi began to work with a committee of Muslims based at the Hamidia Mosque in Johannesburg to oppose the legislation. A rally of the Indian community was called at a local theatre. During the course of the meeting, one of the senior Muslims proposed that the meeting take a sacred oath to refuse to comply with the legislation. Gandhi had not anticipated such a move, but accepted the idea and the whole meeting voted for it. This was, arguably, the crucial moment in the development of Gandhi's strategy of resistance to unjust authority. Gandhi theorized his approach as satyagraha, a neologism meaning 'soul force' or 'firmness in Truth'. The term has sometimes been rendered as 'passive resistance', but to Gandhi there was nothing passive about it. In his conception, the satyagrahi, by refusing to comply with evil and suffering punishment by the state for it, brought the oppressor to a recognition of the wrong he was inflicting. Underlying it was the principle of ahimsa, meaning nonviolence. For Gandhi, political means had always to be consistent with their ends, and the satayagrahi could thus never act in a violent manner.[30]

In January 1908, Gandhi and a number of resisters were imprisoned for resisting registration. After only a few weeks, the negative international publicity that the Transvaal government was receiving led Smuts to summon Gandhi to Pretoria for negotiations. They agreed to a solution by which the community would register voluntarily rather than under legal compulsion, in exchange for the release of those arrested. Not all of Gandhi's supporters accepted this compromise, and he was beaten to within an inch of his life by a disgruntled volunteer. When Smuts reneged on his promise by going ahead with legal compulsion, Gandhi renewed the campaign with a mass burning of the registration certificates, and went to jail with his volunteers twice more in October to December 1908 and February to May 1909.[31] But as the Transvaal government continued to resist change, support for the satyagraha gradually collapsed. And when the Union of South Africa was formed in 1910, not only were the old anti-Indian policies maintained, but the new government went on to impose restrictions on the movement of Indians between provinces.

Yet the campaign was a breakthrough in Gandhi's conception of the Indian nation. In Natal, although he had taken up some of the grievances of indentured labourers, he had primarily represented the much more prosperous Muslim traders, who the Natal colonists treated somewhat less harshly. But in the Transvaal, all Indians were affected equally by the new racial legislation. All were insulted by the taint of criminalization represented by fingerprinting. By creating a common grievance, Smuts had given them a common interest. Gandhi was thus able to mobilize the Transvaal Indians around a single national identity, which overcame religious, ethnic, and caste divisions. Gujarati and Pathan Muslims, Telugu and Tamil Hindus, Parsis, and a handful of Christians were drawn into the campaign. This was made somewhat easier by the way in which the upheavals of migration inevitably disrupted the entrenched divisions of Indian daily life. Gandhi was able not only to envision, but also to put into practice, the ideal of a united Indian nation in a way that would have been much more difficult to do in India itself. In the motherland, 1905 to 1908 had seen the rise of a mass protest movement against the partition of Bengal, of anti-British terrorism, and the growing influence of the Maharashtrian radical B. G. Tilak. All of these developments were taking place largely within a violently Hindu chauvinist, anti-Muslim framework. Gandhi's inclusive and peaceful militancy offered a coherent and inspiring alternative. In an important sense, his practice of Indian nationalism began in Johannesburg.

And despite its apparent failure, the campaign was a political triumph for Gandhi in establishing him as a transnational public figure. The 1908 events made him internationally known; the *Times* of London for example gave extensive coverage to the campaign and discussed Gandhi, not unsympathetically, in its editorial columns. The Transvaal campaign took on immense symbolic significance for Indian nationalists, and Gandhi brilliantly publicized his activities in the Indian press, syndicating *Indian Opinion*'s stories on the struggle. The Government of India was keen to placate Indian elites by demonstrating sympathy with the southern African Indians. Gandhi sought to exploit the moment by making extended visits to England in 1906 and again in 1909, in which he was received by senior officials. He gained the support of a number of prominent experts on colonial policy in India, including Lord Ampthill, a former Acting Viceroy.

But the commitment of the Liberal government to conciliating the Boers and stabilizing a new 'white man's country' in southern Africa was too great to be offset by these efforts. Returning on the *R.M.S. Kildonan Castle* in late 1909, Gandhi drafted his manifesto *Hind Swaraj*, which synthesized his outlook and made bold new claims. *Hind Swaraj* is in the form of a debate between an 'editor' and a 'reader', the editor representing Gandhi's own views and the reader, the position of the violent terrorist nationalists who had become important in Bengal, and were even attracting some attention among Indians in southern Africa. In London, Gandhi had held discussions with the terrorist intellectual V. D. Savarkar. Perhaps driven by a sense of rejection in Britain, and influenced by Ruskin, Tolstoy, and Thoreau, Gandhi delivered a sweeping condemnation of modern Western civilization. It was based on violence, he charged; he deplored its form of state, its industrialism, and its militarism; he condemned its means of communications, its medical services, and its legal system. But, for Gandhi, the terrorist movement was ethically wrong because it simply wanted to create an Indian version of the same modern order. By using violent means, terrorists were accepting the values of their opponents. They would merely replicate the modern form of civilization, under Indian control. The alternative was the Indian civilization of old, based on rural virtues, small-scale production, and decentralization. To get there, the crucial means was swaraj (self-government) in the sense of personal self-control, which was essential to the practice of the satyagrahi. Only through a purity of political means and personal self-control could political self-rule be created.[32] The anti-modernist claims of *Hind Swaraj* were full of hyperbole and self-contradiction. Gandhi's political project depended on the modern technologies, which he denounced. But the book's statement of the means–ends question and its defence of the simple life were powerful, and placed Gandhi on the ethical high ground in relation to all possible competitors.

In writing *Hind Swaraj*, Gandhi had begun to position himself as a leader who presented a new path for Indian nationalism. He was at once providing a forceful denunciation of the terrorists and (more gently and respectfully) an alternative to the moderate leadership of the Congress around Gokhale, by questioning their modernist world views. By asserting that only the morally pure and self-governed could offer real political guidance, Gandhi was converting his acceptance of poverty, chastity, and communal living into essential qualifications for leadership. Gandhi was astute in his timing. Western power was under question as never before. The defeat of Russia by the Japanese in the war of 1904–5 had produced great nationalist enthusiasm across Asia and insecurity in the ranks of the colonial powers. The Bengal anti-partition movement had inaugurated a new era of mass participation in Indian nationalism. The time of the Indian National Congress's genteel lobbying was clearly over.

Over the next few years, Gandhi advanced his project further, with the development of the Tolstoy Farm project and continued lobbying of issues of racist legislation. He further raised his prestige in India in 1912 when he hosted a visit by Gokhale to South Africa. By early 1913, though, the crisis over the conditions of the Indians in South Africa came to a head. During his visit, Gokhale had met Botha and Smuts, and believed that they had agreed to address the Indian grievances through abolition of the Black Act and the £3 tax and new, deracialized immigration legislation. But in the new year, the draft bill showed no real improvement in the position, and the £3 tax was still in operation. On top of that, a High Court decision withdrew legal recognition of Hindu and Muslim marriages, which was felt as a tremendous insult by the Indian community. Because of the issue of marriages, Gandhi decided to initiate a new campaign in which women satyagrahis would take the lead, by crossing illegally from Natal into the Transvaal. The women's imprisonment sparked a mass strike by Indian mine workers in the Natal coal area, around the town of Newcastle. Gandhi moved to Newcastle to lead the protest, mobilizing his merchant supporters to feed the strikers. Gandhi was somewhat taken aback by the success of the movement, and clearly felt a certain class discomfort with his sudden elevation to the role of proletarian leader. But he was determined to lead the workers into action. The strikers and members of their families, numbering several thousand, set off for the Transvaal border. In the meantime, Gandhi met with the coal owners, getting them to pressure the government to relent on the £3 tax. Faced with such a substantial protest, the authorities did not attempt mass arrests, and the procession crossed the border at Volksrust on 6 November 1913. The march was about half the way from the border to Johannesburg when Gandhi was arrested. At the town of Balfour, the protestors were stopped, arrested, and returned by train to Natal. There, the government proclaimed the mines as prisons and subjected the workers to a punitive regime of forced labour. Simultaneously, strikes and protests spread amongst the Natal sugar plantation workers, galvanized by millenarian narratives of the coming of a powerful rajah, and were put down with considerable violence. Gandhi was imprisoned in Bloemfontein. Despite the suffering it involved, the protest was in the short term a triumph for Gandhi. The *Indian Opinion* office kept Gokhale supplied by telegraph with bulletins, and the elder statesman ensured that the situation of the South African Indians became again a central issue in Indian nationalist politics. Gandhi achieved remarkable success in his strategy of playing off the different components of the imperial structure against one another when Lord Hardinge, the Viceroy, made a speech condemning the South African government and even supporting the satyagrahis. The government proposed to appoint a commission to look into the grievances. Gandhi was released after only six weeks in prison. However, Smuts tried to solve the problem by appointing a commission to look into Indian grievances. The satyagrahis found the commission unacceptable and planned a revival of the campaign at the beginning of 1914. Gandhi was aware that Hardinge was against a renewal of the campaign and that Gokhale for that reason did not support it. But Gandhi saw an opportunity in Smuts's difficulties with white workers. In mid-1913, there had been a major strike by white miners on the Rand, culminating in arson, gun battles, and the shooting of twenty protestors by the British Army, and the government had been forced to concede the strikers' demands. By early 1914, Smuts, who genuinely believed that the white worker leaders were engaged in a syndicalist revolutionary conspiracy, was secretly preparing to crush the unions. Gandhi went to Pretoria to meet Smuts. Simultaneously, the railwaymen went on strike and a new white labour general strike erupted; Smuts decided to impose martial law. This enabled Gandhi to make an offer to assist the government by standing down his campaign, leaving Smuts to deal with his white labour opponents. In an agreement between Gandhi and Smuts, the abolition of the £3 tax and the legal recognition of Indian marriages were conceded. This was, however, at the price of an effective acceptance by Gandhi of an end to large-scale emigration from India, and abandonment of the attempt to end restrictions on interprovincial migration.[33]

The campaign saw the final stage in Gandhi's self-presentation of his persona as humble penitent. At Tolstoy Farm, Gandhi had replaced the smart suits he wore in his law office with European-style workers clothing; a statement of egalitarianism but not indigeny. It was during the 1913 campaign that he first appeared in public shaven headed and in the traditional Indian garb in which he is usually imagined. Far from this being a private decision, Gandhi was projecting his bodily appearance into the public arena as a political statement. The rise of photojournalism and the beginnings of the movies meant that he was able to stamp this image on the imagination of the world. And this involved a brilliant play with gender. Unlike other anti-colonial leaders, who aimed to portray themselves as masculine, modern, and (often) militaristic, Gandhi produced an image of his body that played on the British stereotype of the weak and feminized Hindu. Gandhi in his physicality and teaching, instead of conceding the coloniser's version of gendered identity, affirmed complex indigenous forms of masculinity, femininity, and ambiguity, and a new form of strength, that of the satyagrahi. His physical self-presentation was one with which the Indian poor could identify and which made repression of his movement by the authorities appear as bullying of the humble and vulnerable. Churchill's later notorious denunciation of Gandhi as a "naked fakir" was not just a rhetorical device, but represented frustration at the political problems that Gandhi's very appearance and his confounding of gender identities posed to his antagonists.[34]

Gandhi felt his work in South Africa was over. He travelled to England. With the outbreak of World War I, he offered again to raise an ambulance corps, but eventually made the voyage home. By 1913, he had become a charismatic figure, appealing to followers on the basis of his personal authority. Drawing on intellectual resources and political techniques that he had mastered in a campaign that spread across the world, he emerged as not only an Indian, but a global public figure.

Notes

1 N. C. Chaudhuri, *The Autobiography of an Unknown Indian* (first pub. in 1951; Mumbai, India: Jaico, 2000), p. 467.

2 C. Markovits, *The Un-Gandhian Gandhi: The Life and Afterlife of the Mahatma* (Delhi, India: Permanent Black, 2003).

3 For an overview of the literature by one of its more prominent authors, see B. R. Nanda, *Gandhi and His Critics* (New Delhi, India: Oxford University Press, 1985).

4 The term comes from E. Goffman, *The Presentation of Self in Everyday Life* (London: Penguin, 1990).

5 M. K. Gandhi, *An Autobiography* in *The Selected Works of Mahatma Gandhi*, vols. 1 and 2 (Ahmedabad, India: Navajivan, 1968).

6 Markovits, *Un-Gandhian Gandhi*, p. 51.

7 A. Yagnik and S. Seth, *The Shaping of Modern Gujarat: Plurality, Hindutva and Beyond* (New Delhi, India: Penguin, 2005), pp. 158–61.

8 The leading psychoanalytic account of Gandhi is E. H. Erikson, *Gandhi's Truth: On the Origins of Militant Nonviolence* (London: Faber and Faber, 1970). See also Gandhi, *An Autobiography*, pp. 40–4.

9 A. Burton, *At the Heart of the Empire: Indians and the Colonial Encounter in Late-Victorian Britain* (Berkeley: University of California Press, 1998).

10 Gandhi, *An Autobiography*, pp. 71–4.

11 L. Gandhi, *Affective Communities: Anti-Colonial Thought, Fin-de-Siecle Radicalism, and the Politics of Friendship* (Durham, NC: Duke University Press, 2006), pp. 67–114.

12 Gandhi, *An Autobiography*, pp. 156–74.

13 *Ibid.*, pp. 175–204.

14 *Ibid.*, pp. 205–8.

15 *Ibid.*, pp. 209–29.

16 M. Swan, *Gandhi: The South African Experience* (Johannesburg, South Africa: Ravan, 1985).

17   C. A. Bayly, *The Making of the Modern World 1780–1914: Global Connections and Comparisons* (Oxford, England: Blackwell, 2004), pp. 451–87.

18   M. Lake and H. Reynolds, *Drawing the Global Colour Line: White Men's Countries and the International Challenge of Racial Equality* (Cambridge, England: Cambridge University Press, 2008).

19   Gandhi, *An Autobiography*, pp. 275–91. Both ships were owned by Dada Abdulla.

20   *Ibid.*, pp. 320–3.

21   E. Itzkin, *Gandhi's Johannesburg: Birthplace of Satyagraha* (Johannesburg, South Africa: Witwatersrand University Press, 2000).

22   J. J. Doke, *M. K. Gandhi: An Indian Patriot in South Africa* (first pub. in 1909; Delhi, India: Government of India, 1970), p. 3.

23   M. Chatterjee, *Gandhi and his Jewish Friends* (Houndmills, England: Macmillan, 1992).

24   Gandhi, *An Autobiography*, pp. 102, 157.

25   *Ibid.*, pp. 443–9.

26   *Ibid.*, pp. 186–207.

27   U. Dhupelia-Mesthrie, *Gandhi's Prisoner? The Life of Gandhi's Son Manilal* (Cape Town, South Africa: Kwela Books, 2004).

28   M. K. Gandhi, *Satyagraha In South Africa, The Collected Works of Mahatma Gandhi* (New Delhi, India: Publications Division of the Government of India, Navajivan, 1958–94, 100 vols), vol. 29, pp. 466–73. (Hereafter, *CWMG.*)

29   M. C. Nussbaum, *The Clash Within: Democracy, Religious Violence and India's Future* (Cambridge, MA: Harvard University Press, 2007), pp. 94–108.

30   Gandhi, *An Autobiography*, pp. 86–93.

31   *CWMG*, vol. 29, pp. 93–178.

32   *Gandhi: Hind Swaraj and Other Writings*, ed. A. Parel (Cambridge, England: Cambridge University Press, 1997).

33   *CWMG*, vol. 29, pp. 183–269. Because Gandhi scholars have generally not understood the seriousness of the white labour challenge to the state in 1913–14, they have tended to underestimate its importance in Gandhi's ability to extract concessions from Smuts: see E. Katz, *A Trade Union Aristocracy: A History of White Workers in the Transvaal and the General Strike of 1913* (Johannesburg, South Africa: African Studies Institute, 1976).

34   R. C. Young, *Postcolonialism: An Historical Introduction* (Oxford, England: Blackwell, 2001), pp. 326–7.

3 Gandhi as nationalist leader, 1915–1948

JUDITH M. BROWN

INTRODUCTION

This chapter deals with Gandhi's life and work in India, from 1915, when he returned from South Africa, to his assassination in January 1948. This was the phase in his life when he became of central importance to the Indian nationalist movement, and a truly global political and moral figure. The chapter also provides readers with much of the historical evidence they need to know in order to progress to the following thematic chapters on aspects of his life and thought. One of the main messages of this collection of discussions about Gandhi is that, in his life, thinking and action were inseparable; this chapter considers both, alternating its vision between what Gandhi thought about his life and role and about the nature of the Indian nation for which he worked, and his specific activities. At the outset, it is helpful to consider the sources for this chapter, and also the broad chronological outline of Gandhi's activities in these years.[1]

SOURCES

The student of Gandhi's life and thought has access to a wealth of published primary sources. Some of these are the books and pamphlets that Gandhi wrote himself. These are discussed in the following chapter on his key writings. Amongst them are his *Autobiography*, his original pamphlet on what he meant by home rule for India (*Hind Swaraj*: 1909), and his exposition of his so-called constructive programme (1941).[2] We also have access to many of his letters, speeches, and articles in newspapers, as well as comments by his contemporaries in their written accounts of their times and their private papers, and the discussions on Gandhi's role in politics and how to deal with him by the British rulers of India, now accessible in the archives of the imperial government in India and the UK.[3]

CHRONOLOGY

Gandhi returned to India early in 1915. Although he had a significant reputation as the champion of Indians in South Africa, he was considered by many Westernized Indians to be a strange figure, someone who lived a deliberately simple life, and had strange fads about food and sex. He himself had no apparent wish for a political career, and settled down to establish a religious community or ashram around him in Ahmedabad in his native Gujarat. Here, he wished to practise a life of simplicity and prayer, where people of all backgrounds would be welcome. However, he increasingly felt drawn to comment on public affairs and to offer to those who seemed to be suffering from different kinds of oppression the technique of nonviolent resistance to wrong, which he had pioneered in South Africa and to which he had given the name satyagraha or truth force. (He led in 1917 a personal campaign of resistance on behalf of farmers forced to grow indigo in the province of Bihar, and in 1918 in his home region campaigns against the land revenue demand and the employers in the Ahmedabad cloth mills. It was significant that the 'wrongs' in each case were perpetrated by Indians, as well as by the British rulers.) However, in 1919–20, he was drawn into national politics and into the deliberations of the Indian National Congress, the major political organization that attempted to speak for the Indian nation and to claim political reform culminating in some form of home rule. In 1920, Gandhi suggested to Congress that it should support a nationwide campaign of non-cooperation with the British Raj in protest against two major political issues: the massacre of more than 300 bystanders at a meeting in Amritsar on the command of a British army officer; and the treatment, in the aftermath of World War I, of the Sultan of Turkey, revered as worldwide Khalifah by many Muslims, including those in India. Somewhat surprisingly, Congress agreed to this proposal, and a widespread campaign of protest ensued, bringing people on to the streets in hundreds of thousands, and causing the withdrawal of Indians at least temporarily from schools and courts. Ultimately, Gandhi called off the campaign early in 1922 because of outbreaks of violence among Indians themselves, which he felt was the negation of true satyagraha. There followed for him a period in prison, and then of comparative political quiescence, when he concentrated on building his ashram and influencing people through his speeches, writings, and letters. Most Congress supporters were not prepared for a long campaign of self-denial, and many wanted to work in the reformed legislatures that the British had set up in 1919, which offered them real political power, particularly in the provinces.

Gandhi's political career was in many ways rather like a switch-back, with periods of continental influence succeeded by times of quiet local work, particularly for socio-economic reforms on a small scale. In 1928–9, Congress again looked to him for inspiration when it seemed as if the British were not prepared to accede to Indian demands for more political reform and representation. Again, Gandhi was prepared to offer his compatriots the technique of satyagraha as a way of protesting and also putting pressure on a system of government that relied heavily on Indian cooperation. This time the issue he chose was to break the government's salt monopoly by making salt illegally. (This was an issue that touched all Indians regardless of religion, caste, class, or gender, and it seemed unlikely to precipitate violence such as that in 1922.) He began the action by his long march early in 1930 from his ashram to the coast of Western India, where he ceremoniously and in the glare of global newspaper publicity picked up salt on the beach. This campaign took on continental dimensions and was remarkable for it spread and depth. It lasted, with a break in 1931, until 1934. During the gap in campaigning in 1931, Gandhi was freed from prison and went to England for the second of a series of Round Table Conferences to discuss political reform. He was the only representative sent by the Congress and attracted huge publicity in the Western world. This second campaign, known as civil disobedience, petered out eventually, and it became evident that most Congressmen wanted to return to constitutional politics, particularly in the light of impending changes that would have enabled India to become a dominion within the British Empire and Commonwealth. It seemed as if Gandhi's overtly political role was at an end, and he concentrated on his programme of village reconstruction and on a campaign against Untouchability, the practice of treating those at the base of Hindu society as literally untouchable because they were perceived by the higher castes as ritually polluting. This seemed to him a great blot on Hindu tradition and society, and needed to be ended if India was to achieve real and moral self-rule. However, the outbreak of World War II provided the occasion for renewed civil resistance to the British, which culminated in the 1942 Quit India campaign, calling on the British to leave India. But India was of great material and strategic importance to Britain at war, and to her American allies, and the imperial government had no compunction about banning the Congress and locking up its leadership. When the war ended and the political prisoners were released, Indian politics were transformed. Britain, victorious in battle but financially crippled, had promised independence to India as early as 1942 in a bid for Indian wartime cooperation, and now the imperial rulers tried to disentangle themselves from their Indian Raj with haste yet decorum. Their major problem was the resistance by increasingly large numbers of Muslims to the idea of a single India where they might be dominated by a predominantly Hindu Congress. As hostile words turned to bitter violence on the streets, particularly of northern India, the British reluctantly conceded the idea of a partition on religious lines, which Indian politicians, also often with much reluctance, accepted. Gandhi was devastated. For him, India's identity had never been defined by religion, and he believed that all who had made their home in India over the centuries were Indian. He worked tirelessly to stop outbreaks of violence. But months after India was partitioned and the two states of India and Pakistan became independent, he was himself shot by a young Hindu man who believed Gandhi had betrayed his motherland by agreeing to partition. He died immediately on his way to conduct public prayers. Gandhi's death was greeted by a global outpouring of sorrow, but particularly from those such as Nehru who had worked so closely with him and knew that he was a man of profound vision and indomitable spirit, as well as a leader of the nation, the like of which they would not see again.

I. SELF-IMAGE AND GOALS

During Gandhi's lifetime and after his death, many 'Gandhis' developed in people's minds; many images of him took shape, as individuals and groups interpreted his work and teaching and appropriated him to further their own agendas. This was perhaps inevitable, considering how important and singular a figure he was. However, to understand Gandhi, it is important to go back to his own understanding of himself and his life, and to his fundamental goals.

The turning point in Gandhi's life occurred in the first decade of the twentieth century during his time in southern Africa. At this point, as an increasingly successful lawyer, he had discovered a vocation to public life in the service of the Indian community there and also to the pursuit of spiritual goals. As he was later to write, he had gone to South Africa for professional advancement, but instead found himself "in search of God and striving for self-realization".[4] Although he had been brought up in the Hindu tradition, he had increasingly learnt about other great world religions, and began to understand religion as the search for God, or, as he put it, Truth, rather than adherence to a particular religious tradition. He saw his own life as the search for Truth in personal matters of belief and practice, as well as in public and political participation in pursuit of morality. In his private life, this meant a drastic simplification of lifestyle and the development of simple communities of prayer and public service (ashrams) under his leadership, which became his home and professional base first in South Africa and then in India. His Indian ashrams in Ahmedabad, Gujarat, and then at Sevagram in central India were the powerhouses of his later movements, where he welcomed supporters and trained people who wished to follow his teaching and his nonviolent methods of action. For him, they were places akin to laboratories where he could attempt to solve in microcosm problems that afflicted India on a much larger scale.[5]

Gandhi's self-image was of a pilgrim searching for Truth. This was no private piety, though Gandhi paid great attention to personal discipline and religious devotion through prayer and study of scriptures. For him, Truth or God was to be sought in the wider world of human relations and societies, in working for the integrity of each individual and the fight against discrimination, deprivation, and violence. This took him into struggles to reform Indian society, on behalf of those who were despised or denied opportunities, particularly women and Untouchables. He believed passionately that God was to be found amongst the poor, and that service of all humanity and particularly the poor was the only way to personal salvation, moksha, or deliverance from self-bondage into the realization of one's true self in the service of Truth. Gandhi's embracing religious vision made him into a champion of simple village societies and economies where there should be sufficiency for all rather than great variations of wealth. It also took him into the world of nationalist politics, because he believed that British imperial rule was impeding Indians in their search for a moral polity and socio-economic order. He soon came to be called a Mahatma or great soul. However, when asked about himself, he would deny that he was a prophet or a holy man, or that there was such a thing as 'Gandhism' that he wished to spread. Rather, he was a man who was striving for personal integrity and salvation, someone who was constantly experimenting with ways of following Truth, whether this meant physical self-denial such as celibacy or a very limited diet, or involvement in small-scale social and economic experiments in reform, or in great public affairs.

Gandhi is principally known as a champion of nonviolence.[6] This was a central part of his self-image and his goals. He believed that non-violence was the only way to resolve any sort of conflict, from the smallest in his ashram to the great contest with imperial rule. Violence denied the integrity of those against whom it was used and also harmed the violent person, whereas nonviolence safeguarded the integrity of all involved and brought about true transformation in relationships and true 'change of heart'. It was the only way to lasting resolution of conflict. However, it demanded of the protagonist courage and discipline, as it might well involve hardship, particularly if it involved principled and peaceful breaking of the law. Gandhi first experimented with this in public life in South Africa, and called it satyagraha or truth force. He became convinced that it was his role in life to practice and teach satyagraha. When he returned to India with his little ashram community, he seemed to have had no idea that he would become involved in national politics. However, through the practice of nonviolence in local, small-scale conflicts in Bihar and in Gujarat, he not only became known in political life but began to sense that this might be an arena where he could and should suggest the practice of satyagraha. By 1920, he was convinced that British rule in India was such a serious public 'wrong' that he launched his first major campaign of non-cooperation with the British Raj through the Congress party.

2. VISION OF THE NATION AND SELF-RULE: WHAT IS SWARAJ (SELF-RULE)?

Gandhi's vision of an Indian nation and what might be meant by swaraj or self-rule differed greatly from the views held by many of his contemporaries. There was no universal or commonly accepted idea of what was meant by a 'nation' in India. The British denied such a political community existed because of the many differences of region, language, religion, and social division on the subcontinent. Some Indians defined the nation by reference to religion. In the early twentieth century, a significant body of opinion held that 'being Indian' rested on Hindu culture and society, and that many of the minorities in India such as Muslims or Christians did not belong to that nation – despite the fact that the vast majority of such people were descended from people who had lived in India for centuries, if not millennia. Some Muslims by contrast began to argue that they constituted another complete nation with its own claims to political autonomy. Others – and probably the majority – agreed that all those who lived in India were potential members of an India in the process of finding a modern national identity. Jawaharlal Nehru spoke passionately of India as a composite nation, while Gandhi believed that all those who lived in India were brothers and that no nation was ever defined by religious identity.[7] He poured his energy into fostering what he called communal unity. For him, perhaps the greatest tragedy of the end of British rule was the partition of the subcontinent and the rending of the community that he thought constituted the nation.

For most of Gandhi's contemporaries, swaraj – self-rule – meant simple political independence from British imperial control, and when they opposed British rule, they did so on the basis that the British ruled India in British rather than Indian interests. They believed that India had a right to self-determination, but also that once she had achieved that goal, she could use the powers of the state to achieve desirable social and economic goods for her people. For Gandhi, the problem of British rule was a moral one – not the denial of self-determination but the fact that British rule, as he saw it, trapped India in a world where violence was rampant and where society was organized on competitive lines as people scrambled for wealth and power. He longed for what he saw (unhistorically and erroneously) as India's spiritual civilization where people lived in small-scale, self-sustaining communities, where cooperation replaced competition, and community prevailed against dominance and exploitation. Consequently, he was far less interested than many of his contemporaries, in particular political arrangements as part of swaraj, though he agreed that, at least as an interim measure, some form of parliamentary democracy free from British rule should be India's goal. For him, true swaraj was a construction by Indians themselves of a new society and polity whose hallmarks would be nonviolence, harmony between people of different religious traditions, the abolition of Untouchability, and the development of an economy based on simplicity and self-sufficiency, whose symbol was the use of khadi, or hand-spun cloth. This broad-based programme of practical construction lay at the heart of his vision of swaraj.[8] He returned to it time and again when he parted company with his political colleagues on questions of policy and strategy, and when there seemed to be no place for him in the Congress and no appetite amongst his compatriots for the practice of satyagraha.

3. THE POLITICS OF NATIONALISM

The discussion so far shows how ambiguous a figure Gandhi was in Indian public life. We need to explore this further to understand Gandhi's role in the politics of nationalism. Right from his return from South Africa, the educated leaders of the growing nationalist movement commented how strange he seemed, with his insistence on the simple life and his apparent desire to do away with many of the benefits, as they saw them, of a constructive modernity ushered in by British rule – such as modern transportation including the railways, a more industrial economy, and many of the modern professions such as medicine and law. For Gandhi, these were the signs of a false civilization; for many others, they were the tools that would help India become a powerful state in the modern world. Nonetheless, Gandhi achieved a position in Indian political life like no politician before him. Very few of his contemporaries became true 'Gandhians', though he attracted much interest, affection, and at times popular adulation, which distressed him. Amongst some of the less educated, he acquired a reputation akin to that of a wonder-working religious figure. Even among the highly educated and Westernized, there was a sense of huge excitement and hope at what he offered Indians. Jawaharlal Nehru gives insight into this excitement and the prospect of release from the moderate politics of cooperation with the British, which Gandhi gave his generation in the first movement of non-cooperation. "Many of us who worked for the Congress programme lived in a kind of intoxication during the year 1921. We were full of excitement and optimism and a buoyant enthusiasm ... Above all, we had a sense of freedom and a pride in that freedom. The old feeling of oppression and frustration was completely gone. There was no more whispering, no roundabout legal phraseology to avoid getting into trouble with the authorities. We said what we felt and shouted it out from the house-tops".[9] Prison in pursuit of the cause held no fears. Moreover, they had a real sense of moral superiority over the British, in terms of their goal and their non-violent methods, and a pride in their new leader and what seemed his unique method of resistance to the imperial ruler.[10] From then until his death, nobody in India could make major all-India political decisions without reference to Gandhi's position and likely reactions – whether they were the British themselves, Gandhi's opponents, or those who were potentially if not permanently his followers.

By the second decade of the twentieth century, India under British rule had a very complex political system; it was within this system that Gandhi achieved a particular and unprecedented political role. India was made up of a number of distinctive regions, fashioned by geography, language, and history, and each had its own patterns of dominance that fed into emerging modern styles of politics. Like a palimpsest, over these older patterns of power were laid new patterns of wealth and influence by the presence of Western rulers and the career opportunities offered to those who took to English medium education and went into a variety of new professions such as teaching, medicine, law, and government service. Gandhi himself and Nehru had both received some of their education and professional training abroad in order to take advantage of such opportunities and sustain their family fortunes in a time of transition. Perhaps the most striking political change was the development of new political institutions from all-India level to the province and down to the localities, as the imperial rulers engaged in political reforms to attract Indian allies in the processes of legislation and governance. The numbers of British in India were tiny by comparison with the millions of their Indian subjects; so were their financial resources for government. So they needed the active support of Indian taxpayers, Indian officials at low levels of government, Indian soldiers, Indian professionals of many kind, and increasingly educated Indian men who would work through the new legislatures at provincial and continental level, thereby giving the British Raj legitimacy and wide support. However, increasingly, the educated, who were so vital to British rule, were drawing on their knowledge of Western patterns of politics and Western ideals of nationalism, and were making demands for increased power to Indian hands. Drawn together by common professional ties, as well as skills, and a common language, English, they founded numerous political organizations, which had as their apex the Indian National Congress. By the time Gandhi returned from South Africa, it was a successful umbrella organization, speaking in the name of Indian nationalism. However, there was always tension within it between the local priorities of groups of members, coming from their own regions with their particular power structures, and potential all-India strategies to gain concessions from the British. So far, it had only engaged in the politics of cooperation or petition and demand, and it had no way of exerting direct and significant leverage on the British. It was Gandhi who provided this means of leverage at various times between 1920 and 1947, when India gained independence.

Gandhi's aim, as we have seen, was to build a swaraj or self-rule that had broad socio-economic implications, as well as political independence. His chosen means were his constructive programme and, on occasion, the use of satyagraha, nonviolent resistance to perceived wrong or injustice. He was above all an all-India leader. He was not rooted in any regional structures of power, and had no solid power base in any particular locality, from which he might have exerted continental influence. Rather, he offered a combination of attributes and skills to his compatriots, which persuaded many of them at distinct times that an all-India alliance with him made good political sense, both in terms of their own regions and in terms of a pan-Indian struggle with the imperial rulers. As we saw in the chronology at the start of this chapter, there were three main times when Congressmen turned to Gandhi and what he could offer them when their own more conventional politics seemed to have brought them to a political dead end, in the sense of failing to put pressure on the British over very important issues. In 1920-2, Congressmen took the most unusual step of agreeing to a strategy of non-cooperation with the British when the issues of the Amritsar massacre and the treatment of the Khalifah indicated that, despite the 1919 constitutional reforms that had just extended considerable power to elected Indian representatives in expanded central and provincial legislatures, the British were unwilling to listen to Indian protest. The campaign only ended when Gandhi himself called it off for fear of violence amongst Indians. In 1930-4, Congress, after a period of cooperating in constitutional politics, again turned to satyagraha, in this case, forms of civil disobedience, as a way of pressurizing the British into further constitutional reform. Then, during World War II in 1940-2, they turned to Gandhi again to find ways of protesting against Indian implication in the war, and eventually to demand that the British quit India completely. In each case, as in 1922, once the immediate crisis was over, Congressmen reverted to constitutional politics, successfully exploiting the opportunities of successive constitutional reforms, and building a political machine and culture, deeply rooted in their regions, which brought them to power at independence. Once the British had made clear that India would be independent after the war, even though this meant the partition of the country, Gandhi really had no further political role to play, and a younger generation of men led India into independence. Independence for Gandhi was not true swaraj, and when a young Hindu assassinated him in January 1948, he was tired and distressed at the route his country had taken.

What was it that Gandhi had to offer his fellow Indians during those key phases when he exerted such power in Indian politics? Of course, in the first place, he offered them a new strategy – that of nonviolent resistance to the British. We shall turn to this in more detail later in this chapter, but for the moment, it is important to remember that this was an innovative way of dealing with a regime that relied heavily on Indian cooperation, and which might be seriously shaken by the withdrawal of key aspects of that cooperation. Gandhi was also a deeply creative politician, and developed many ways to participate in satyagraha (such as making salt, boycotting foreign cloth, and withdrawing from schools, colleges, and courts), which opened political participation up to a far wider social span of Indians. The practice of satyagraha was not an elite educated enterprise as earlier politics had been. So thousands more people were involved in the political process, which in its turn put pressure on the regime, particularly when so many went willingly to prison. Gandhi involved people of humble background, young people and women in their thousands, who now felt they could come on to the streets with propriety. Not only was Gandhi a strategist, he also played other major and valuable roles in the Congress, as a fund-raiser and organizer of what had, until 1920, been a loose connection of disparate allies rather than a functioning political party. He was also a peacemaker and concilator among Congressmen of very different political backgrounds and persuasions. He believed passionately in Indian unity – and in the need for unity in Congress – and he did all he could to hold the Congress together by his choice of techniques of satyagraha, as well as his profound personal influence on those who gathered round him. This was not only important as a precondition to a strong political campaign; it also worked to convince the British that Congress really spoke with a legitimate national voice rather than being an educated and isolated pressure group.

Gandhi's growing public image in India and abroad was also significant in what he could offer Congressmen. In India, he was known far more widely than any earlier politician, and his fame had reached deep into the countryside, as well as into towns and cities. He was often seen as a holy man, a miracle worker, a great soul, and became the object of popular adulation and veneration.[11] But this meant that he could bring the message of swaraj to a far wider swathe of the Indian people. He travelled widely, as often as possible spoke in a vernacular language, and described swaraj in practical terms, which ordinary people could understand. As a publicist, he was immensely important for Congress because he brought to the organization and its campaigns and demands popular backing that the British could not ignore. Further, Gandhi was becoming well known abroad, from his writings, the reports by foreign journalists of his activities and teachings, and from his visit to England in 1931. In England itself, there was a group of people who were his supporters or were concerned at the regular imprisonment of such a holy figure; and they pressed their concerns on the British government. His wider repute and support, particularly in the United States, increasingly meant that the British had to consider their Western allies when they made policy for India.

Gandhi realized that many Congressmen viewed nonviolence as a utilitarian strategy rather than as a moral imperative as he did. Consequently, he was realistic about the temporary and limited commitment of most of those who 'followed' him in nonviolent campaigns to satyagraha. He was prepared to end campaigns when he realized that the majority were no longer with him; and while they reverted to constitutional politics and plucked the fruits of political collaboration with the British,[12] he returned to his constant commitment – building swaraj from the bottom up from his ashram base.

So far, we have discussed Gandhi's contribution to the politics of nationalism, and the ambivalent and conditional support of many in Congress for him and his strategies. But we need to note the opposition to him as well, and the fact that many did not share his vision of the Indian nation. One small but significant group were those who shared his hopes for independence and his vision of a nation that was inclusive, but were concerned about his methods. They were essentially moderates in politics who feared the breaking of the law, even without violence, because they believed it would build a popular contempt for the law, which boded ill in independent India. One such person was the noted South Indian, Srinivasa Sastri, highly regarded in India and in Britain, whose letters to friends and to Gandhi himself showed his anguish at Gandhi's methods.[13] There were also those who disputed Gandhi's vision of an inclusive nation. Those who saw India as a Hindu nation opposed his commitment to cooperation with Indian Muslims and his vision of India's future where all minorities would be welcome. They believed he was falsely claiming to be a committed and devout Hindu, and at least some blamed him for partition – as did his assassin. Many Muslims for their part were increasingly fearful of a politics couched in the language of religion by a Hindu Mahatma, and believed that once the British had gone, they would be at the mercy of the Hindu majority and a well-organized Congress that was largely Hindu in composition. The claim that Muslims were a second nation on the subcontinent had compara-tively little support until World War II, but it drew for its success on a swell of fear that Gandhi had been unable to prevent, despite his personal commitment to partnership with Muslims in a new India. Yet others who feared Gandhi were many of the Untouchables, despite his campaign for their better treatment in India. They saw him as a paternalist Hindu who would never agree to social revolution of the sort that would really trans-form their position. The ambiguity of public response to Gandhi demon-strated not only the difficulties of his position as a nationalist leader; it also underlined the contested nature of the Indian nation itself, particu-larly in the final years of British rule, when the shape of the nation-state to succeed imperial rule was becoming a real and urgent issue.

4. THE PRACTICE OF CIVIL RESISTANCE
IN LATE COLONIAL INDIA

Gandhi's later reputation as an Indian leader rests largely on his role as the initiator of civil resistance. It is therefore important to remember that Gandhi himself thought that civil resistance was only part of his far broader work of constructing swaraj from the grass roots upwards, though of course nonviolence was a central principle of his life. In his late exposition of his constructive programme in 1941, he spelt out the particular functions civil resistance could perform in this broader framework, and in a memorable phrase concluded, "For my handling of civil disobedience without the constructive programme will be like a paralysed hand attempting to lift a spoon".[14] Nonetheless, civil resistance was such a distinctive hallmark of the Indian nationalist movement in the final decades of British rule that we should examine it more closely, in particular the dilemmas its practice posed for Gandhi.[15]

In South Africa, and then in a number of local movements in India in 1917–18 and 1928, Gandhi offered in person, or as the leader of a group of protesters, civil resistance in response to very specific issues. These were issues where the opponent (whether the government or a group such as employers or landlords) could in fact resolve the issue by specific action. They involved only small close-knit groups of protesters who could be disciplined or could discipline themselves during the campaigns. This was very different, as Gandhi soon found, from trying to use nonviolence in the service of pan-Indian issues and as part of the broader campaign for swaraj. However, in broad strategic terms nonviolent non-cooperation with the British imperial regime made sense because of its particular nature. It relied very heavily on Indian cooperation and acceptance for its key civilian and military personnel, its finance, and its legitimacy. Moreover, it always had an eye to its democratic masters at home in London, the British public and Britain's international allies, and could not afford to be seen as an imperial regime that held on to power by violent repression. Therefore, nonviolent resistance was an ideal way to probe its particular vulnerability. Even so, to put nonviolent resistance into practice on an all-India scale posed Gandhi serious dilemmas, particularly given the political system we have already considered.

For Gandhi, the first dilemma was that of the issue or set of issues on which to launch civil resistance. He believed these had to be relatively small-scale or symbolic issues where the British could be expected to take action to meet Indian demands rather than on the great issue of freedom itself. "Civil disobedience can never be directed for a general cause such as for independence. The issue must be definite and capable of being clearly understood and within the power of the opponent to yield".[16] They had to be issues that would appeal to people across India and through as many levels of society as possible. If they were purely sectional, they would not generate enough support to put pressure on the British or substantiate the claim that this was a national and popular protest. They also had to be symbolically effective both in India and abroad. At home, this meant choosing issues that reflected an aspect of freedom and symbolically displayed swaraj in ways ordinary people, as well as the educated, could understand. Abroad, they had to enable Indian opponents of the British to claim the high moral ground in their resistance and generate foreign sympathy. They also had to be issues that were unlikely to generate violence among Indians themselves: this was something Gandhi recognized painfully after he had to call off his first major campaign in 1922 because of violence against Indian policemen. For these complex and interlocking reasons, Gandhi often chose unusual and unexpected issues – the boycott of foreign cloth and government liquor shops in 1920–2, resistance to the government salt monopoly in 1930, or, in 1940, individual protests against Indian involvement in the war effort. Although they differed significantly from the issues round which constitutional politics crystallized, many of his contemporaries quickly realized Gandhi's creativity and popular touch in choosing them.

The next set of problems confronting Gandhi was how to educate and discipline the much larger numbers of protagonists in all-India satyagraha campaigns compared with the small-scale local ones. This was vital in order to protect nonviolence – important for itself in Gandhi's eyes, but also to preserve Indian unity and to remove the excuse for a crackdown on protest, which violence and disorder would have given the British. Gandhi threw himself into the role of educator and publicist, using his speeches, personal letters, and writings in his two newspapers, *Young India* and *Navajivan*, to spread his message about the nature of nonviolent resistance, the characteristics expected of campaigners, and the sort of actions that could and could not be undertaken.[17] He masterminded the way campaigns were conducted and escalated, and on occasion he actually vetted the people who were allowed to participate, as in 1940 during the individual protests against the war effort. Moreover, if violence broke out (as in 1922) or if popular support was clearly ebbing (as in 1934) he was prepared to call off the campaign or to pronounce that he alone would continue it. Problems in enforcing discipline reflected not just the large numbers now involved in popular protest, but the regional nature of Indian politics and the weakness of existing political organizations. Gandhi had to rely to a large extent on the Congress organization as the means to organize nonviolent resistance. But despite his attempt to streamline the party and give it local substance in 1920–2, by 1928 when another campaign of nonviolence was imminent, he discovered that the Congress in the provinces was often little more than a group of lawyers for whom politics was a part-time occupation, or even a nameplate on a door. As a party, it was also poor, often too poor to sustain a long drawn-out campaign, particularly when activists were anxious to return to constitutional politics. So Gandhi had to rely on his personal reputation and energy, and on his closest adherents in his ashram communities to set examples and be the hub of nonviolent campaigns. However, in retrospect, when civil resistance became truly popular, this was not because of good organization or mass commitment to Gandhi's views and strategies, but rather the dovetailing of all-India programmes with regional and local movements of protest. Where local people saw Gandhian nonviolence as a vehicle for their own needs and protests, the movements 'took off' locally. But the consequence was that they were less controllable, less amenable to discipline, and more likely to break the rules that Gandhi set for real satyagraha.

The final question we must address is one of 'efficacy'. Did nonviolence work politically and what did it achieve? These are not of course questions that Gandhi would have asked. He believed that if someone really practised nonviolence, this inevitably changed a situation of conflict by its effects on the protagonist and opponent. When satyagraha appeared not to work, he maintained that it had not been real satyagraha. This was his response at the end of his life, when his last pan-Indian movement disintegrated in violence and a government crackdown, and when simple political independence, rather than true swaraj, was achieved in 1947. For the historian, as opposed to a Gandhian, it is, however, possible to ask what nonviolence achieved in the context of India's nationalist movement. It clearly gave Indian activists a method of opposition to the British, which helped to make the movement relatively peaceful compared with other movements for the ending of imperial rule.[18] But it did not make the British Raj impossible, except in rare instances in specific places. Government effectively broke down on the Malabar Coast, for example, in the 1920–2 non-cooperation movement when Gandhi's movement drew strength from an anti-landlord protest. Or again, in Bihar in 1942, government communications had to be carried on with small planes borrowed from a local flying club because activists had cut normal communications by rail and telegraph. But on a broad scale, the British imperial regime kept functioning and retained the loyalty of sufficient of its Indian employees and allies in paid employment and in the political institutions it had set up. However, in some ways, nonviolent protest was a profound nuisance for the government, cutting its revenue streams (e.g. from its liquor monopoly), clogging city roads with protestors, and of course filling the prisons with political prisoners who were delighted to stay there causing government expense and inconvenience. In the longer term, Gandhi's nonviolent campaigns did not bring about the British decision to leave India. This was a decision precipitated by wartime politics, but also reflective of the declining significance, over a longer period, of India to Britain and its Empire. However, as the British government in London was contemplating the timing of British withdrawal from India, it was aware that any further large-scale campaigns of civil resistance would be politically and practically impossible to combat given the declining power of the British regime in India. There were other domestic repercussions of Gandhi's campaigns. The experience of campaigning together and going to prison together bonded a whole political class, and increasingly gave them public repute as those who had suffered in the cause of independence. For at least a decade after independence, the cachet of having been a Gandhian worker or a prisoner for nonviolent protest was a powerful resource for those who sought election to the legislatures. The shared experiences of protest, prison, and working with Gandhi also helped to bind together a generation of Congress politicians, thus helping to give Indian politics stability and some unity in the turbulent times of 1947 and beyond – a rare characteristic for new nation-states emerging from the processes of decolonization.

CONCLUSION: IMAGE AND REALITY

Gandhi's public image at the time of Indian independence was unparalleled. Despite the limitations of his pan-Indian campaigns, the ambivalence of most of his contemporaries to his deepest views and hopes for India, and the outright hostility of many to him, he had become the symbol of India's campaign for freedom. His colleagues in the Congress and the representatives of the departing British regime alike treated him in some sense as the father of the new nation of India. He had never been elected as a representative of Indians at any level in the country's political system; he had held no public office except briefly in the Congress itself. His home was a simple religious community where he was likely to be found praying, keeping days of silence, and writing. He made no profit from public work and had no political power in ordinary terms. But he had become a magnet for millions, a symbol of something they hoped for, a figure of meaning and stability in a fast-changing world. When he was assassinated, the country was plunged in grief, and the circumstances of his death only increased his reputation, lifting him for decades beyond criticism or rigorous historical analysis. Sixty years after his assassination, when historical records are open for examination, and the legend can be assessed against reality, the image against practical achievement, it is possible to see how Gandhi came to achieve a unique position of influence and leverage in Indian public life. We can also assess the nature of popular support for him, the ambiguities of his political career, and the limitations of his nonviolent movements. Nonetheless, he remains a crucial figure in the history of Indian nationalism. Perhaps more significantly, he remains to a far wider audience an example of an idealist in politics, a man with deeply held values and a religious vision who insisted that these demanded of him political involvement and action. For him, personal and public life could not be divorced, means and ends were intimately connected, and public life was an arena for service rather than achievement and gain. His is an example that challenges our contemporaries, as it did his own.

Notes

1 For a detailed account of Gandhi's life, see Judith M. Brown, *Gandhi. Prisoner of Hope* (New Haven and London: Yale University Press, 1989).

2 A convenient selection of Gandhi's writings, which includes sections of these works, is Judith M. Brown (ed.), *Mahatma Gandhi. The Essential Writings*, new edition (Oxford, England: Oxford University Press, 2008). His letters, speeches, and also many key writings are available in *The Collected Works of Mahatma Gandhi* (New Delhi, India: Publications Division of the Government of India, Navajivan, 1958–94, 100 vols). (Henceforth, *CWMG*.)

3 For official government sources and private papers, see those cited in the footnotes of my works on Gandhi; e.g., *Gandhi. Prisoner of Hope*. An example of a contemporary who wrote much about Gandhi is Jawaharlal Nehru: see his *An Autobiography* (London: John Lane, The Bodley Head, 1936).

4 M. K. Gandhi, *An Autobiography or The Story of My Experiments with Truth*, trans. Mahadev Desai, first pub. in serial form in 1927, part II, chapter XXII.

5 For a selection of texts on Gandhi's ashrams, see Judith M. Brown (ed.), *Gandhi. Essential Writings*, pp. 105–32.

6 For a selection of texts on what Gandhi meant by nonviolence and how it should be practised, see *ibid.*, pp. 309–73.

7 *Gandhi: Hind Swaraj and Other Writings*, ed. A. J. Parel (Cambridge, England: Cambridge University Press, 1997), pp. 52–3.

8 On Gandhi's vision of swaraj, see the texts in Judith M. Brown (ed.), *Gandhi. Essential Writings*, pp. 133–307. This section contains significant parts of two key texts, *Hind Swaraj* (1909) and the *Constructive Programme* (1941).

9 Nehru, *An Autobiography*, p. 69.

10 *Ibid.*, p. 70.

11 For an excellent case study of Gandhi's popular image in one locality, see S. Amin, 'Gandhi as Mahatma: Gorakhpur District, Eastern UP, 1921–2', R. Guha (ed.), *Subaltern Studies III. Writings on South Asian History and Society* (Delhi, India: Oxford University Press, 1984), pp. 1–61.

12 A detailed study of Congress and the priorities of its members is B. R. Tomlinson, *The Indian National Congress and the Raj, 1929–1942* (London and Basingstoke: MacMillan, 1976).

13 See, e.g., Sastri to P. Kodanda Rao, 10 October 1932, and to Gandhi, 27 August 1933, T. N. Jagadisan (ed.), *Letters of the Right Honourable V. S. Srinivasa Sastri* (Bombay, India: Asia Publishing House, 1963), pp. 237–9, 258–60.

14 Judith M. Brown (ed.), *Gandhi. Essential Writings*, p. 184.

15 For a detailed discussion of Gandhi's civil resistance movements, see Judith M. Brown, *Gandhi's Rise to Power: Indian Politics 1915–1922* (Cambridge, England: Cambridge University Press, 1972); *Gandhi and Civil Disobedience: The Mahatma in Indian Politics 1928–34* (Cambridge, England: Cambridge University Press, 1977); 'Gandhi and Civil Resistance in India, 1917–47: Key Issues', A. Roberts and T. Garton Ash (eds.), *Civil Resistance and Power Politics: The Experience of Nonviolent Action from Gandhi to the Present* (Oxford, England: Oxford University Press, 2009), pp. 43–57.

16 Judith M. Brown (ed.), *Gandhi. Essential Writings*, p. 183.

17 See the rules for satyagrahis he issued in 1930, *ibid.*, pp. 332–4.

18 Where violence by nationalists and the imperial regime was a feature of movements for decolonization, this was often in situations where there was white settler regime in place (as in Kenya) or where there was a Communist movement (as in Malaya). The Indian experience clearly set a pattern for potentially peaceful ends to empire, which was to be very important in the next two decades.

Part II

Gandhi: Thinker and activist

4 Gandhi's key writings: In search of unity

TRIDIP SUHRUD

M. K. Gandhi in his autobiography wrote, "What I want to achieve – what I have been striving and pining to achieve these thirty years – is self-realization, to see God face to face, to attain moksha. I live and move and have my being in pursuit of this goal".[1] Gandhi asserted that all his speaking, writing, political work, and experiments in the spiritual realm were directed towards the attainment of this desire. As this desire became stronger with the passing years, he increasingly gave himself up to *Ramanama* (recitation of the name of the god, Rama, conceived as Truth). In the weeks preceding his assassination, Gandhi repeatedly spoke of his desire to submit and surrender to *Ramanama* and have Ram's name on his lips at the moment of death.[2]

If this was his principal quest, we must ask how it informs his seven books.[3] There is no apparent thematic unity among these works. *Hind Swaraj* is a dialogue between Indian civilization and modern Western civilization, between civilization and its reverse, between those who see ends as justification of means, and those who see means and ends as inviolably related. *Satyagraha In South Africa* is an account of the struggle for dignity and equality of the Indian people in South Africa. The autobiography is the story of a soul in quest of Truth. *From Yeravda Mandir* and *Ashram Observances in Action* are a reflection on ashram vows and the experiences of the ashram community in leading a life committed to these vows. *Constructive Programme: Its Meaning and Place* is best described as a handbook, a guide to action meant for those seeking a nonviolent, non-exploitative society for India. *Key to Health* is a reflection on the nature of the body, disease, and healing, while *Anasakti Yoga* is a translation of the Bhagavad Gita.

Thematic unities and disjunctions become apparent only when we examine each work separately and discern an underlying concern that unites them.

HIND SWARAJ

Hind Swaraj was written aboard the *Kildonan Castle* in 1909. It was originally written in Gujarati and published in two instalments in the Gujarati section of *Indian Opinion*.[4] It was soon banned in India, not because it advocated revolt or the use of physical force against British rule in India, but because it advocated a 'dangerous thought', that of passive resistance or satyagraha. In March 1910, Gandhi published an English rendering – 'hurriedly dictated' to a European friend, Hermann Kallenbach – as *Indian Home Rule*.[5] *Hind Swaraj* is philosophically located at a fleeting, tantalizing moment in human history. It is located at a moment where it is still possible to conceive of life outside the realm of the modern universe. In this moment, two modes of life and thought are present simultaneously. A mode of life that we call a-modern. A-modern is not anti-modern. It is not non-modern in the sense that it signifies absence of modernity. It is something that lies outside the modern realm and has to be conceptualized without a necessary and inevitable referent to the modern. The other mode of life and thought that is present is modern civilization. *Hind Swaraj* should be read as a text that was written at a moment in history where both the a-modern and modern universe exist simultaneously, however fleeting that moment might have been.[6]

Gandhi's deep unease with modern civilization stems from his argument that the purpose of a civilization is to make possible for those who live under it to know themselves. It is this capacity for self-understanding that defines civilization for Gandhi. "Civilization is that mode of conduct that points out to man the path of duty. Performance of duty and observance of morality are convertible terms. To observe morality is to attain mastery over our mind and our passions. So doing, we know ourselves".[7] A civilization that makes possible knowledge of oneself is *Sudhar* and one that precludes that possibility is *Kudhar* or 'reverse of civilization'. Gandhi was clearly invoking *Sudhar* in two senses, which have been latent in Gujarati. *Su-dhar* not just as good path, but one that holds, bears; from the Sanskrit root *dhri*. One that holds and bears human society is *Sudhar*, and only such *Sudhar* could point out to man the path of duty and open the possibility of self-knowledge. *Sudhar* is civilization in this sense. Second, *Sudhar* suggests a movement towards virtue. It entails a choice in favour of the good and active shunning of all that is undesirable. It is this active, choice-enabling, virtue-enhancing possibility of *Sudhar* that Gandhi desired from civilization.

For Gandhi, the essential character of modern civilization is not represented by either the Empire, or the speed of railways, the contractual nature of society brought about by Western law, nor by the vivisection practised in modern medicine. It is also not represented by use of violence as a legitimate means of expressing political dissent and obtaining political goals, even though these are significant markers of modern civilization. The essential character of modern civilization is represented by denial of a fundamental possibility, that of knowing oneself. Describing modern civilization Gandhi says, "Its true test lies in the fact that people living in it make bodily welfare the object of life".[8] This is an inadequate rendering of the original Gujarati, which could be rendered as "Its true identity is in the fact that people seek to find in engagement with the material world and bodily comfort meaning and human worth". When the main goal of life becomes the search for meaning and fulfilment in the material world and bodily comfort, it shifts fundamentally the ground of judgement about human worth. It is for this reason that Gandhi characterized modern civilization as 'irreligion', 'Satanic', and the 'Black Age'. By shifting the locus of human endeavour to objects of bodily welfare, modern civilization also precludes the possibility of swaraj. "It is Swaraj when we learn to rule ourselves".[9] This capacity to rule oneself is different from Home Rule or political freedom.[10] Swaraj is predicated upon *Sudharo*, a civilization that makes self-understanding its central concern.

Gandhi argues that Swaraj cannot be obtained so long as Indians and Britons remain in the grip of modern civilization. *Hind Swaraj* claims that this civilization is self-destructive. Anything that leads one away from oneself cannot be permanent for Gandhi. Despite decrying modern civilization and its emblems, *Hind Swaraj* does not display or provoke hatred. In fact, it is moved by deep love and empathy for those caught within modern civilization. *Hind Swaraj* is a theory of salvation, not only for India but also for Britain. Gandhi is at pains to point out that India's struggle cannot be against the British but against the civilization that they represent. He reminds the British that they are a religious people, that their fundamental identity is therefore not flawed. Gandhi's plea is that Britons be Christian in the true sense, and suggests that if they become moral and recognize that their current priorities are both irreligious and destructive, then they can stay in India. They can stay as moral people, but not as followers of modern civilization and upholders of an empire that this civilization sustains. *Hind Swaraj* is a rare document of contemporary thought that seeks the salvation not the annihilation of the oppressor. In Gandhi's thinking, the duty of India is unique. It must not only realize swaraj for itself but also save the British from the fire of modern civilization.

Hind Swaraj is also a meditation upon the question of means and ends. Violence for Gandhi is indelibly linked to modern civilization. Violence has to be shunned not only because ahimsa (nonviolence, love) is superior morality, but also because violence creates a distance between the self and the pursuit of Truth. "The more he took to violence, the more he receded from Truth".[11] Violence for Gandhi makes the possibility of knowing oneself even fainter. He, therefore, decries the argument that the end justifies the means. He says, "'As is the God, so is the votary' is a maxim worth considering".[12] He likens means to a seed and the end to a tree, "and there is just the same inviolable connection between the means and the end as there is between the seed and the tree".[13] Not only is the relationship between means and the end inviolable, Gandhi argues for purity of both the means and the end. One cannot worship God by evil means. This emphasis on the purity of the means and the end and their inviolable relationship is a unique contribution of *Hind Swaraj*.

THE BHAGAVAD GITA

The means are mediated through human agency; in the final analysis, the pure means are those that are wielded by a pure person. It was this relationship between objects of senses and the attachment for them that attracted Gandhi to the Bhagavad Gita. He read the Gita first in Sir Edwin Arnold's translation, *The Song Celestial*, with Theosophist friends in England. The poem struck him as one of "priceless worth". The verses 62 and 63 of the second discourse made a deep impression on him.

> *If one*
> *Ponders on objects of the sense, there springs*
> *Attraction; from attraction grows desire,*
> *Desire flames to fierce passion, passion breeds*
> *Recklessness; then the memory – all betrayed –*
> *Lets noble purpose go, and saps the mind,*
> *Till purpose, mind, and man are all undone.*[14]

At the time of writing his autobiography, they were clearly in his mind. They claim that those who make bodily welfare their object and the measure of human worth are certain to be ruined. Gandhi would have agreed in relation to individuals and civilizations. The verses describe a state that is opposed to that of brahmacharya. The year was 1888–9, and

Gandhi was far from making brahmacharya, even in the limited sense of chastity and celibacy, a central quest of his life. But what awakened in young Gandhi was a religious quest that was to govern the rest of life. The Gita became his lifelong companion. He translated it as *Anasakti Yoga* in Gujarati.[15] Gandhi's engagement with the Gita, though deep, was in no way unique. India's national movement displayed a marked preference for the Gita.[16]

This translation posed the questions of authority and qualification (*adhikar*) before Gandhi.[17] The question of authority was acute in the case of translation of the Gita, revered by many as sacred and having a long history of scholastic commentaries and translations. He was, by his own admission, the son of a Vanik or bania, and had very limited knowledge of Sanskrit, while his Gujarati was "in no way scholarly".[18] He made a unique claim; he and his associates at the satyagraha ashram had made an attempt to lead their lives in accordance with the teachings of the Gita, which he described as their 'spiritual guide book'. Gandhi invoked his *adhikar* in the following terms: "But I am not aware of the claim made by the translators of enforcing the meaning of the Gita in their own lives. At the back of my reading there is the claim of an endeavour to enforce the meaning in my own conduct for an unbroken period of forty years. For this reason I do harbour the wish that all Gujarati men and women wishing to shape their conduct according to their own faith, should digest and derive strength from the translation here presented".[19]

The path of the Gita for Gandhi was neither that of contemplation nor of devotion but that of *anasakta* (desireless, unattached) action. This idea is embodied in the Gita in the image of the *sthitpragnya* (one whose intellect is secure); who acts without attachment to either the action or fruits thereof.[20] Gandhi adopted two modes of self-practice to attain the state where one acts and yet does not act. These two modes were yajna (sacrifice) and satyagraha; both were deeply personal and simultaneously political.

The Gita declared that: "Together with the sacrifice did the Lord of beings create".[21] Gandhi saw this idea of sacrifice – of the self and not a symbolic, ritualistic sacrifice – as the basis of all religions. The ideal, of course, was Jesus; Gandhi said that the word yajna had to be understood in the way Jesus lived and died. "Jesus put on a crown of thorns to win salvation for his people, allowed his hands and feet to be nailed and suffered agonies before he gave up the ghost. This has been the law of yajna from immemorial times, without yajna the earth cannot exist even for a moment".[22] But how is one to perform such sacrifice in daily life? Gandhi's response was twofold; for one, he turned to the Bible, and the other was uniquely his own. "Earn thy bread by the sweat of thy brow", says the Bible. Gandhi made this central to the life at the ashram and borrowed the term 'bread labour' to describe it. The other form of yajna was peculiar to his times: spinning. Spinning was an obligatory ashram observance, each member being required to spin one hundred and forty threads daily, each thread measuring four feet.[23] This spinning was called *sutra-yajna* (sacrificial spinning). During his public debate with poet Rabindranath Tagore, Gandhi responded to his criticism of the 'cult of the charkha' by an essay called 'Charkha in the *Gita*'. He asserted that in the context of his India, "I can only think of spinning as the fittest and most acceptable sacrificial body labour".[24] He further clarified: "If here we understand the meaning of yajna rightly, there will be no difficulty in accepting the interpretation I have put upon it . . . Spinning is a true yajna".[25] As his conviction regarding spinning as the true yajna deepened, his ashram, hitherto called satyagraha ashram, was renamed Udyog Mandir (literally, temple of industry); explaining the term Udyog, Gandhi said; "Udyog has to be read in the light of the Bhagavad Gita".[26] Spinning even came to occupy the place of the Gita. During his imprisonment at Yeravda prison in 1932–3, his close associate and disciple, the English woman Mirabehn, sought an English translation of his commentaries on the Gita. Gandhi agreed that prison would be the most appropriate place for such a task, but if he were to do it, he would be required to give up spinning, a more sacrosanct activity: "For the spinning is the applied translation of the Gita; if one may coin that expression".[27]

If the Gita and the state of *sthitpragnya* informed and guided his spiritual quest to attain self-realization, satyagraha was his chosen means to attain swaraj. Gandhi believed that the model of satyagrahi was a *sthitpragnya*, who performs all actions with purity of heart and mind, unattached to both the actions and fruits thereof. He claimed that the first glimpses of satyagraha had come to him, not on 11 September 1906 in that fateful meeting at the Empire Theatre in Johannesburg, but much earlier when he read the Gita for the first time. He wrote: "It is certainly the Bhagavad Gita's intention that one should go on working without the attachment to the fruits of work. I deduced the principle of satyagraha from this. He who is free from such attachment will not kill the enemy but rather sacrifice himself . . . As far back as 1889, when I had my first contact with the *Gita*, it gave me a hint of satyagraha, and as I read more and more, the hint developed into a full revelation of satyagraha".[28] A satyagrahi like the *sthitpragnya* has to know the self, as satyagraha is not only a method based on the moral superiority of self-suffering, but also a mode of conduct that leads to self-knowledge. In the absence of a quest to know oneself, satyagraha is not possible, as it is based on the inviolable relationship between means and end, and its essence lies in the purity of both. Pure means are means adopted by a person who, through a process of constant self-search, cleanses and purifies the self; whose only true aim is to be a seeker after Truth and swaraj.

SATYAGRAHA IN SOUTH AFRICA

Hind Swaraj only introduces the theory and practice of satyagraha. In *Satyagraha In South Africa* (*Dakshin Africa Na Satyagraha No Itihas*),[29] Gandhi gives an account of the struggle of the Indian people in South Africa. He faced a serious problem. How does one write a 'history' of satyagraha? It was not a methodological problem but a philosophical one. It is best captured by the titles of the book in Gujarati and in English. The Gujarati title would have to be translated as 'A History of Satyagraha In South Africa'. The title of the book in English reads *Satyagraha In South Africa*. To understand the omission of the term 'history', we will have to understand the meaning that he attached to two terms: the Gujarati term *Itihas* and the English term 'history'. Gandhi in fact saw these two as different. In *Hind Swaraj*, there is a discussion about the historical evidence of satyagraha. His argument was that soul-force was the basis of the world. Brute force was an aberration and a break in the even flow of soul-force. It is here that he makes a fundamental distinction between *Itihas* and history. *Itihas* means 'It so happened'.[30] History means the doings of kings and emperors. "History, as we know it, is a record of the wars of the world, and so there is a proverb among Englishmen that a nation which has no history, that is no wars, is a happy nation. How kings played, how they became enemies of one another is found accurately recorded in history".[31] Thus he makes a crucial distinction between *Itihas* and history. He argued that it is impossible for history to record instances of the use of satyagraha. "You cannot expect silver-ore in a tin mine".[32] He thus could use the word *Itihas* in the Gujarati title but not in the English title, as history was not for him a translation of the term *Itihas*. He was not willing to employ two terms as convertible terms, even if their usage had become customary, as for him they represented two divergent traditions.[33]

Gandhi wanted *Satyagraha In South Africa* to be read alongside his autobiography, almost as a companion volume. "I need hardly mention that those who are following the weekly chapters of *My Experiments with Truth* cannot afford to miss these chapters on satyagraha, if they would follow in all details the working out of the search after Truth".[34] Gandhi clearly saw his spiritual quest and political striving as one, and stemming from the same root. Satyagraha has its roots in a pledge, a pledge taken in the name of God and with God as witness.[35] Satyagraha as a philosophy and a practice recognizes the humanity of others. In *Hind Swaraj*, while making a severe condemnation of lawyers, Gandhi stated: "there is something good in everyone".[36] Satyagraha recognizes the universal possibility of goodness and virtue.

ASHRAM OBSERVANCES IN ACTION
AND FROM YERAVDA MANDIR

Gandhi increasingly came to believe that a person who wields such a pure means had to be pure. In *Hind Swaraj* and *Satyagraha In South Africa*, this aspect is recessive, though he does mention the need for voluntary poverty, brahmacharya, and fearlessness. The reason for this lies in the fact that during his South African years, his understanding of the ashram and ashram observances had not fully matured. He had established two 'ashram-like' communities in South Africa, but one was a 'settlement' (Phoenix Settlement) while the other was a 'farm' (Tolstoy Farm). The initial impulse for Phoenix was provided by Ruskin's *Unto This Last*. Though it had a religious basis, "the visible object was purity of body and mind as well as economic equality".[37] Celibacy was not regarded as essential; in fact, co-workers were expected to live as family men and have children. Gandhi began to look upon Phoenix deliberately as a religious institution after 1906 when he took the vow of brahmacharya, and celibacy became an imperative for a life devoted to service. In 1911, the establishment of Tolstoy Farm was a recognition that satyagraha required a community where the families of satyagrahis could live and lead a religious life.

Gandhi as a satyagrahi can be understood only when we understand him as an ashramite. Gandhi wrote two works, *Ashram Observances in Action* (*Satyagraha Ashram No Itihas*) and *From Yeravda Mandir* (*Mangal Prabhat*)[38] to explain the philosophy and practice of ashram life. On his return to India, Gandhi established an ashram in Kochrab, Ahmedabad in 1915. It was later shifted to the banks of the Sabarmati River in Ahmedabad in 1917. It was called satyagraha ashram, as it owed its very existence to the "pursuit and attempted practice of Truth".[39] Gandhi described the ashram as a community of men of religion. The emphasis was on both community and religious life. The word 'religion' indicated a non-denominational idea of dharma.[40] What gave members a sense of being part of a religious community was a set of eleven vows (*ekadash vrata*),[41] of which three were Gandhi's response to his times and context (removal of Untouchability, equality of all religions, and swadeshi), while the inclusion of bread labour was an innovation in the Indian context where notions of social and ritual purity and impurity are determined also by the materials that one deals with. The other seven were part of many Indic traditions. Gandhi's originality lay in the fact that he made them central to the political realm. Ashram observances were essential for those who wished to wield the pure means of satyagraha.

Thus *Hind Swaraj, Satyagraha In South Africa,* and the autobiography make sense only when read along with these two works on ashram observances. In the last lines of *Hind Swaraj*, Gandhi made an assertion and a dedication: "In my opinion, we have used the term 'Swaraj' without understanding its real significance. I have endeavoured to explain it as I understand it, and my conscience testifies that my life henceforth is dedicated to its attainment".[42] The true meaning and significance of a life dedicated to attainment of swaraj can be understood only when one understands Gandhi as an ashram member.

CONSTRUCTIVE PROGRAMME: ITS MEANING AND PLACE

Gandhi had elevated bread labour to an ashram observance, and spinning was for him a sacrifice; but for the Congress and a large part of the country, the relationship between the attainment of *purna swaraj* (complete independence) and sacrificial work remained obscure. The relationship between swadeshi and swaraj, between freedom and the creation of a nonviolent social order, and between sacrifice and swaraj become clear when we read a small tract *Constructive Programme: Its Meaning and Place*.[43] After 1932, Gandhi came to regard the constructive programme as central to his quest for Swaraj. The salience of this increased as he came to view civil disobedience as an aid to constructive work and not as a primary means of attainment of swaraj. "For my handling of civil disobedience without the constructive programme will be like a paralyzed hand attempting to lift a spoon".[44] Gandhi rooted his vision of *purna swaraj* in the idea of a nonviolent society, where every unit, even the most humble, was independent and interdependent. He was convinced that violence could not lead to even an imaginary independence nor could it create equality. A movement for freedom, in the absence of a programme, such as his eighteen-point constructive programme, that would enable each Indian to be free, was inconceivable for him. He had said in *Hind Swaraj* that swaraj had to be experienced by each person.

Therefore, there was no question of swaraj being obtained by some on behalf of others.

KEY TO HEALTH

What could be the relationship of swaraj, *sthitpragnya*, swadeshi to mud poultice, hip bath, and exhortations to eat food without condiments? Long before he became a satyagrahi, sought swaraj, and aspired to be a brahmachari, Gandhi began to experiment with food, diet, and naturopathy. It was only much later that he was to realize the importance of control over the palate to the practice of brahmacharya. "Control of the palate is the first essential in the observance of the vow. I found that complete control of the palate made the observance very easy, and so I now pursued my dietetic experiments not merely from the vegetarian's but also from the brahmachari's point of view".[45] Brahmacharya was also a necessary observance for a satyagrahi and the one seeking the state of *sthitpragnya*. Thus the experiments in dietetics and more fundamentally the conception of body were related to the three principal quests.

Gandhi saw the body as both an enabler and an obstacle. It was the body that allowed one to serve others. Service to others and, through them, of God was the reason for human existence. In his widely read *Key to Health*,[46] Gandhi said: "Man came into the world in order to pay off [the] debt owed by him to it, that is to say, in order to serve God and (or through) His creation".[47] Hence, he argued one has to act as a guardian of the body, exercise self-restraint, and serve the world. Indulgence, on the contrary, harms not only the self but others also. Gandhi's *Key to Health* is a primer on the body and healing, written for those who wish to serve through a body trained in self-restraint. Health for Gandhi is not a state free of disease but it is a relationship between mind and body. It is a state of harmony. He characterized a healthy person thus: "His mind and senses are in a state of harmony and poise".[48] During the last years of his life, Gandhi came to be convinced that disease originates in the mind and not the body. During his experiments in naturopathy at a clinic in the village of Uruli-Kanchan, Gandhi prescribed *Ramanama*, the recitation of the name of Rama as Truth, as the only infallible remedy. His conviction grew to the extent that he came to believe that if his own recitation of the *Ramanama* were pure and perfect and if he had succeeded in installing Rama in his heart, even those around him would be free of disease and passions. During the last two years of his life, Manu Gandhi, a young relative, had become his constant companion and a partner in his yajna. Her frail health, her illness, which finally required her to be operated upon, plunged Gandhi into a deep crisis. He took Manu's illness as a sign that *Ramanama* had not yet taken root in his heart. He shared his despondency with Manu and others. Her appendicitis operation was for him a proof of his own incompleteness. "After all I have made her my partner in this yajna. If *Ramanama* is firmly rooted in my heart, this girl should be free from her ailments".[49] He told Manu: "Since I sent you to the hospital, I have been constantly thinking where I stand, what God demands of me, where He will ultimately lead me...I know my striving is incomplete; your operation is a proof".[50]

The body, though it allowed for service, was an impediment in the larger quest to attain perfect brahmacharya and to see God face to face. He was painfully aware that no one can be regarded as really free as long as one lives in the body. In his autobiography, Gandhi spoke of the 'unbroken torture' that the separation from Truth as God caused him. This desire to be close to God governed every breath of his life, but "I know that it is the evil passions within that keep me so far from Him, and yet I cannot get away from them".[51] It was this idea of the body as the root of passion that made Gandhi transpose a saying of Tulsidas in *Hind Swaraj*. Gandhi wrote: "Of religion, pity or love is the root, as egotism of the body. Therefore we should not abandon pity so long as we are alive".[52] The more widely prevalent rendering of it is: "Of religion, pity or love is the root, as egotism of the sin".[53] This introduction of the term 'body' in place of sin was not an error. It was a deliberate choice, which encapsulated Gandhi's own unease with the passions of the body, which may lead to sin and hence away from God. The *Key to Health* expresses both his unease with the body as the seat of the passions and his appreciation of the body's role as an indispensable instrument in the service of fellow human beings.

AN AUTOBIOGRAPHY

Autobiography in India is essentially a nineteenth-century form. Its emergence was linked with two processes. One was the process of colonial, Western education. The second was the movement for social and religious reform in the second half of the nineteenth century in various regions of India. Two very powerful literary forms emerged in nineteenth-century India: the novel and the autobiography. In a culture that had a long tradition of storytelling, the novel as a form did not pose many cultural problems. It was the autobiography that was deeply troubling as a literary form. Major Indian philosophical systems had advocated the self-effacement of the individual. It was argued that only by the subjugation of the individual ego could the soul be sublimated and eventually be one with the Creator. In such a culture, autobiography as a story of the self was seen as introducing major cultural transitions. Therefore, almost all individuals who wrote autobiographies in various Indian languages in the nineteenth century wrote about the difficulty of writing about the self in an alien form.[54]

When Gandhi decided to write his autobiography in 1925 at the instance of Swami Anand, he had to face the same dilemma. How was he to speak about his life in a form that was seen as Western? He narrates his perplexity: "But a God-fearing friend had his doubts, which he shared with me on my day of silence. 'What has set you on this adventure?' he asked. 'Writing an autobiography is a practice peculiar to the West. I know of nobody in the East having written one, except amongst those who have come under Western influence... Don't you think it would be better not to write anything like an autobiography, at any rate just as yet?'"[55]

Gandhi's response to this criticism is most creative. He responded: "This argument had some effect on me. But it is not my purpose to attempt a real autobiography. I simply want to tell the story of my numerous experiments with Truth... But I should certainly like to narrate my experiments in the spiritual field which are known only to myself, and from which I have derived such powers as I possess for working in the political field. If the experiments are really spiritual, then there can be no room for self-praise. They can only add to my humility".[56]

He distinguishes between what he calls a real autobiography and an autobiography that he would write. A real autobiography is a Western form, a form that can lead to self-praise. But what he wanted to write was not that. A narration of spiritual and moral experiments can only make him and his readers more aware of his limitations and make him humble.

The Gujarati word for autobiographical writings is *Atmakatha*. The term *Atmakatha* translates not as autobiography but as 'the story of the soul'. In its original Christian sense, autobiography was a story of a soul in search of God. Gandhi, by employing autobiography as *Atmakatha*, opens up the possibility of speaking of his striving and pining for self-realization. As *Atmakatha*, he could speak of his spiritual and moral quest. There is an interesting transposition that happens in the actual act of translating Gandhi's autobiography from Gujarati into English.[57] In the original Gujarati, the main title of the story is *Satya Na Prayogo*, which literally means experiments with Truth. The word *Atmakatha* appears as a subtitle. It signifies two things: that it is the story of experiments that is primary, and that it has autobiographical context. The title thus matches with Gandhi's original intention. In the English translation, the process is reversed. *An Autobiography* becomes the main title, while *Experiments with Truth* is rendered as a subtitle. It indicates not a failure of translation but a much deeper cultural failure. It indicates the difficulty of speaking about the soul in an alien tongue.

Gandhi chooses to call his method 'experiments'; in Gujarati he uses the term *Prayogo*. This choice of term is very significant. He had another term available from the spiritual tradition. This term is 'sadhana'. Sadhana is a difficult term to translate into English. It has been variously translated as 'spiritual practices', as 'penance', and as 'striving'. He indicates why the term experiment was chosen over sadhana in the following way. "There are some things which are known only to oneself and one's maker. They are clearly incommunicable. The experiments that I am about to relate are not such".[58] He is saying that if his striving was such that it was communicable only to him and to his God, they would be sadhana. He in fact refers to the scientific method. He says: "I claim for them nothing more than does a scientist who, though he conducts his experiments with the utmost accuracy, forethought, and minuteness, never claims any finality about his conclusions, but keeps an open mind regarding them. I have gone through deep self-introspection, searched myself through and through, and examined and analysed every psychological situation . . . For me they appear to be absolutely correct, and seem for the time being to be final".[59] As experiment, his quest for Truth could be taken as a guide, as an illustration by other seekers. He urges us to read the autobiography not as a personal history but as a story of a soul in quest of Truth.

It is important to ask if Gandhi's autobiography or his other experiments not narrated in the text give us a glimpse of what his sadhana could have been like. Because this sadhana is the unstated part of the *Atmakatha*, it in fact provides the basis to his claim that his principal quest was to see God face to face, to attain self-realization. He worshipped God as Truth. He did not ever claim that he had indeed found Him, or seen Him face to face but could imagine that state: "One who has realized God is freed from sin forever. He has no desire to be fulfilled. Not even in his thoughts will he suffer from faults, imperfections, or impurities. Whatever he does will be perfect because he does nothing himself but the God within him does everything. He is completely merged in Him".[60] This state was for Gandhi the state of perfect self-realization, of perfect self-knowledge. Although he believed that such perfect knowledge may elude him so long as he was imprisoned in the mortal body, he did make an extraordinary claim. This was his claim to hear what he described as a 'small, still voice', or the 'inner voice'. He used various terms such as the voice of God, of conscience, the inner voice, voice of Truth or the small, still voice.[61] He made this claim often and also declared that he was powerless before the irresistible voice, that his conduct was guided by this voice. The nature of this inner voice and Gandhi's need and ability to listen to the voice becomes apparent when we examine his invocation of it.

The first time he invoked the authority of this inner voice in India was at a public meeting in Ahmedabad, where he suddenly declared his resolve to fast. This day was 15 February 1918. Twenty-two days prior to this date, Gandhi had been leading the strike of the workers of the textiles mills of Ahmedabad. The mill workers had taken a pledge to strike work until their demands were met. They appeared to be going back upon their pledge. Gandhi was groping, not being able to see clearly the way forward. He described his sudden resolve thus: "One morning – it was at a mill-hands' meeting – while I was groping and unable to see my way clearly, the light came to me. Unbidden and all by themselves the words came to my lips: 'unless the strikers rally', I declared to the meeting, 'and continue to strike till a settlement is reached, or till they leave the mills altogether, I will not touch any food'".[62]

He was to speak repeatedly of the inner voice in similar metaphors; of darkness that enveloped him, his groping, churning, wanting to find a way forward, and the moment of light, of knowledge when the voice spoke to him. Gandhi sought the guidance of his inner voice not only in the spiritual realm, but also in the political realm. His famous Dandi March came to him through the voice speaking from within. Gandhi's search for moral and spiritual basis for political action was anchored in his claim that one could and ought to be guided by the Voice of Truth speaking from within. This made his politics deeply spiritual.

Perhaps the most contentious invocation of the inner voice occurred in 1933. In 1932, Gandhi had undergone a fast from 20 September to 25 September as a prisoner of the Yeravda Central Prison. This fast, done in opposition to the decision of the British Government to conduct elections in India on basis of communal representation, had proved dangerous for his already frail body and brought him precariously close to death.

Even before he had fully regained his strength, he shocked the nation by announcing a twenty-one-day fast in May 1933. On 30 April 1933, he made a public announcement to go on an unconditional and irrevocable fast for self-purification. The fast was to commence at noon on Monday 8 May and end at noon on Monday 29 May.[63] He declared that this resolution was made in submission to an irresistible call of inner voice. This announcement caught even his closest associates and fellow prisoners unaware; they did not know that a tempest had been raging within him. He described this act of listening to his fellow prisoner, Vallabhbhai Patel: "as if for the last three days I were preparing myself for the great deluge! On many occasions, however, the thought of a fast would come repeatedly to my mind and I would drive it away . . . but the same thought would persistently come to my mind: 'If you have grown so restless, why don't you undertake the fast? Do it'. The inner dialogue went on for quite sometime. At half past twelve came the clear, unmistakable voice, 'You must undertake the fast'. That was all".[64] Gandhi knew that his invocation of the inner voice was beyond comprehension and also beyond his capacity to explain. He asked: "After all, does one express, can one express, all one's thoughts to others?"[65] Not all were convinced of his claim to hear the inner voice. It was argued that what he heard was not the voice of God, but it was hallucination, that Gandhi was deluding himself and that his imagination had become overheated by the cramped prison walls.

Gandhi remained steadfast and refuted the charge of self-delusion or hallucination. He said, "not the unanimous verdict of the whole world against me could shake me from the belief that what I heard was the true Voice of God".[66] After the fast, he explained the nature of divine inspiration. "The night I got the inspiration, I had a terrible inner struggle. My mind was restless. I could see no way. The burden of my responsibility was crushing me. But what I did hear was like a Voice from afar and yet quite near. It was as unmistakable as some human voice definitely speaking to me, and irresistible. I was not dreaming at the time when I heard the Voice. The hearing of the Voice was preceded by a terrific struggle within me. Suddenly the Voice came upon me. I listened, made certain that it was the Voice, and the struggle ceased. I was calm".[67] He argued that his claim was beyond both proof and reason, the fact that he had survived the fiery ordeal was the proof. It was a moment for which he had been preparing himself. He felt that his submission to God as Truth was so complete, at least in that particular instance of fasting, that he had no autonomy left. Such a moment of total submission transcends reason. He wrote in a letter: "Of course, for me personally it transcends reason, because I feel it to be a clear will from God. My position is that there is nothing just now that I am doing of my own accord. He guides me from moment to moment".[68]

Gandhi's claim to hear the inner voice was neither unique nor exclusive. The validity and legitimacy of such a claim was recognized in the spiritual realm. The idea of perfect surrender was integral to and consistent with ideals of religious life. Although Gandhi never made the claim of having seen God face to face, the inner voice was for him the voice of God. He said: "The inner voice is the voice of the Lord".[69] But it was not a voice that came from a force outside of him. Gandhi made a distinction between an outer force and a power beyond us. A power beyond us has its locus within us. It is superior to us, not subject to our command or wilful action but it is still located within us. He explained the nature of this power. 'Beyond us' means a "power which is beyond our ego".[70] According to Gandhi, one acquires the capacity to hear this voice when the "ego is reduced to zero".[71] Reducing the ego to zero for Gandhi meant an act of total surrender to *Satya Narayan.* This surrender required subjugation of human will, of individual autonomy. It is when a person loses autonomy that conscience emerges. Conscience is an act of obedience not wilfulness. He said: "Willfullness is not conscience ... Conscience is the ripe fruit of strictest discipline ... Conscience can reside only in a delicately tuned breast".[72] This capacity did not belong to everyone as a natural gift or a right available in equal measure. What one required was a cultivated capacity to discern the inner voice as distinct from the voice of the ego because "one cannot always recognize whether it is the voice of Rama or Ravana".[73]

What was this ever wakefulness that allowed him to hear the call of Truth as distinct from voice of untruth? How does one acquire the fitness to wait upon God? He had likened this preparation to an attempt to empty the sea with a drainer as small as a point of a blade of grass. And yet, it had to be as natural as life itself. He created a regime of spiritual discipline that enabled him to search himself through and through. As part of his spiritual training, he formulated the eleven vows. The ashram was constituted by their abiding faith in these and by their prayers.

Prayer was the expression of the definitive and conscious longing of the soul; it was his act of waiting upon Him for guidance. His want was to feel the utterly pure presence of the divine within. Only a heart purified and cleansed by prayer could be filled with the presence of God, where life became one long continuous prayer, an act of worship. Prayer was for him the final reliance upon God to the exclusion of all else. Such a prayer could only be offered in the spirit of non-attachment, *anasakti.* Moreover, when the God that he sought to realize is Truth, prayer, though externalized, was in essence directed inwards. Because Truth is not merely that we are expected to speak. It is That which alone is, it is That of which all things are made, it is That which subsists by its own power, which alone is eternal. Gandhi's intense yearning was that such Truth should illuminate his heart. Prayer was a plea, a preparation, a cleansing that enabled him to hear his inner voice. The eleven vows allowed for this waiting upon God. The act of waiting meant to perform one's actions in a desireless or detached manner.

CONCLUSION

Now we have some understanding of Gandhi's experiments and his ultimate quest: to know himself, to attain moksha, that is, to see God (Truth) face to face. In order to fulfil his quest, he must be an ashramite, a satyagrahi, and a seeker after swaraj. He added two other practices to this search: one was fasting, the other brahmacharya. Fasting in its original sense is not mortification of flesh, but a means to come closer to God. In this sense, there could be no fast without a prayer and indeed no prayer without a fast. Such a fast was both penance and self-purification.

The ultimate practice of self-purification is the practice of brahmacharya. For Gandhi, realization of Truth and self-gratification appears a contradiction in terms. From this emanate not only brahmacharya but also three other observances: control of the palate, poverty, and non-stealing. Brahmacharya came to Gandhi as a necessary observance at a time when he had organized an ambulance corps during the Zulu rebellion in South Africa. He realized that service of the community was not possible without observance of brahmacharya. In 1906, Gandhi took the vow of brahmacharya. This was not without a purpose. He was later to feel that they were secretly preparing him for satyagraha.[74] It would take him several decades, but through his observances, his experiments, Gandhi developed insights into the interrelatedness of Truth, ahimsa, and brahmacharya. He came to regard the practice of brahmacharya in thought, word, and deed as essential for the search for Truth and the practice of ahimsa. Gandhi, by making observance of brahmacharya essential for Truth and ahimsa, made it central to the practice of satyagraha and the quest for swaraj. This understanding allowed Gandhi to expand the conception of brahmacharya itself. He began with a popular and restricted notion in the sense of chastity and celibacy, including celibacy in marriage. He expanded this notion to mean observance in thought, word, and deed. But it is only when he began to recognize the deeper and fundamental relationship that brahmacharya shared with satyagraha, ahimsa, and swaraj that Gandhi could go to the root of the term brahmacharya. (*Charya* or conduct adopted in search of *Brahma*, that is Truth is brahmacharya.) In this sense, brahmacharya is not denial or control over one sense, but it is an attempt to bring all senses in harmony with each other. Brahmacharya so conceived and practised becomes that mode of conduct that leads to Truth, knowledge, and hence moksha. Thus the ability to hear the inner voice, a voice that is "perfect knowledge or realization of Truth",[75] is an experiment in brahmacharya.

It is therefore possible to seek a unity in what appear to be varied writings. This unity exists not in any apparent theoretical continuity but in Gandhi's life and his strivings – political and spiritual – which were moved by a quest for Truth as God, which worked out in the practice of satyagraha and swadeshi, and the struggle for swaraj.

Notes

1 M. K. Gandhi, *An Autobiography or The Story of My Experiments with Truth*, trans. Mahadev Desai, first pub. in serial form in 1927, second revised edition 1940 (Ahmedabad, India: Navajivan, 1999), p. x.
2 *The Collected Works of Mahatma Gandhi* (New Delhi, India: Publications Division of the Government of India, Navajivan, 1958–94, 100 vols) vol. 40, p. 489. (Henceforth, *CWMG*.)
3 The seven books under consideration are: *Hind Swaraj, Satyagraha In South Africa, An Autobiography or The Story of My Experiments with Truth, From Yeravda Mandir, Ashram Observances in Action, Constructive Programme: Its Meaning and Place*, and *Key To Health*. We shall also consider his translation of the Bhagavad Gita as *Anasakti Yoga*. The term 'book' has to be understood in a broad sense in the context of Gandhi's writings. *From Yeravda Mandir* is a set of letters. Large parts of *Satyagraha In South Africa* were dictated to a fellow prisoner and serialized in his journal, *Navajivan*. His autobiography also appeared first in a serialized form in both Gujarati and its English translation.
4 For a note on the history of the text, see A. Parel (ed.), *Gandhi: Hind Swaraj and Other Writings* (New Delhi, India: Foundation Books, 1997), pp. lxiii–lxiv. All references to *Hind Swaraj* are to the Parel edition.
5 All the works under consideration except *Constructive Programme* were originally written in Gujarati. *Hind Swaraj* is the only work that Gandhi himself translated into English. All his other works were translated by his close associates and co-workers under his watchful eye, and bear his testimony to the translation's faithfulness to the original. *Ashram Observances in Action* was published and translated after his death.
6 In chapter XII, 'What is True Civilization?', Gandhi draws a picture of India unsullied by modern civilization and its emblems; the railway, doctors, and lawyers. It is this India that Gandhi often characterized as 'ancient civilization' and even as 'real civilization'. It is significant that the forty-year-old author was a very modern Indian migrant. It is thus possible to read *Hind Swaraj* as a dialogue anchored in this migratory experience.

7   *Hind Swaraj*, p. 67.

8   *Ibid.*, p. 35.

9   *Ibid.*, p. 73.

10 The term *swaraj* occurs fifty-six times in the Gujarati text. The English rendering alternates between home rule and swaraj, the choice being guided by the context of usage and the distance from or proximity to his own vision. In half of the fifty-six occurrences of the term *swaraj* in Gujarati, it has been rendered as home rule.

11 M. K. Gandhi, *From Yeravda Mandir*, trans. Valji Govindji Desai. (Ahmedabad, India: Navajivan, original edition 1932, new edition 2005), p. 5.

12 *Hind Swaraj*, p. 81.

13 *Ibid.*

14 Sir Edwin Arnold's translation. Gandhi's own rendering in contrast reads: "In a man brooding on objects of the senses, attachment to them spring up; attachment begat craving and craving begets wrath. Wrath breeds stupefaction, stupefaction leads to loss of memory, loss of memory ruins reason, and the ruin of reason spells utter destruction". M. Desai, *The Gospel of Selfless Action or The Gita According to Gandhi* (Ahmedabad, India: Navajivan, original edition 1946, new edition 2004), p. 163.

15 The translation was done in 1926–7. He wrote the introduction to the translation two years later at Kosani in Almora and finished it on 24 June 1929. The *Anasakti Yoga* was published on 12 March 1930, the day he left the ashram at Sabarmati on his historic salt march to Dandi. Mahadev Desai translated the *Anasakti Yoga* as *The Gospel of Selfless Action* in English, during his imprisonment in 1933–4. The translation could not be published until January 1946, as Gandhi did not have time to read the translation. Mahadev Desai died as a prisoner in the Aga Khan Palace on 15 August 1942, and as a tribute to his memory, Gandhi hastened the publication soon after his release from prison. In 1936, he published a concordance to the Gita (*Gitapadarthkosha*), and he also composed a primer on the Gita, popularly known as *Ram-Gita* for his son, Ramdas.

16 Among the major commentators, translators of the *Gita* were Sister Nivedita, Bankim Chandra Chatterjee, Annie Beasant, Sri Aurobindo, and Bal Gangadhar Tilak. The tradition continued up to Vinoba Bhave.

17 Gandhi was keenly aware of the question of *adhikar*. In 1920, during the non-cooperation movement, he established a university that was then called the Gujarat Mahavidyalaya. Gandhi was appointed its chancellor for life. In his inaugural address, Gandhi raised the question of *adhikar*. "I fulfilled a function of a rishi, if a Vanik's son can do it". *CWMG*, vol. 21, p. 482.

18 M. Desai, *The Gita According to Gandhi*, p. 126.

19 *Ibid.*, p. 127.

20 *Gita* II, pp. 54–72 deals with the characteristics of a *sthitpragnya*. They were recited daily in the ashram evening prayers. During the morning prayers, the recitation of the *Gita* was so arranged that the entire work

was recited every fourteen days. Later, this was changed so that the recitation was completed every seven days. The schedule of the recitation of the *Gita* was distributed among the days as follows: Friday, 1 and 2; Saturday, 3, 4, and 5; Sunday, 6, 7, and 8; Monday, 9, 10, 11, and 12; Tuesday, 13, 14, and 15; Wednesday, 16 and 17; Thursday, 18.

21 *Gita* III, p. 10.

22 *CWMG*, vol. 20, p. 404.

23 Initially, spinning was for half an hour; later the measure was changed to threads spun.

24 *CWMG*, vol. 24, p. 435.

25 *Ibid.*, pp. 464–5.

26 *Ibid.*, vol. 43, p. 203.

27 *Ibid.*, vol. 49, p. 357.

28 *Ibid.*, vol. 18, pp. 50–1.

29 To say 'written' is an inexact description of composition. He began to *dictate* this account to his fellow prisoner, Indulal Yagnik, in the Yeravda Central Prison on 26 November 1923. By the time he was released on 5 February 1924, he had completed thirty chapters, which appeared serially in *Navajivan* from 13 April 1924 to 22 November 1925. The remaining twenty chapters were written after his release. They appeared in a book form in two parts, in 1924 and 1925. The English translation as *Satyagraha In South Africa*, done by Valji Govindji Desai, which was seen and approved by Gandhi, was published in 1928 by S. Ganesan, Madras. A second revised edition of it was published by Navajivan Press in December 1950.

30 *Hind Swaraj*, p. 89.

31 *Ibid.*

32 *Ibid.*

33 This distinction was carried into other translations as well. He wrote an *Itihas* of the Satyagraha Ashram as *Satyagraha Ashram No Itihas*. It was rendered into English by Valji Govindji Desai as *Ashram Observances in Action*. This distinction became part of the Gandhian thought. Mahadev Desai writes an *Itihas* of the Satyagraha in Bardoli as *Bardoli Satyagraha No Itihas*, which he rendered in English as *The Story of Bardoli*.

34 M. K. Gandhi, *Satyagraha In South Africa*, trans. Valji Govindji Desai. (Ahmedabad, Navajivan, 1950, 2003), p. vii.

35 *Ibid.*, p. 97.

36 *Hind Swaraj*, p. 59.

37 *CWMG*, vol. 50, p. 189.

38 Gandhi commenced writing the *Itihas* of the Satyagraha Ashram in Yeravda Central Prison on 5 April 1932. This work was written intermittently and the last instalment was written on 11 July 1932. It was never completed. It was published after his death in May 1948, and the English translation by Valji Govindji Desai was published in 1955. *Mangal Prabhat* was written as weekly letters to the Satyagraha Ashram during his imprisonment in 1930. It was translated into English by Valji

Govindji Desai and published in 1932. The last chapter in this work on Swadeshi was written after his release from prison. He did not write it in jail as he felt that he could not do justice to the politics of Swadeshi without encroaching upon his limits as a prisoner.

39 M. K. Gandhi, *From Yeravda Mandir*, p. 3.

40 In *Hind Swaraj*, also, Gandhi had this non-denominational idea of religion. He wrote: "Here I am not thinking of the Hindu, the Mahomedan, or the Zoroastrian religion, but of that religion which underlies all religions". *Hind Swaraj*, p. 42.

41 They are satya (Truth), ahimsa (nonviolence or love), brahmacharya (chastity), *Asvad* (control of the palate), *Asteya* (non-stealing), *Aparigraha* (non-possession or poverty), *Abhaya* (fearlessness), *Ashprushyata Nivaran* (removal of untouchability), *Sharer Shrama* (bread labour), *Sarva Dharma Samabhav* (tolerance or equality of religions), and swadeshi.

42 *Hind Swaraj*, p. 119.

43 This was the only work under consideration that Gandhi wrote in English. It was written in 1941, and revised and enlarged in 1945. M. K. Gandhi, *Constructive Programme: Its Meaning and Place* (Ahmedabad, India: Navajivan, revised edition 1945, new edition, 2006).

44 *Ibid.*, p. 29.

45 M. K. Gandhi, *An Autobiography or The Story of My Experiments with Truth*, trans. Mahadev Desai (Ahmedabad, India: Navajivan, 1940, 1999), p. 175.

46 M. K. Gandhi, *Key to Health*, trans. Dr. Sushila Nayyar. See *CWMG*, vol. 77, pp. 1–48.

47 *Ibid.*, p. 3.

48 *Ibid.*

49 *CWMG*, vol. 86, p. 486.

50 *CWMG*, vol. 86, pp. 521–2. This sense deepened with his own fast. The last fast affected both his kidneys and liver, a sure sign that the purity that he had wished and prayed for still eluded him.

51 Gandhi, *An Autobiography*, p. xii.

52 *Hind Swaraj*, p. 88.

53 In Hindi it reads:

> "*Daya dharma ka mool hain, pap mool abhiman*
> *Tulsi daya na chandiya, jab lag ghatmen pran*".

In Gandhi's rendering, the word *deha* (body) was introduced in place of *pap* (sin).

54 For the relation between social reform and the emergence of autobiographical writing, the novel, and history, see T. Suhrud, *Writing Life: Three Gujarati Thinkers* (New Delhi, India: Orient Blackswan, 2008).

55 Gandhi, *An Autobiography*, p. ix.

56 *Ibid.*, pp. ix–x.

57 For a history of the translation and a comparison of the two editions of the English translation, see T. Suhrud, *An Autobiography or The Story*

of My Experiments with Truth: A Table of Concordance (New Delhi, India: Routledge, 2009).

58 Gandhi, *An Autobiography*, p. x.
59 *Ibid.*, pp. x–xi.
60 *CWMG*, vol. 55, p. 255.
61 *Ibid.*
62 Gandhi, *An Autobiography*, p. 359.
63 For the statement on the fast, see *CWMG*, vol. 55, pp. 74–5.
64 *CWMG*, vol. 55, p. 76.
65 *Ibid.*
66 *Ibid.*, p. 256.
67 *Ibid.*, p. 255.
68 *Ibid.*, vol. 52, p. 244.
69 *Ibid.*, vol. 53, p. 483.
70 *Ibid.*
71 *Ibid.*
72 *Ibid.*, vol. 25, pp. 23–4.
73 *Ibid.*, vol. 52, p. 130.
74 Gandhi, *An Autobiography*, p. 266.
75 *CWMG*, vol. 56, p. 182.

5 Gandhi's religion and its relation to his politics

AKEEL BILGRAMI

Gandhi was a deeply – and avowedly – religious man, in particular, a Hindu. His religiosity was eclectic and individual, a product partly of what was given to him, but partly too a matter of his instincts, which were then consolidated over the years by his haphazard reading and his highly personal and searching reflection.

What was given to him was the particular kind of Vaishnavism that was pervasive in his native Gujarat, ranging from the temples to which his mother took him as a child[1] to the Gujarati sant-poets such as Narsin Mehta and Shamal Bhat whom he read from an early age. To this, he added a great variety of elements – religious, moral, and philosophical. These included: Advaita-Vedantin ideas; Bhakti ideals of devotion (ideals through which he read his beloved Bhagavad Gita and made it, as he himself would say, his constant moral guide); the Jainism of his mentor Raychandbhai; Buddhism and an admiration for the person of the Buddha that he acquired after being moved by Edwin Arnold's biography *The Light of Asia*;[2] theosophical notions (shorn of their occultism) that he got from exposure in England to Annie Besant, and Christianity – particularly the New Testament and what he took to be the moral instruction that comes from the very life and example of its founder – which he filtered through his admiring, though selective, reading of Tolstoy's writings, as well as what he took from his frequent encounter with missionaries both in South Africa and in India. He even made something religious out of what he learnt from his study of Ruskin and Thoreau who, like all the other influences on him, contributed to the shaping of a life of spiritual dedication and service and conscience.

To the extent that we may talk of a 'high' Hinduism, this, by its lights, would be a very maverick mix. But Gandhi's convictions were such that, despite – somewhat perversely – calling himself a sanatani (an orthodox Hindu), he was very sceptical of the idea that there *was* a high or canonical Hinduism. The appeal of Hinduism for him was precisely that there was no such thing, by way of neither doctrine nor authoritative institutions, allowing him to make of it what his temperament wished, while allowing others to embrace it in quite other forms deriving from the many influences available in a diverse land and its history.

If there was any method underlying Gandhi's eclectic religious probings, it is to be found in these words. "I am not a literalist," he wrote. "Therefore I try to understand the *spirit* of the various scriptures of the world. I apply the test of *'satya'* (Truth) and *'ahimsa'* (nonviolence) laid down by these very scriptures for their interpretation. I reject what is inconsistent with that test, and I appropriate all that is consistent with it" (*Young India*, 27-8-1925). This puts a great burden on the two notions that provide the criteria for applying the crucial test, the notions of Truth and nonviolence, and I will return to them in a moment – but for now, I want to stress Gandhi's interpretative ideal of focusing on the spirit rather than on the letter of religious texts. So, for instance, he says that of all the versions of the Ramayana, the one to which he most turns is Tulsidas because "it is the spirit running through the book that holds me spellbound" (*ibid.*). And, according to Gandhi, the Bhagavad Gita (the most widely read and the most widely inspiring fragment of the Mahabharata), even though it famously presents a sustained argument for war, if properly read for its spirit, reveals, among other things, the *futility* of war. The methodological proposal, then, seems to be this: two underlying commitments (to 'Truth' and to 'nonviolence') are found in all great religious books and they provide the criteria for a test for how to detect the spirit that informs their own detailed narratives and normative injunctions. One need not be a literalist (nor what is sometimes called 'fundamentalist') about those narratives and norms, one need only take from them what passes the test provided by these two fundamental criteria, since that will be what captures the spiritual wisdom in these great works.

So, whatever sanatani means for him, it does not mean someone who commends a strict adherence to a textually articulated doctrine. When characterizing a sanatani Hindu, he explicitly mentions four things: (1) belief in the ancient Hindu texts; (2) belief in the *varnashrama dharma* (though not, he hastily adds, 'the caste system' as widely understood in his time, but an early scripturally based system of caste differentiation conceived on personal qualities and forms of work, and not on birth); (3) a commitment to cow protection in what he also describes as a much larger and more symbolically important sense than is widely understood; and (4) a firm refusal of idol worship.[3] He then crucially adds: "The reader will notice that I have purposely refused from using the word 'divine origin' in reference to the Vedas or any other scriptures . . . My belief in the Hindu scriptures does not require me to accept every word and every verse as divinely inspired. Nor do I claim to have any first-hand knowledge of these wonderful books. But I do claim to know *and feel* [italics mine] the essential truths of the essential teachings of the scriptures. I decline to be bound by any interpretation, however learned it may be, if it is repugnant to *reason* or *moral sense* [italics mine]. I do most emphatically repudiate the claim (if they advance any such) of the present *shankaracharyas* and *shastris* to give the correct interpretation of the Hindu scriptures" (*Young India*, 6-10-1921). It is not as if he denies that there are a few things that all Hindus must believe (one assumes that ahimsa and satya figures in what all must believe), but what he is most keen to allow is the greatest possible freedom for each person to get, as he puts it, a *'feel'* for the texts' wisdom. So, when he goes on to use words like 'reason' and 'moral sense' to describe how he and each person must ratify the scriptures for himself, he means something much more instinctive than those words meant on the lips and pens of philosophers such as Bentham, the Mills, Macaulay, Morley, and so on who also spoke of reason and the moral sense from within the quite different liberal tradition of India's colonial masters.

But, above all, the distinctiveness of his own understanding of Hinduism was a certain nested relationship that it offered between personal life and the public life of service to one's fellow human beings – that is to say, it could inspire the daily practices of his life, but also allow him to view those practices as essentially continuous with the remarkable political actions by which he transformed a series of lawyerly demands made to the British for incremental constitutional rights into the most prodigious mobilization of a people towards total freedom from colonial rule. It is not surprising, therefore, that he should have declared that he could never make sense of the notion of keeping religion sequestered from politics. What religion should mean in, and for, a life, is so comprehensive that it could not conceivably be kept out from any aspect of it at all: " . . . for me there are no politics devoid of religion. They subserve religion. Politics devoid of religion are a death-trap because they kill the soul" (*Young India*, 24-3-1924). Remarks like this were often addressed to those politicians around him who had a more purely instrumental view of politics. But he was equally concerned to convince the stricter Hindus around him, suspicious of all politics, of this point. "I know that many of my *Sanatanist* friends think that this is a deep political game. How I wish I could convince them that it is purely religious" (*Harijan*, 6-5-1933).

The eclecticism of Gandhi's religious thought that I have been trying to convey vexes any attempt to write about it in a systematic essay and raises challenges of creative interpretation. There are apparent inconsistencies that would stop a less creative, less inspired and instinctive thinker than Gandhi, but in him they point to very interesting and novel directions of thought.[4] Thus, for instance, he pronounces a commitment to both advaita and dvaita (monism and dualism), saying that he sees no inconsistency in this at all. "The world is changing every moment and is, therefore, unreal, it has no permanent existence. But though it is constantly changing, it has something about it which persists, and is therefore to that extent, real. I have therefore no objection to calling it both real and unreal, and thus being called an *anekantavadi* or a *syadvadi*. [Both Jain notions, the first connoting pluralism, the second, roughly, a form of internalism regarding Truth, whereby the truth of a doctrine is judged entirely from within the point of view of the doctrine itself.] But my *syadvada* is not the *syadvada* of the learned, it is peculiarly my own. I cannot engage in a debate with them. It has been my *experience* [italics mine] that I am always true from my point of view, and am often wrong from the point of view of my honest critics. I know that we are both right from our respective points of view" (*Young India*, 21-1-1926).

This unblushing relativism, indeed subjectivism, would be less than satisfactory were it not for the fact that Gandhi is saying clearly that it is matter of his *experience* that he is always true from his point of view. So the notion of Truth (satya) that is so central to his religion is not a cognitive notion that holds of propositions. It is an experiential notion. If Truth is a predicate of one's experiences, not of propositions, the subjectivism becomes more believable. A patient elaboration of what it amounted to and what its implications are in his overall religious and moral thought should help bring out the originality of his thought.[5] The initial idea upon which the details are built is that Truth carries the conviction it does for those who experience it, and not for others. When his critics are, as he puts it 'honest', and what they say by way of criticism of him, reflects and expresses some deeply felt experience, they too must be right – by the lights of that experience, of course.

Thus, in this passage, he uses the conflict and reconciliation between monism and dualism – a metaphysical issue – to move seamlessly to the more religious and moral issue of reconciling the conflict between pluralism on the one hand and the conviction in the universalizable truth of one's own moral and religious convictions. A world of diverse personal religious and moral commitments and experiences is vital to his political and religious pluralism, but at the same time, the acknowledgement (indeed, the insistent assertion) in the passage of this pluralism must do nothing to dampen the confidence in his own convictions of the truth as he judges it. Everyone judges with conviction the moral and religious Truth in the experiential sense, by the lights of their own experience.

However, this raises a fundamental question. It is one thing to assert that relativism and pluralism need not have the effect of making one hold one's own religious and moral convictions with diffidence. There are some who think that if others who oppose one also have Truth on their side, everyone – they and we – should be less than confident in holding our own religious views. Gandhi was keen to deny this, and in this, he is surely right: one should be diffident only if one was *not* a relativist, if one thought that not all these opposing views could be right and so *one might oneself be wrong*. But the point of the pluralist relativism in *syadvada* is precisely that *all* genuinely experienced views *had* the right (relative right) on their side, so there was no reason to think that any of these views is wrong and therefore no need for anyone to be diffident in holding them. Still, another much harder question remains: if religious and moral Truth is a matter of experience and personal conviction, always Truth by one's own lights, how are we to assert the centrality and importance of religion and morals in social life? How are we to give ourselves the right to *universalize* our own moral and religious convictions to others? If we did not see our own personal convictions as universalizable, as having a wider relevance for all other human beings, we would not be able to capture what is distinctively humanistic and universal about religious and moral Truth. We would relegate it to the relatively trivial realm of personal taste (a flavour of food, say) in which one does not particularly care that someone else has the taste for things other than what one likes. Thus the *syadvada* (internalism, implying subjectivism even, as we have seen) needs to be supplemented if religion and morality are not going to deteriorate into frivolous matters of taste. How, then, does he achieve the reconciliation between the pluralism that subjectivity of experience allows, and the universality, the universal relevance, of the religious and moral Truths that one's experience presents to one? Gandhi's religion was, as he repeatedly said, a 'humanistic' creed. It would not do to have the personal and experiential aspect of religion fail to be of relevance to a wider and more universal humanity. If one did not see such a wider relevance, one would have trivialized religion to matters of taste, and Gandhi's entire life was a religious life because he was utterly driven to universalize the personal convictions that he describes so well in his interpretative ideas about the sacred books of Hinduism.

As in all reconciliations of seeming opposites, the intellectual task here is not easy. One wants to preserve what is important in both or each of irreconcilable elements. I have just said why it is important for Gandhi to stress the element of *universalizability* of one's religious convictions. Without it, one would not see the human relevance of the truth as one sees it and experiences it. But why is the opposing element so important for him, why is it so important for him to insist that religious convictions are primarily a matter of personal experience and that satya or Truth itself is an *experiential* notion? Why can't Truth be seen as the truth of universal propositions, as it generally is, in moral and religious thought? After all, religion (indeed, all morality) has certain *principles* that they consider to be truths. So why is he so keen to remove from our religious life any place for doctrines, propositions, and principles that require a wholly different notion of Truth from his? It cannot just be because he wants to make possible a flexible reading of texts; it cannot be motivated merely by his ideals of interpretative freedom, as in those passages cited at the outset. Something deeper must underlie it.

It is here, I think, that ahimsa first enters as a very fundamental religious ideal for him, and then pervades his entire religious and political life. In many passages (see, e.g., *Young India*, 4-10-1928, and some of the weekly discourses known as 'Ashram Vows' sent from Yeravda Prison),[6] Gandhi is keen to say that himsa and ahimsa, when understood in their full religious sense, as opposed to strategic political sense, must not be thought of in narrow terms. It is not just a matter of physical violence and its avoidance. In fact, physical violence is, as he says there, the 'least expression' of himsa. It comes in much more, as he puts it, 'insidious' and indirect forms. It goes much deeper as an attitude of mind and interpersonal behaviour; and it is at this deeper realm of violence in which the very idea of principles and propositions and doctrines are subtly and *indirectly* implicated.

The conceptual links of this implicated relation are roughly as follows. In saying that violence is much more than physical, the point is not merely to say that it can be also be psychological or emotional. That, as a general truth, is obvious, but it is underdescribed. The specific and striking idea he has in mind is that himsa is present even in criticisms made of individual human beings. Why? Because such criticisms are the originary basis of negative attitudes of contempt and ill will towards others that are often the basis of violence and lead to violence in action. (Gandhi was not against criticism of institutions and policies and even of whole civilizational tendencies and himself made such criticism frequently as, say, in *Hind Swaraj* where he is harshly critical of the modern

West. But he tried throughout his life to avoid criticism of individuals. And the fact is that even if he was often critical of individuals, that does not overturn his intellectual opposition to such criticism. Failing to live up to what one thinks one should and shouldn't do is not to be inconsistent in one's *thinking*.)

What has this deeper notion of violence that is found even in criticism of others got to do with his opposition to a religion and a morality based on principles and doctrines? It is in the nature of principles that when someone fails to live up to them or falls afoul of them, he or she become subject to criticism. That is why principles should not be an essential part of religion and morals. This does not mean that individuals must cease making moral judgements and choices. What it means is that when one makes a choice or a judgement, one should not set it up as generating or issuing from a principle or a doctrine of what is sacred or righteous or virtuous. Making a choice and a judgement is a reflection of one's *conscience*, not of principles. (Gandhi used the term '*antaratman*' for conscience, thus registering an Indian and religious moral notion rather than a secular moral one, owing to Greek and Western sources.) It is a matter of living up to the truth in the experiential sense (satya), not truth in a propositional and doctrinal sense. Others may, therefore, come to *other* truths in this experiential sense without contradicting one's own experience, and that is how *syadvada* allows that they too are genuinely *truths* – criticism of them, therefore, is beside the point. It is only if one's moral judgements and choices generated principles and truths in a quite different sense (i.e. if truth was a predicate of principles and not one's experience) that others who fell afoul of the principle could be subject to criticism and be seen as failures, from our point of view.

Propositions and principles and doctrines can clash with one another and be inconsistent with one another, and each side, then, can blame the other when that happens. And that is what sets one on the path to the wrong mentality; a mentality of negative attitudes leading up to contempt and even, eventually, violence. Thus one's own moral and religious choices should really be seen only as matters of one's conscience and experience, not as issuing from or generating principles and doctrines.

A question now arises: can one have a religion and ethics with no principles and truths in that propositional sense? What does Gandhi intend to put in their place? We know that he wants to introduce the notion of satya, or Truth in its experiential sense, but that cannot be all there is to satya. It cannot be exhausted by the experiential because, as we have already seen, that, without further supplementation and elaboration, leads to a purely subjective religious and moral conception. And Gandhi certainly did not want to sequester the relevance of one's religious and moral convictions to oneself, just because their truth was a matter of one's experience rather than the truth of a doctrine. In a most interesting, if sometimes harsh, profile of Thoreau, Robert Louis Stevenson says of him, after describing the great virtue of the man, "...Thoreau was a skulker. He did not wish virtue to go out of him among his fellow men, but slunk into a corner to hoard it for himself. He left all for the sake of certain virtuous self-indulgences".[7] Well, for Gandhi, in spite of his admiration for Thoreau, virtue should be the exact opposite of a *self*-indulgence. The virtuous person should be the exact opposite of a 'skulker'.

Those, then, are the two claims of his conception of religious and moral virtue that pull in different directions and need to be reconciled. On the one hand, there is his repudiation of the idea that one's religious and moral convictions generate principles that apply to everyone because that leads to a moral psychology of criticism and contempt for those who fall afoul of those principles. On the other hand, there is his insistence that one's own judgements and convictions are of universal human relevance.

The reconciliation would be possible if there was *another way* of establishing the general human relevance of the moral and religious truth based on one's own experiences, than by erecting them into principles. There is a well-known slogan, which says, "When I choose for myself, I choose for everyone". Gandhi's commitment to the universal human relevance of one's personal choices would applaud this principle, but *only* if it was *not* read as saying: "*When I choose for myself, I generate a principle for everyone to follow*". That is not a satisfactory way of reconciling personal experience and choice with universal relevance of that choice and experience. So how else would one read the slogan, if this *principled* way of reading it is not allowed?

At this point, one has to introduce Gandhi's notion of satya and his ideal of the satyagrahi. Literally, the term means someone who holds firm to the truth. There is much that has been said about the role of the satyagrahi in politics, especially in the freedom movement, which Gandhi led for three decades after his return to India from South Africa. But I am appealing to something rather more general and profound that Gandhi conceived in talking of the satyagrahi as the ideal of the public individual. The clue to its centrality in his thought is that such an individual was someone possessed of the right religious understanding of the life of the individual. It was to be the life of service to others.

That is well known, and service while India was colonized often took the form of nonviolent resistance to the colonial power. But service also meant something much more general, and so the satyagrahi's actions had a much more general significance. He or she represented the ideal of an individual's life because the actions of such an individual were self-consciously conceived by him or her as *exemplary*. This is the vital element in the conceptual transition from individual choice in the realm of religion to a public and universal relevance of one's choices. I had said that we needed a reading of the slogan "When I choose for myself I choose for everyone" that did not erect principles out of one's personal choices and convictions and amount to saying, "When I choose for myself, I generate a principle for everyone". We are now given such a reading: "*When I choose for myself, I set an example for everyone*". In Gandhi's mind, this reading, despite the replacement of only one crucial word, conveyed a wholly different understanding of the nature of one's religious commitments. To set an example is not at all to generate a principle.

When one generates a principle, one sets up something normative of a kind that releases a whole set of moralistic attitudes towards those who transgress the principle, more specifically criticism and its woeful implications – the downward path to interpersonal hostility and possibly even violence. By contrast, if in one's individual choices and actions one is merely setting an example and not pronouncing a principle that can be transgressed, the moral psychology of response to those who fail to follow one's example is much weaker. It is not criticism but something altogether more humane, perhaps best described as 'disappointment'. And often, as Gandhi would say, the disappointment is in oneself that one's example hasn't set. The entire psychology of exemplary action is such that the notion of *transgression* or violation of something that is normative in the imperatival sense of principles does not figure in it at all. That is crucial to him if ahimsa is to be achieved at its deepest level. At this level, there is no criticism of other individuals who have run afoul of our moral convictions. At best, there is disappointment and a striving of the satyagrahi in each individual to do better by way of setting an example. A truly religious person in this world is someone who has come to live with this level of ahimsa, and, in that ideal of religion, the very idea of principles (or doctrines) is replaced by the idea of exemplarity.

In making the distinction between propositional/principled notions of faith and exemplary conceptions of it, Gandhi says, "Faith does not admit of telling. It has to be lived and then it becomes self-propagating"

(*Young India*, 20-10-1927). Even more explicitly, in a letter to Ramachandra Kahre (11 February 1932, see *Collected Works of Mahatma Gandhi*, vol. 55), he says: "The correct reasoning, however, is this. If we do our duty, others also will do theirs some day. We have a saying to the effect: If we ourselves are good, the *whole world* will be good". This is not just a casual remark in a letter. It is an idea that surfaces in many places in his thought and is the basis of an entirely different way of thinking about religion and the moral life. The good, conceived in this way as exemplarity, breaks out of the subjectivity of one's own conscience and truth, in the experiential sense. Goodness begins in that subjective experience, but by exemplary action, it asserts its humanistic relevance of what begins there, no longer now something subjectively limited (as matters of taste are) but reaching out to 'the whole world', making possible a humanistic universalism – the very opposite of what Stevenson describes as 'skulking' in one's own moral 'self-indulgence'. Yet being goodness in the form of exemplarity rather than in the form of a principle, it remains at the same time embedded in one's experience, and so doesn't float free of that experience in some reified notion of universality. Thus it is that the ideal of exemplarity, which is most ideally achieved in the actions of the satyagrahi, but something that all must aspire to, provides the last step in the argument by which the seeming inconsistency that I registered at the beginning of the exposition of this argument is resolved.

The entire argument constitutes a conception of religion and morality that is remarkably original. It is not as if notions of exemplarity did not exist in religious thought before him. One finds it in Erasmus, among others. But with Gandhi it is the basis of a wholesale transformation of the very idea of religion from its doctrinal and textual form to its experiential *yet* universal form. It's not (quite obviously) as if Gandhi was the first to suggest that religion should be less doctrinal and more experiential. Such ideas go as far back as Buddhism, as is well known, but Gandhi provided a new and explicit *argument* for them that is detailed in its dialectic and systematic in its implicit structure, and which I have been expounding in these last few pages.

Like Kant, a word that Gandhi often used to describe a righteous world was 'kingdom'. For Gandhi it was, among other things, a world of far-reaching ahimsa and satya, as I have been describing it, and his favourite description of it was *Ramarajya*, the kingdom or rule of Rama. Kant's ideal of a kingdom of *ends* is something with which Gandhi completely agreed – famously having claimed both that the fruits of action were irrelevant to the righteous act, and that no person should be treated as a means. But, entirely unlike Kant, in Gandhi's kingdom of righteousness, one's duty or dharma (another word often on his lips and pen) was not dictated by the rule of principles implying imperatives that set up obligations for each and all persons. Rather, duty, though issuing from a conviction whose Truth was experienced by each person as something personal, was the task of making this Truth plain to all by its display in the conduct of exemplary action.

Some of the tense dialectic between individual and universal aspects of religion that we have elaborated in Gandhi's thought was echoed in his social ideas as well. Dharma (a notoriously vague notion spanning connotations of faith on the one hand and duty on the other) constituted the universal sense of duty that held society together, but there was a contrapuntal notion of *swadharma* as well, which was the *distributed* potentiality of each individual in society. Self-knowledge consists in gradually coming to understand what one's unique *swadharma* is and living by it, not pretending one could do whatever one pleased in life. This idea of *swadharma* was just a highly individualized instance of a quite general tendency in Gandhi to shun shallow forms of ambition in which we imagine that we can just simply overthrow what was *given to one*, be it one's faith or one's family or whatever. (In fact, he compares the givenness of his faith, despite its flaws, to his wife, whom he says he loved, despite hers.) One should not easily discard what is given to one and only do so if deep inner reflection gave one highly considered grounds for doing so. "Believing as I do in heredity, being born a Hindu, I have remained a Hindu. I should only reject it if I found it inconsistent with my moral sense and my spiritual growth" (*Young India*, 6-10-1921). That is why he was opposed to the idea of missionary forms of conversion. If there were to be change of faith, it should only come from an inner experience, it could not be, to use a term from a passage cited earlier, a matter of someone else's *telling*. One may apply one's 'moral sense' and 'reason' and be selective in embracing what was given to one, as he himself certainly was in his own Hinduism. But that was not the same as being susceptible to conversion.

This point was not restricted to *swadharma* and to *individuals*. He was at least as consistent as someone like Burke in the insistence that one cannot be cavalier with what was given to one as a *civilization* and a *people*. Burke's consistency in this matter was remarkably to be found in the fact that he was prepared to be (what people have considered highly) 'conservative', as well as (what people have considered highly) 'progressive' if that is where his respect for what is given would take him. Thus his 'conservative' stand on the French Revolution and his 'progressive' stand on British rule in India was motivated by the *same argument*, which was this: whether it is done by a revolutionary mobilization in France or by an imperial presence in India, it is a form of insolence to think that you may upturn a great existing civilization. *He* was perfectly consistent in this argument, even if *we* respond to Burke's stances differentially (applause for the latter stance, but not for the former). In Gandhi too, the commitment to what was given was so consistently applied by him that it has brought him the severest of criticism in one very controversial case to which he applied it – some of his remarks on caste. His writings (and his political stances and actions) have been confusingly varied on this subject, but two things consistently underlie and motivate them all.

The first is just this Burkean thought that one shouldn't easily and entirely overthrow what is given to one, and the other (also to be found in Burke) is that *heterogeneity* should not, as far as possible, be erased for some abstract and homogenizing uniformity.

Preserving heterogeneity is one of the motivations for the very idea of *swadharma*, and that is why dharma, which provides the cement of society, should not be conceived as issuing from some abstract, universalist, homogenizing ideal, but rather, as I've already conveyed, via the universal relevance of truths conceived experientially by each person. Gandhi, however, boldly and perhaps recklessly extends this point beyond heterogeneities issuing from the fact of each individual in society possessing a unique *swadharma*, and asserted that the heterogeneities that are given to Hindu society in caste are not to be erased by the abstractions of a homogenizing ideal of citizenship in a nation-state, nor even by willful conversion to another faith without any inner experience for oneself (i.e. for each individual) of its Truth.

It has to be said, in fairness, that he was as opposed as anyone among the political leaders of India, including Ambedkar and Nehru, to the hierarchical aspects of caste, and wrote with fervent passion in direct and eloquent prose against it. But though its hierarchy and its attitudes of contempt and its violence must be discarded, its *heterogeneities* should not be eradicated along with the hierarchy, no more than Muslims should cease to be Muslims, nor Sikhs, nor Christians, nor Hindus, in the name of an abstract national citizenry. For him, unity and homogeneity were not the same thing at all. He was firm in his claims for the unity of all life in God's creation (in the spiritual force of *Brahman*), and wished to include animals too in this unity. His vegetarianism, derived from the Jainism that he was taught by an early mentor, was philosophically grounded in this idea of a unity of all living creatures, and his endorsement of cow worship as a commitment of the sanatani Hindu was a symbolic assertion of this capacious notion of unity. But nothing in such a notion of unity could possibly give rise to ideas of legislating a social homogeneity that deprived one from the diverse forms of life and work that were given in Indian society. These heterogeneities, like all pluralisms, enriched society, and society should not be impoverished by its loss, even if one removed the hierarchical aspects of caste. I give this exposition of him not to defend Gandhi from criticism on this subject, but to make plain what his underlying (more or less Burkean) motivations were. He sometimes wrote as if the hierarchies of caste were simply not a part of Hinduism. But I think he realized that this did not sit well with his own understanding of religion as a matter of experience and practice. Caste, the most resilient form of social inegalitarianism in the history of the world, and Hinduism, the religion, are indeed inseparable. Still, he urged that one's moral sense should distinguish between the hierarchy of caste and its heterogeneity. He wished for a selective Hinduism here, one that retained the latter without the former. Whatever one thinks of this as a possibility, no one can deny that the *actual politics* that this understanding of Hindu religion generated during his own lifetime (and often in his own political stances, as for instance during the controversial Poona Pact) was confused, confusing, and highly problematic.

Part of the difficulty with his religious outlook, when it came to the social practices of a religion, was that he did not think that deep and abiding social change came by legislation, but rather by changes in mentality. The importance of mind (and heart, which the Vaishnavism of his region particularly stressed) in both religion and in politics was already evident, as we saw, in his understanding of violence as far deeper than physical violence. It is also evident in another aspect of his religious thinking and practice: the ideals of brahmacharya or sexual abstinence. This is, of course, a familiar aspect of some religious traditions, and much has been written on the subject both in general and with regard to Gandhi. There is no space to discuss it at length here, but it is worth linking it to this deeper level of mentality to which he thought all religious issues must lead if they are to capture the experiential aspects of Truth that he described with the term 'satya'. Here too, Gandhi wanted to see brahmacharya as a discipline not merely of the body but of the mind, and the implications of this were indeed very deep for him. The source of the depth, once again, is the governing ideal of ahimsa.

He liked to say that violence is a form of impatience in one's actions. One indulged in it to arrive at ends by means that one perceived to be quicker than the means that the highest religious ideals would find to be suited to those ends. The achievement of ahimsa in one's life, therefore, was at least partly a result of the cultivation of a form of *patience*. But he knew perfectly well the standard (and, as he would even sometimes say, 'understandable') question that many would raise for such a philosophical outlook of nonviolence. Since the suffering wrought by political or economic or social oppression sometimes leaves people with feelings of utter *desperation*, can one not find impatience in one's action, sometimes quite understandable? He received many verbal and written queries along these lines. The brahmacharya ideal was intimately connected with the response he wished to give to such a question. The response was roughly this. For him, just like violence was not merely a physical phenomenon, impatience too was not restricted to impatience *in action*. It was possible to be impatient in one's *mentality* too, not just one's action. And desperation was the mental counterpart to impatience in action. Feelings of desperation were a form of *mental* impatience. And the most basic site of one's desperation, so conceived as an inner experiential and mental phenomenon, was in one's sexuality. Sexual arousal produced the most familiar and pervasive site of such interiorized desperation. Thus brahmacharya was the cultivation of patience along the entire spectrum of the inner life where desperation surfaced. It was by no means a training into *merely* physical abstinence. But Gandhi, true to many familiar traditions in India, knew that the body and its training was the technical path to the achievement of higher ideals, in this case the deeper forms of a *cultivated patience* needed for ahimsa. There is no understanding the daily role of spinning and the periodic role of fasting, in Gandhi's religious and social thought, without seeing this link between bodily techniques and the cultivation of the dispositions and habits of virtue. They were primarily personal efforts not outward ones directed to the worship of idols, which, as he says in the passage cited earlier, was quite inessential to the Hindu religion. They were directed to one's own person, working through one's body to the mind and soul. We may find his ideas about brahmacharya quaint and reject them, but even as we do so, it should be on record that, like his ideas about how it was shallow to restrict the notion of violence to physical violence, the idea of abstinence for him was not restricted to sexuality alone. He had in mind by it something with far wider reach that underlay the possibility of ahimsa at the deepest level.

These, then, are some of the implications of the stress on satya and ahimsa in the religious sensibility of a man who had permitted himself to be highly susceptible to a variety of influences within Hinduism and outside of it. Hinduism itself, we must recall, in its broadest historical description, first emerged as a result of the combination of very ancient religious texts (the Vedas) on the one hand and, on the other, a range of pagan, including animist, popular religious practices that had existed for centuries. We have mentioned some of Gandhi's attitudes towards those ancient texts, as well as the somewhat later books beloved of Hindus – the great epics (the Mahabharata and the Ramayana) and the Puranas. But the specifically Jain and Bhakti influences, as well as elements of the local Vaishnavism and the poet saints, also spoke to the more *popular* forms of religion that were vital to the syncretist Hindu culture that shaped his thinking; and it was really *this* aspect of his religious thinking that made him far more *systematically sceptical* of Western civilization than other Indian leaders, both religious and political.

Unlike some others, who shared his scepticism, he was not hostile to the modern West because it was an alien and imperialist presence on Indian soil. Even though he was the greatest anti-imperialist theorist who ever wrote (greater, in my view, despite his rather impoverished understanding of the concepts of class and race, than Lenin or Fanon or Said), Gandhi often said that he would be happy to have the English presence in India if the English overcame the shortcomings of their civilizational tendencies. His critique rather owed to a very clear-headed genealogical understanding of the *mentality* (and eventually, therefore, the materiality too) of the modern West and his anxieties about India's *cognitive* enslavement to it. This was, of course, a political critique, but it could not have been made in the form that he made it (first in *Hind Swaraj*, but supported at length in the many despatches to *Young India* and in various other writings) without the broader *religious* influences on his thinking I just mentioned, that shaped his thinking about nature and its relation to its inhabitants, and the essentially ethical and practical rather than intellectualized relations we bear to the world we live in. This last point and distinction need careful elaboration.

The scepticism that Gandhi displayed about the modern West was over two very basic and seemingly quite distinct ingredients, which he profoundly saw as conceptually linked and owing to a single genealogical fault line. Some of the rhetoric by which he described the fault line was crude and conflated, especially when he laid the blame on modern science rather than on some of the *outlooks* that emerged with the rise of modern science. The two ingredients were both transformations that emerged in the West sometime in the late seventeenth century, and it is interesting to see Gandhi's anxieties for India in the early twentieth century, echoing the anxieties that were first generated in Europe in that period of early modernity. This is not surprising, since he had a strong premonition that India was at the sort of crossroads that early modern Europe had been in the late seventeenth century and that it was quite uncompulsory for Indians to think that India should, as a sort of inevitability, go down the path of European modernity in these two different domains: the political economy of the West that had emerged in that period, and the Westphalian ideal of nationhood that also more or less emerged just then. His writings offer a subtle and *integrated* diagnosis of each of these transformations.

The criticisms of the outlooks of modern science that lay behind Gandhi's extensive remarks about industrialization, modern medicine, and the apparatus of modern statehood are worth exploring explicitly because they show his *religious* ideas in their most penetrating critical power. The clearest way to present them is roughly as follows. The two transformations I mentioned owe to changes in two of our most fundamental concepts to which the popular religious ideas that influenced him speak: the concept of nature and the concept of human beings as inhabitants of nature.

In those ideas, owing originally to pagan, animist conceptions of the world but consolidated by many subsequent religious ideas within Hinduism, a sacral presence and stamp was everywhere in the world, in all of nature and humanity. The idea of a human body suffused with atman as continuous with and responding to a world around it, suffused with the sacred, was a frequent occurrence in Gandhi's articulations of his religious outlook. It was this world view that was first undermined with the rise of a form of science that was modern in conception (unlike, say, Aristotelian science) and method and that lay behind first, the 'decline of magic' and only much later 'the death of God' – I put these expressions in quotation marks because they are the two forms of rhetoric by which the 'disenchantment' wrought by modern science is most often described.

Gandhi implicitly but insightfully understood that, well before the death of God, there was something much more significant brought about by the outlooks generated by some ideologues around modern science, what I think might rightly be called the *exile* of God by a specifically deist conception that placed God outside the universe, responsible for its motion by a push from an *external*, archimedean point and controlling it providentially, with all the familiar metaphors of a clockwinder, and so forth to describe it. This contrasted with the popular religious outlooks in Europe that echoed Gandhi's own Bhakti and Vaishnavite conception of the world, the neo-Platonisms and pantheisms prevalent in everyday religious understanding, which asserted a quite different conception of motion, one that came from a sacralized nature that contained an *inner* source of dynamism within the universe that was divine.

For Gandhi, like for a number of scientific dissenters in Europe, the denial of his omnipresence, that is, the exile of God to a place of inaccessibility from the visionary temperaments of ordinary people, had two disastrous consequences for culture and for politics. First, it desacralized nature and made it prey without impunity to the most ruthlessly systematic extractive political economies – of mining, deforestation, plantation agriculture (what we now call 'agribusiness'), and so on. Human beings had, of course, taken from nature ever since they first began to inhabit it. But in many social worlds, such taking as occurred was accompanied by attitudes of respect for nature in rituals of reciprocation offered before cycles of planting, and even hunting. What happened in the seventeenth century that was distinctive was that for the first time explicit alliances were formed between scientific communities (e.g. the Royal Society in England) and commercial interests, and established religious interests (e.g. the Anglicans in England) to make the idea of a desacralized nature, the ideological basis for capital's systemic predatory transformation of the very idea of nature into the idea of *natural resources*.[8]

Without knowing it, Gandhi joined a long tradition (going back to late seventeenth-century radical freethinking in England, which invoked the radical sects of the mid-century, such as the Diggers, who had valiantly resisted 'enclosures') of those who wrote with passion against this turn in religious outlook and rightly diagnosed it as an originary fault line for a predatory conception of political economy. The point is not that God was everywhere conceived as immanent before modern science promoted a specific form of deism that exiled him. God was frequently also conceived in transcendentalist rather than immanentist terms (Gandhi spoke of God in both terms himself). But at no point till the seventeenth century was God's inaccessibility made the source of a transformed conception of nature by the systematic alliances I have just mentioned. As I said, even though Gandhi did not understand the concept of class with any depth or analysis, he understood that the rise of capital came not only because of what Weber presented – emerging Protestant notions of work– but because of radically revised notions of nature around which certain crucial worldly alliances were formed. And when he wrote of the 'evils of modern science',[9] it was the devotional

Hinduism of populist religiosity and its views of the natural world we inhabited that moved him as much as anything else.

It is interesting that this very form of religiosity was also the basis of Gandhi's temperamental rejection of Hinduism's hierarchies of caste. In his ideal of *varnashrama dharma*, it was natural and right that some among one's people should be learned in the scriptures of one's religion, while others kept the peace, and yet others worked the fields, worked the crafts, and so on; all this was part of the heterogeneous distribution of any humane society and syncretic Hinduism was its living instance. This syncretism reflected the distributions of work in the *earliest varna* conception that were based on one's personal qualities and abilities that shaped one's specific dharma. In many writings, Gandhi opposed the prevalent interpretation of the varna system, which he saw as an utter corruption of the earlier ideal of caste into a hierarchical system based on birth. But, quite apart from this well-known point about his views on caste, what I want to stress now is that he was shrewd and perceptive about something much more subtle and just as consequential in the Brahmanical ideologies that had erected these corrupted interpretations into an orthodoxy. What he saw was that the privilege accorded to scriptural knowledges would and *had* made alliances with other worldly forces to corner (much more generally than in just scriptural matters) for the privileged in society, the knowledges by which *governance* is made possible. It is this *vanguard of rule* that *Shramanical* (ascetic) ideals of popular Hinduism opposed, for it is the notion of God's availability to the visions of all who inhabit his earth (conceived as sacralized by his immanent presence) from which Gandhi's democratic tendencies grew, and they were fortified by his reading of the New Testament with its expression (especially in the Sermon on the Mount) of noble sentiments of trust in the judgement of ordinary (rather than privileged) people.

The deracination of God in early Modern Europe from availability to the visions of ordinary people had similar effects in Europe, where now only university-trained divines could possess the learning and scriptural judgement that gave access to a God put away in exile for safekeeping (that is the literal meaning of *Deus Absconditus*, a term frequently used to describe this exiled conception[10]), and this elitism proceeded to spread outward from the religious sphere, by the very alliances mentioned above, shaping oligarchies around the monarch and his or her courts who possessed the privileged knowledges and values by which a centralized state emerged for the first time in the modern period in the newly emerging nations after the Westphalian peace. The monarch and the propertied elites around him ruling over a brute populace, thus, came to be viewed as the *mundane* version of an external God ruling over a brute, desacralized nature.[11]

The idea of these knowledges and values as the possession of a ruling elite first emerged in notions of *civility*, which have been well studied by Norbert Elias and more recently by Keith Thomas. But neither make much of the fact that Gandhi saw implicitly: one function of the notion of civility was that it hid from the ruling courts the cruelties of their own perpetration, because the entire semantic point of notions of civility as possessed by the propertied elites around a monarch was that cruelty could only occur in the lifestyles and behaviours of the brute and ignorant populace, lacking the knowledges and values by which humane rule is possible. This is precisely what Gandhi's Bhakti sensibility found repugnant and the New Testament's valorization of the meek and the humble over the privileged spoke directly to this recoil on his part. And he saw that this screening function of civility that generated such self-deception carried over to the more abstract morphing of ideals of civility into the idea of rights and constitutions.

It is widely known that Gandhi did not speak with the same enthusiasm as many of his Congress colleagues did for the entire panoply of principles and codes, rights and constitutions that emerged out of the political Enlightenment. The grounds for this indifference were essentially religious. He understood that what lay behind these political codes was a much more basic, indeed I would say *the* most basic, commitment of the Enlightenment, namely, that what is bad in us can be constrained by *good politics*. In other words, we can be made to be better *people* by being made over into *citizens* of a nation state. Gandhi simply did not believe this, and he thought it a massive form of secular impertinence to believe it. And, even more ambitiously, indeed brilliantly and profoundly, he was convinced that this belief in the transformation of human beings into citizens erupted from the same fault line as the transformation of the concept of nature into the concept of the natural resources. They both were the product of an outlook of modern science that, once it had desacralized the world, could not see the world itself as containing anything that made moral or normative demands on one. Nature was defined now as what the natural sciences study by a detached method, as were *people*, who now became *populations* and *citizenry*, also the objects of intellectualized study.[12] Thus the desacralized world, whether it is nature or humanity, could be *made over* by the norms that all now came from the vanguards of governance and were to be defined in terms of gains and utilities that could be imposed on the world (now conceived as natural resources and populations), shaping it to pursue these gains and utilities.

He felt that he saw more clearly than the eager modernists in the Congress party, how in such a transformed world, rights had the same function for a later time that civility did in the early modern courts; in other words, for all the good that rights and constitutions have done and are justly celebrated for, they hide from the countries who have erected them the cruelties of their own perpetration on distant lands, because, by the semantic stipulation implied by such codes, cruelties are supposed to happen only in those places where there are no rights and constitutions (i.e. among the behaviours and lifestyles of the natives of colonized lands, or in our own later time in Saddam's Iraq, or Mugabe's Zimbabwe, etc.). This was partly, at least, the source of his scepticism about rights, but what went deeper in him by way of diagnosis of all this, was the emergence of this entire way of thinking of nature and of humanity as the sorts of thing that can be improved and politically domesticated and made over, respectively, into resources and citizens.

So also, because he diagnosed the fault line where he did, he found the entire idea of a secularism that followed such a desacralization of the world, to be a hapless remedy for unredeemable damage that had already been done in the European West and which he did not want repeated in India. The entire trajectory of the Westphalian ideal of a centralized *nation*-state, for him, was based on a shift of the source of the legitimacy of the state from the divine rights of Kings to nationalisms based on feelings for a nation generated by majoritarian sentiment, consistently created in Europe via the subjugation within national territories, of minorities. (In this respect, Savarkar's ideas, rather than Nehru's, most clearly represented this Westphalian ideal in India.[13]) Ideals of secularism and multiculturalism, by Gandhi's lights, were then introduced later (and quite ineffectively), to try and undo the damage that had been done in building the ideal of the nation along these majoritarian lines. When he wrote *Hind Swaraj*, he wrote in a harshly critical tone because he was anxious to fend off the assumption that this entire disgraceful trajectory was inevitable for India. He was convinced that it was only the passing of sacralized conceptions of nature and religious conceptions of human conduct and conscience, and the rigours of devotion, that could give rise to the cast of mind that would make such a future seem compulsory for India. A secular, pluralist society should not be built at the end of a lamentable living out of the political and economic consequences of a desacralized world. It should be the proud possession of a thoroughly religious society, a Hinduism capacious enough to accommodate all the wisdom and practices of Islam, Christianity, Sikhism, Jainism, and Buddhism, (even, bizarrely, atheism[14]), an *un*self-consciously pluralist society rather than a *self-conscious* pluralism introduced too late, with the damage already done by the cognitive enslavement of a people to a decadent and utilitarian modernity.

Notes

My references to Gandhi's despatches to *Young India* and *Harijan* are specified by the date. This is the most convenient way of doing it since passages from these despatches occur in many different anthologies, apart from *The Collected Works of Mahatma Gandhi*. In all these sources, they are most easily surveyed by checking for the date.

1 In fact, according to his biographer Pyarelal, in the first volume of his biography, *Gandhi: The Early Years* (Ahmedabad, India: Navjivan Press, 1965), Gandhi recalled to him that he was not so much impressed by the haveli (the Vaishnavite temple in his vicinity) as with the Pranami Temple his mother, Putali Bai, would sometimes take him to, which was more congenial to him because more ecumenical, even taking in Islamic faith and displaying what seemed to him to be writing from the Quran on its walls.

2 Both Jainism and Buddhism are obvious influences on Gandhi's commitment to ahimsa. Yet, for all the self- and world-denying claims he made in the name of the moral appeal of brahmacharya, the fact is that he wielded and wished to wield ahimsa as a force in public life, in bringing about change and good quite directly *in the world*. It was a principle of action for him and not, as ideas of nonviolence had historically tended to be both in the Indian tradition and in the West, something that is restricted to *contemplative* ways of religious life. In this respect, he was combining (and partly shedding) Buddhism and Jainism with other influences, such as what he read in Thoreau about civil disobedience, and he then went on to make something entirely his own.

3 A word of qualification regarding his own statement here in this fourth clause. Gandhi, despite this statement, did not condemn idol worship with any zeal, and would even defend it against the zealous condemnation of some reformers. I think the right thing to say about his attitude was that he did not think it essential to Hinduism, but he was not willing to join any campaign against it and in fact found those campaigns to be wrong-headed.

4 In general, it is foolish to think that there is a definitive interpretation one can give to a religious thinker as unsystematic and yet as creative and individual and eclectic as Gandhi. The ideas are too various and too instinctively presented to contain a single and rigorous and consistent argument. Readers simply have to get an overall sense of the theoretical

instincts and of the *implicit* arguments and systematic structure and make it explicit for themselves.

5 I conjoin 'religious and moral' deliberately and frequently through this essay. Nothing short of this conjunction is appropriate for an essay on Gandhi's religious thought. As he often said, he could never separate religion from morals, and he was an unrelenting moralist all his adult life. It is, I think, because his understanding of religion was so shaped by his moral instincts and reflection, that it is so distinctive. In this, he was more like Spinoza among Western thinkers than anyone else.

6 *From Yeravda Mandir* (Gandhi referred to that prison as temple) also published in *Young India*, 30-11-1947.

7 Robert Louis Stevenson, 'Henry David Thoreau: His Character and Opinions', *Cornhill Magazine*, June 1880.

8 As is well known, the idea that nature was brute and desacralized was there in mechanistic views of a slightly earlier period than Newton, in the work of Galileo and Descartes; so also, the idea that nature was now to be seen as natural resources was something that Bacon had asserted a few decades before the 'Newtonianism' of the Royal Society. But it was only after Newton that the Royal Society came into the act and forged the alliances that ensured that other *worldly* interests were mobilized to silence the sacralized metaphysics of nature of the dissenters, whom they often stigmatized with the term 'enthusiasts'.

9 I use here a frequent phrase in Gandhi: 'the evils of modern science'. I had said earlier that Gandhi's rhetoric was crude on this point, conflating the metaphysical outlook that desacralized nature, which emerged in the seventeenth century with the rise of modern science, with science itself. I am a little uncertain about how much and how sharply to press this distinction, which he frequently conflated in this way. It is a real (and a very interesting) question as to whether this metaphysical outlook was not a *built-in* disposition of modern science. All the same, I make the distinction between science itself and this metaphysical outlook generated by science for two reasons. First, as I have written elsewhere (see my 'Gandhi, Newton, and the Enlightenment' in Aakash Singh Rathore, ed., *Indian Political Thought: A Reader*. London and New York: Routledge 2010), a number of *scientists* (then, of course, called 'natural philosophers') of the late seventeenth century (John Toland, for instance) vocally dissented from the understanding of Newtonian science as being interpreted along lines that made the divine *source* of motion external to the universe rather than an inner source of dynamism. This was a debate *within* the community of scientists and it was over a metaphysical matter, since both sides of the dispute *agreed* on the *science*, that is, on all of Newton's laws and his basic scientific notions, such as gravity. The disagreement was really only over where to place God, with the dissenting side keen *not* to desacralize matter and nature by exiling God, insisting instead on the immanentist idea of the source of motion. All this clearly suggests that one should distinguish between science and

the metaphysical outlook. The second reason is that Gandhi himself sometimes spoke as if he had nothing against science, or even technology, so long as it was in the service of the needs of ordinary people and not in the control of elites whose purpose was to exploit it (and nature) for profit. Indeed, he would say, if people wanted to see how science is done, they should come and see how effectively the problem of waste management had been studied and effectively dealt with in the life and organization of his ashram.

10 This idea is not to be confused with the more familiar cliché about how Protestantism's victories over popery had released one to have an individual relation with God without the mediation of church institutions. That had the effect of creating the 'possessive individualism' that commentators on orthodox Protestantism's influence on politics have stressed. The point being made here stresses something quite different – the thought of the radical scientific dissenters and the radical sects such as the Levellers and Diggers they often invoked were actually *opposed* to this orthodox Protestantism that had repudiated popery, not because they had any affection for Catholicism but because it was the Protestant establishment that was very much behind the Newtonian metaphysics and the political and economic ideology it had generated. In fact, these radical sects emphasized *collective* cultivation of the common rather than individualism, as well as collective governance in local, egalitarian communities.

11 This is not the idea of the 'divine *right* of kings'. That older and more familiar idea was, as is explicit in the phrase, an idea about what gives *legitimacy* to the monarchical state. The idea I am discussing here is not about legitimacy, but rather about the kind of role monarchs and their courts had in their relation to the populace, a providential role, with a very clear understanding of the nature of the brute populace over which they rule, in analogy with God ruling over a brute universe.

12 There is a disambiguation needed with the terms 'engagement' and 'detachment' when one writes of Gandhi. He wrote consistently of the importance of detachment. But he wrote with equal consistency of the harms that form of detachment that *intellectualized* relations to the world bring – that is, a view of nature as mere natural resources and people as mere populations and citizens. So the detachment he wished for was a detachment *within* one's *engaged* (i.e. moral rather than intellectual) responses to the world of others.

13 For a clear and forceful statement of this, see Ashis Nandy's forthcoming article on Savarkar's politics in *Public Culture*. One should not be misled by the fact that Gandhi was killed by someone who is described as a *Hindu* fanatic, that Gandhi was killed *because* he was not Hindu enough or a highly maverick Hindu, even if these latter two descriptions are perfectly good descriptions of him. He was killed by someone who subscribed to an ideology that secretly despised Hinduism more than it despised Islam (which, it perhaps even secretly admired in some respects). He was killed by a self-proclaimed modernist in the Savarkar

mode who wished nothing more than to transform India away from
what he perceived to be a traditional and namby-pamby Hindu ethos.
Nandy is very convincing on this point.

14 Indeed, when Gandhi later in life inverted his own famous dictum "God
is Truth" to "Truth is God", he did so partly to include even atheism in
his capacious ideal of Hinduism for India.

6 Conflict and nonviolence

RONALD J. TERCHEK

Gandhi is rightly known for his advocacy of nonviolence and love and for his dedication to the autonomy, dignity, and freedom of everyone, as well as his quest for individual and social harmony. Yet, as in so many areas of his life and writings, he seeks both harmony and conflict.[1] This joint quest is not a paradox, and the two do not invariably stand as opposites. For Gandhi, harmony comes with neither passivity nor blindness in a world beset by the domination and humiliation of the strong over the weak. Gandhian harmony stems from the free choices of autonomous individuals in the many realms of their lives. Unfortunately, what ought to be freely chosen choices are often hampered or denied by the more powerful who would have others forego their own deepest aspirations and moral commitments,[2] and Gandhi wants to change the situation of those who are dominated and humiliated. Although he, and the rest of us for the most part, would prefer to have change come through reasoned, calm dialogue with those we want to reach, those with superior power frequently decline to listen, much less change, because of rational argument.[3]

To disturb this state of affairs, Gandhi challenges the current order of things, usually by introducing a crisis that leads to conflict, albeit nonviolently. He urges those who have been dominated to protest actively and to struggle for their autonomy.[4] For Gandhi, harmony and autonomy are intertwined with eliminating injustice, and the conflicts that he pursues aim at all three. These Gandhian contests are self-limiting, eschewing violence, hatred, and a thirst for vengeance.[5] Gandhi wants nonviolence to be much more than a political tactic but a way of life that rests on an understanding about the inherent worth and dignity of all life.[6]

He ties nonviolence to the Truth, and he calls his civil disobedience campaigns expressions of satyagraha, that is, truth force. He tells us that he strives to live by the Truth, that Truth is God, and that nonviolence serves the Truth.[7] At the same time, he argues that no one knows the whole Truth (including him), that each of us is capable of knowing fragments of the Truth,[8] and that we are better off when we live by the Truth rather than reject it. Moreover, he tells us that different people see the Truth differently.[9] What are we to make of this, and how do we proceed in a world of uncertainty?

Gandhi's view of the Truth is embedded in his own religious tradition, and he finds in Hinduism a celebration of all life, a cosmological view of our relationships with one another, and a pervasive sense of duty we owe to one another. At the same time, he acknowledges that other religions and other traditions grasp important elements of the Truth. What fragments does Gandhi take to be reliably true? One aspect has to do with the essential autonomy of each individual, that is, the inherent dignity and worth of everyone regardless of a person's background. He also finds that we are better able to approach the Truth when we love rather than hate, when we forgive rather than seek revenge, when we are guided by rational discourse rather than the passions, and when we confront injustice rather than accept injustice for the sake of a surface order.

For Gandhi, we are all essentially equal as human beings, even though some of us may have more than others, and we are not only fallible but also autonomous: each of us should make our own moral decisions and lead our own moral lives. We ought not to be coerced by others or moulded by convention to act this way or that. Because of the equality premise, what we claim for ourselves we ought also to respect in others. To leave the story of moral choices here would tempt us to make Gandhi into a rights theorist. Although he often speaks of rights, such as the rights of dacoits and women, he emphasizes the duties we have towards each other.[10]

Part of Gandhi's idea of equality rests on the limits that describe all human beings. Because none of us is omniscient or omnipotent, none has leave to dominate others, that is, to deny others their dignity and autonomy. To pretend otherwise is to puff ourselves up with attributes reserved for the divine. However, human limitations do not make us impotent. Gandhi reserves considerable power to individuals to make choices and lead moral lives. As people do so, they must pay close attention to how they proceed; they ought, in Gandhi's language, to pay attention to the means they use to construct their lives. He tells us that we do not have control over ends but only means. So, he insists that we proceed nonviolently. Gandhi holds that violence results from a confusion about means and ends. With violent conflicts, any means are frequently seen as justifiable to serve the ultimate end of victory. Speaking to an exponent of violence, he argues that "by using similar means, we can get only the same thing that they have got ... We reap exactly what we sow".[11] According to Gandhi, people can control the means but not the ends. "They say 'means are after all means'. I would say that 'means are after all everything'. As the means, so the end... Violent means will give violent *Swaraj*... I have been endeavouring to keep the country to means that are purely peaceful and legitimate".[12]

Before Gandhi undertakes a civil disobedience campaign, he insists that it is necessary to prepare for the nonviolent confrontation. He expects that his opponents will use a variety of tactics to stop the campaign, and they often employ violence, intimidation, and imprisonments to achieve their goals. Gandhi wants the satyagrahi to be trained in self-discipline to accept such pains and not return violence with violence.[13]

Even when those who have been dominated succeed in alleviating their situation nonviolently, the autonomy and harmony they seek is not necessarily stable or lasting. One reason is that most of us are subject to many sites of power, and becoming free in one site hardly guarantees freedom in each of the others. This is why Indian national independence is not a sufficient goal for Gandhi throughout his many years of struggle on the subcontinent. He also works nonviolently to dismantle many of the other disabilities confronting various Indians, including dacoits, millworkers, women, and indigo farmers.[14] Another reason is that because the world is not fixed, an autonomy and harmony that seem secure is often later disturbed by those who have gained new power in the changing order of things. As far as Gandhi is concerned, therefore, it is necessary to confront new expressions of power that are used to dominate others.[15] As he sees matters, harmony is an ideal that speaks to our moral aspirations and acts as a beacon that steers us to a better life and a better society, and we need to work at approaching it. Even though harmony is illusive as a permanent condition for both the individual and society, to disregard its importance is to risk that injustices would repeat themselves.

GANDHI, INJUSTICE, AND POWER

Gandhi's conception of justice and injustice parallels contemporary theories of justice that emphasize nondomination and noninterference.[16] There is a tendency in classical liberalism to emphasize non-interference, that is, leaving others be. However, if noninterference is the norm but domination is rampant, then the injustices housed in any society go undisturbed. For Gandhi, justice sometimes means interfering with those who dominate others, and this he makes central to his politics.[17] In practice, Gandhi emphasizes injustice because it is concrete; he thinks we can more readily see present-day suffering, pain, and humiliation rather than agree about abstract, idealized conceptions of justice that might be achieved sometime in the future. As he understands matters, injustice, in its concreteness, robs people of their autonomy and dignity in the here and now. When we see brutality, domination, and the like, Gandhi hopes that we will acknowledge that they are wrong and judge the situation to be unjust. When we talk to others about the meaning of justice, however, we often disagree. Some will emphasize a strong community, others a robust individualism, and still others a combination of the two. Others will debate the ways that markets, a centralized economy, or a welfare state contribute to justice.[18]

Although Gandhi concentrates on injustice, he understands that many do not consider the sufferings and pains they see about them as injustices. Rather they translate them, to use Judith Shklar's phrase, as 'misfortunes'.[19] With misfortunes, the hurts and agonies that crowd the lives of some people are taken to be beyond human design or repair, but rather have origins in the nature of things or because of divine edicts. Shklar shows that many of the injuries that people experience fall into the category of 'misfortunes' but that many other pains are the result of what some human beings do or leave undone to others. Gandhi's purpose in creating many crises is not only to demonstrate the real suffering of people but also to show that these pains are caused by human beings and can be corrected by them.

Gandhi believes that, by and large, many expressions of injustice can be traced to inequalities of power.[20] Because there are many sites of unequal power, there are many possibilities of injustice.[21] They might be found in the family, in gender, class, or caste relationships, or in political, economic, social, or cultural practices. When power relationships are asymmetrical, those holding a preponderance of power are often tempted to use their resources for their own advantages.[22] The powerful often believe that they are entitled to do so because of custom, because of their skills, such as with military personnel or professionals, because of their position, such as in government, or because of the resources they command in the economy.[23] It is the case that many people who have power over others are, in turn, the objects of power by those above them or in other spheres of their lives.[24] This is one reason why Gandhi believes the quest for autonomy, harmony, and justice is never ending.

Not content to leave his discussion of power with those who possess formal power by virtue of their office, wealth, or birth, Gandhi invests individuals with considerable power. He holds that power, wherever it is lodged, rests on the consent, albeit frequently the tacit consent of the members of society. For this reason, he argues that we are responsible for what we tolerate. As he sees matters, "Most people . . . do not realize every citizen silently but none the less certainly sustains the government of the day . . . Every citizen renders himself responsible for every act of his government". With this in mind, he holds that "It is not so much as British guns that are responsible for our subjection as our voluntary cooperation".[25] Because power can be traced back to individuals, men and women should refuse to support power that they find is morally abhorrent. Gandhi claims, "Civil disobedience is the inherent right of a citizen. He does not give it up without ceasing to be a man. Civil disobedience is never followed by anarchy . . . Civil disobedience . . . becomes a sacred duty when the State has become lawless, or which is the same thing, corrupt. And a citizen who barters with such a State shares its corruption or lawlessness".[26]

CRISIS, CONFLICT, AND CHANGE

Too often, ordinary people are expected to know their place in society and to be quiet about matters that deeply trouble them. Their lot is to defer to authority and to submit to the powerful respectfully and humbly. The role assigned to them in life is to accept who and where they are, perhaps hoping to make marginal improvements in their lives but dampening ambitions that seem inappropriate for the likes of them, and certainly not disturbing matters that would challenge those with superior power. When this happens, there is a surface tranquility in society, and people go about their routines as they have previously and probably will in the future. But the order of such a time and place often masks deep injustices and asymmetries of power that routine calm only perpetuates.

Enter Gandhi. He seeks to disturb the routines of the day that frees patterns of domination of their claims of legitimacy. Gandhi calls on people to assert themselves regarding the injustices they personally experience or they witness in their society. The claims of those with little conventional power, however, are unlikely to move those with formal power. To initiate a process that will lead to dismantling injustice requires something more than talk, although talk is vitally important to Gandhi. What is especially necessary is to do something that alerts those with formal power that once-predictable routines have been sundered and that matters cannot quietly continue as they had in the past. Only when the old order is challenged will those with power be prepared to talk seriously with those with grievances.[27] For this to happen, people must act on their own behalf. However, before Gandhi calls for civil disobedience, he insists that a determined effort be made to negotiate with the other side.

Nonviolent confrontation is about more than action: Gandhi's crises ultimately aim at promoting dialogue, which is at the heart of voluntary change. Gandhi's commitment to open, honest speech parallels in some important respects Socrates' reliance on dialogue. Socrates challenges those around him to give good reasons for their ideas and, when their defenses are wanting, to see the need to change their views. Socrates invites us to explore matters in ways that take us away from conclusions that are based on conventions, interests, or the passions. His project is based on mutual, voluntary commitments by everyone to search for the Truth or at least approach it.[28] Gandhi wants to engage in a dialogue with those who are reluctant or opposed to talking to him and taking him seriously. In disturbing the status quo, Gandhi makes it costly, if not impossible, to return to routine ways, as if nothing had happened. For the discussions that Gandhi wishes to promote, Gandhian crises not only disturb old ways but also mobilize power. We see this in *Hind Swaraj*, where he argues that the absence of force or power will make demands to correct injustices unconvincing to the satyagrahi's adversaries.[29]

Even though Gandhi promotes crises, he does so selectively, and one reason is that he believes that some forms of conflict are dangerous. Why can conflict be dangerous? Sometimes it is directed to petty matters that, nevertheless, disturbs the peace and basic order of society, matters that are not Gandhi's highest goods but goods he admires. Even when injustice prevails, conflict can also be dangerous because the civilly disobedient person does not control others who are engaged in the same struggle but who may become violent. We see this in what appeared to be a successful civil disobedience campaign that Gandhi leads in early 1922. Several protestors in the town of Chauri Chaura are attacked by the local police; after the demonstrators regroup, they chase the police back to their station, which they then attack and kill the officers. After this outbreak of violence by Gandhi's followers, he suspends the civil disobedience campaign, explaining, "Suspension of mass civil disobedience and subsidence of excitement are necessary for further progress, indeed indispensable to prevent further retrogression". There is, he admits, a certain 'unreality' in a campaign that had not guarded against potential violence within its own ranks and takes too optimistic a reading of everyone who actively joined its ranks.[30] This is one reason he insists that before any action is taken, it is necessary to assemble all of the facts in order to establish the justice claims of the protesters, and in this way, he hopes to avoid campaigns propelled by passion rather than a drive to correct injustices. He seeks to preclude campaigns fired by emotions, such as revenge, anger, or envy, which proceed blindly, without a sense of limits. When passion, anger, and revenge rule, it is difficult to know how to reason or forgive and proceed nonviolently.

LOVE AND ACTION

Moving beyond conventional views of power, Gandhi offers an expansive and intensive understanding of power. He sees it residing in places and practices ignored, or even denied, by most observers. Even so, his wide-ranging views are shared by some others, and at the present time, this includes many post-modernist writers and feminists.[31] However, where they conclude their discussions of power as practices of domination and humiliation, Gandhi plows further, taking an unexpected direction. For him, love is also a form of power.[32]

According to Gandhi, satyagraha is about conflict but also about love. He wants people not only to love their family and friends, as well as strangers, but also to love their adversaries. According to him, "Love is reckless in giving away, oblivious as to what it gets in return. Love wrestles with the world as with itself and ultimately gains a mastery over all other feelings".[33] For Gandhi, real lovers do not love each other for their own advantage. Lovers do not judge their relationship in pragmatic or utilitarian terms. Gandhian love is giving without demanding conditions. From this perspective, parental love, for example, is reckless; it does not depend on the child's meeting certain expectations. Ideally, parental love is given in good and bad times. Moreover, parental love, from the vantage of this perspective, is forthcoming when the child pleases but withdrawn when the child disappoints. Gandhian love, in other words, can exist alongside of disapproval.

Gandhi makes love one of two forms of power: one "is obtained by the fear of punishment and the other by acts of love". The first is based on force while the latter rests on conversion. "Love never claims, it ever gives. Love ever suffers, never resents, never revenges itself".[34] As Gandhi sees matters, everyone can love as well as respond to love, though it may take time. Love derives its power, he holds, through its ability to change others positively. Margaret Chatterjee finds that Gandhi believes "Love is the power which draws people closer together".[35] The power of love, Gandhi insists, comes with ability to convert others, to have them change their attitudes and behavior voluntarily. To convert others, to have them see matters in new ways, is not just a matter of the good will of the satyagrahi.[36] Gandhi's satyagrahis bring not only their own self-respect, but respect for their opponents, as well as their willingness to suffer freely for their cause without responding to the violence their opponents might employ.

The satyagrahi approaches adversaries not in the spirit of hatred or revenge, which would only confirm in the adversaries' mind the moral inferiority of the satyagrahi but also justify harsh, violent responses. "The appeal [of the satyagrahi] is never to his [opponent's] fear; it is, must be, always to his heart. The satyagrahi's object is to convert, not to coerce, the wrong-doer".[37] One aspect of Gandhi's claim that one's opponent can love comes in his discussion of voluntary suffering by the satyagrahi. "Reason has to be strengthened by suffering and suffering opens the eyes to understanding".[38] Voluntary suffering, Gandhi insists, moves others, showing them the sincerity and commitment of the satya-grahi, and eventually converting their opponents.

Even though Gandhi holds that love can be encompassing and is an ideal to which we should all strive, he does not believe that we will be able to achieve the universalizing ideal of love fully. He reasons that all human life "exists by some himsa [harm, violence]" and remains with us as long as we live. However, that is no reason to think we should not strive to diminish himsa in our lives and cultivate ahimsa, that is, love, nonviolence.[39] For Gandhi, love, not violence, brings out the best in us.

SCEPTICISM, COURAGE, AND HOPE

The powerless often believe that they have no alternative but to acquiesce in their situation. Such people become fatalists who conclude that matters cannot be otherwise, that they have been consigned to a particular lot in life that they cannot significantly alter, and they are best off when they recognize their assigned limits. Fatalists believe that nothing can be done to improve their situation, much less transform it. They think their situation is a dictate of nature, ordained by the gods, or is somehow deserved by them. Fatalism appears generation after generation, taking new shapes and new rationales.[40] The struggle against fatalism never ends, and the need for scepticism and hope remains a necessity for a people who would be free. To have people recognize that they have a dormant power that can be activated to challenge injustice, Gandhi promotes political scepticism and political hope and thus challenges political fatalism.

Gandhian political sceptics raise questions when others think the subject is closed. They nurture doubts about matters that others think settled. They see problems that the apathetic citizen or the routine loyalist does not. The posture of the Gandhian sceptic is not that of a perpetual fault-finder; his sceptics frequently support the proposals of others. But Gandhi's sceptics refuse to be sheep, herded about this way and that at the design or convenience of their shepherd. They use their minds, which often means their common sense and their experiences.[41]

Wanting those trapped by injustice to shun fatalism, Gandhi invites them to question conventional arrangements that deny their autonomy, dignity, and basic rights. For a healthy scepticism to emerge, it is necessary to raise new questions. Answers to the old questions that have been handed to us do not necessarily bring fresh understandings of our condition. Rather, the old questions tend, at best, to produce answers that are variations of what we have heard before. Accordingly, Gandhi wants people to become discontented with the current orthodoxies.[42] As he puts it in *Hind Swaraj*, "As long as man is contented with his present lot, so long is it difficult to persuade them to come out of it".[43] In this way, the remainders, that is, what is left out of the dominant framework and that have been ignored in the old formula, are exposed, and unacknowledged pains and costs can be addressed.[44] It turns out that to initiate political scepticism, it is necessary to be discontented both with one's situation, as well as with the old questions and answers.

Gandhian sceptics carry an abundance of hope that they can change matters.[45] Gandhi's hope is not grounded on a blind optimism that holds that simply by speaking out and challenging injustice matters will inevitably change for the better. For Gandhi's hopeful person, the future is always undecided. Even so, hope is necessary for the kind of nonviolent challenges that he seeks to promote against injustice. But this does not mean that without hope there can be no challenging action. Action against injustice and domination can be driven by entrenched revenge, a gnawing envy, melancholy rancor, deep-seated anger, or other passions that are unlikely to pay heed to Gandhian imperatives of nonviolence. Gandhi's hopeful person surmounts these passions through love and nonviolence.

The hopeful person engages in neither wishful thinking nor blind faith. Gandhian hope departs from pleasant dreams, which are expansive and face no formidable obstacles that cannot be overcome. It is not a self-assured confidence that the righteousness of one's cause assures a triumphant conclusion. Gandhian hope leaves ethereal realms filled with dreams of transformed vistas; it stays with everyday life with all of its opportunities and difficulties in order to ask what can be done. Gandhi's hopeful person seeks to be constructive while adhering to non-violent means. How realistic is Gandhi's hope? After all, it seems to some to ignore the harsh realities of power and the inflexibility of the status quo. It is helpful here to turn to the German theologian, Jurgen Moltmann, who finds that hope is not another name for dreams but is anchored in realism. He writes:

> Hope alone is to be called 'realistic', because it alone takes seriously the possibilities with which all reality is fraught. It does not take things as they happen to stand or to lie, but as progressing, moving things with possibilities of change . . . The celebrated realism of the stark facts, of established objects and laws, the attitude that despairs of its possibilities and clings to reality as it is, is inevitably much more open to the charge of being utopian, for in its eyes there is 'no place' for possibilities, for future novelty, and consequently for the historic character of reality.[46]

In periods buffeted by change, hopeful people expect that they can have a hand in directing some of that change or taking advantage of its most promising possibilities, at the same time seriously responding to new injustices that come with much change. To have no hope at such times is to leave the field open to those who see opportunities for themselves and work to steer matters in their favor, even at the expense of others. Hopeful individuals reject assignments that place them in inferior places where discouragement abounds and helplessness seems to be their lot. Gandhian hope is also about the hope to be heard and taken seriously in politics and the hope to achieve something like political equality among citizens.

The alliance of scepticism, hope, and politics is not unique to Gandhi. The Italian neo-realist political theorist, Norberto Bobbio, is one writer who not only emphasizes the importance of hope, but also ties it to a healthy scepticism. For Bobbio, scepticism is not, in itself, to be feared. Indeed, it "is the ripe fruit of an exuberant culture". The questioning of the sceptic leads to action; the sceptic is "the man of the world *par excellence*". In contrast to the sceptic, Bobbio finds the cynic is an obstacle to action; indeed, the cynic "is incapable of action in the world".[47] For the cynic, nothing is true, everything is not only relative, but also corrupt and destined to remain so.

Focusing on a negative, despairing outlook on life, the person coughed up by cynicism is alone. Bobbio sees such a person as "isolated, shut up in his finiteness, his own prisoner; nor has he outside himself any means of attaining transcendency save in the direction of nothingness". This antisocial entity is left without society, without a concrete world in which to participate. As Bobbio sees matters, cynics "fail to grasp the meaning of society regarded as a union of beings involved in a joint struggle, as *struggle* and *cooperation*".[48] However, scepticism by itself is insufficient; it must be tied to action that is propelled by hope. For Bobbio, "Hope is not enough to win, but if one does not have a little hope, then the game is lost before you even begin".[49]

In addition to scepticism, discontent, and hope, Gandhi insists that people must be courageous.[50] As Bhikhu Parekh puts it, "For Gandhi, courage was one of the highest human virtues".[51] Gandhi holds that frightened people do not rule themselves but let fear direct them, preferring safe ways, even when it means that the person is dishonest to his or her deepest principles and aspirations. Frightened people forfeit their own self-respect, as well as the respect of others.[52] Such people are mere objects of those who stand over them.[53] Having suspended their conscience, cowards are guided by prospects of threatened or real punishments or rewards denied. Why is fear so troubling to someone like Gandhi? John Keane provides an answer in his essay, 'Fear and Democracy', where he argues that "Fear is indeed a thief. It robs subjects of their capacity to act with or against others". Keane goes on to observe that scholars increasingly have come to the conclusion "that fear and its paralyzing effects could be overcome, not just comforted and consoled . . . Fear came to be regarded a thoroughly human problem for which there are thoroughly human remedies".[54] To break out of the confining chains of fear, Gandhi calls on people to summon their courage and act.

Gandhi's conception of courage parallels Aristotle's understanding. In each case, courageous persons are neither rash nor cowardly. They have a sensibility about what is really important, and that is not always their lives, possessions, or status. Courageous persons are directed by their consciences and decide to govern themselves rather than be ruled by fear. Gandhi reasons that people trapped by fatalism, cynicism, and despair are not apt to find the courage to act on their own behalf. For them to shake off such outlooks, people must respect themselves and become their own masters.[55] Those who live in fear are, from Gandhi's perspective, incapable of practicing the other virtues. Driven by their fears, they leave love, compassion, forgiveness, and mutual regard behind as they build barricades around themselves, leading Raghavan Iyer to observe that "Gandhi tended to assimilate all the virtues to that of moral courage".[56]

Neither all political inaction nor the many acceptances of injustice can be traced to fear or fatalism. Many people surrender their autonomy in exchange for something they think more valuable. Or they think they can simultaneously have two different things that they believe are valuable without realizing that they are incommensurable. Or they think they can easily recover what they have forsaken. Such people rent out their consciences to the more powerful for things they see as glittering and enticing. They embrace, so to speak, a Trojan horse with all of its external appeals without sensing the dangers that lie within. Gandhi has this in mind when he writes that "the English have not taken India, we have given it to them". The reason for this, he tells us, is that Indians love British commerce.[57] But in exchange, they have surrendered their freedom.

CONCLUSIONS

Gandhi has frequently been portrayed as an idealist, one far removed from the harsh realities of the world of politics. Yet there is a compelling realism in much that he writes and does. He is acutely aware of power, the many forms it takes, and the excuses it offers for what it does. Gandhi untangles the relationship between consent and power, and argues that tacit consent legitimizes the government of the day. If that consent is withdrawn, Gandhi insists, then government loses not only its legitimacy but also its power, which returns to ordinary men and women. He also works with the premise that the goodness of a cause does not absolve it of constraints, and insists that nonviolence limits what we can and cannot do. In violent conflicts, each of the adversaries seeks to force the other side into submission, generally without regard to the costs, including moral costs, to either oneself or others. Believing that nonviolence dampens the passions, Gandhi holds that it enables the parties to live in harmony without fear of one another after the conflict has ended. If we focus only on our own goodness, we often fail to see any wrongs we commit on behalf of our good cause, and if we do acknowledge the harms we do, we are often tempted to consider them as regrettable but unavoidable collateral damage. As the same time, our opponents, concentrating on their own good cause, proceed down their own violent path, excusing what they do.[58] Gandhi wants the satyagrahi to determine the terrain on which the contest will be conducted, rather than accept the violent grounds preferred by many adversaries. To accept the rules of engagement laid down by their opponents, Gandhi insists, means that we all begin to look like our adversaries, trying to gain the upper hand regardless of costs, including moral costs.[59]

When he promotes conflict, it is to challenge injustice and relieve the suffering of others here and now. Although Gandhi always has his eyes on justice, it turns out that in practice he is concerned about diminishing specific injustices that typically emanate from an unequal distribution of power.[60] There are those who believe that all applications of power are evil. Gandhi is not one of these people. In fact, he seeks to empower people who have been deprived of formal power in their lives so they can gain their autonomy and self-respect. For him, power must always be contextualized, and he is particularly interested in how power is expressed and whether it serves to enlarge or diminish the dignity of human beings. With this in mind, Gandhi rejects a relativistic standard for judging power. He judges power by both the end it serves and the means deployed to achieve its end.

Gandhi's appreciation of power is linked to his emphasis on its uses or purposes. When power is used to dominate, he wants to challenge it. Power, for him, cannot be considered in the abstract but must be evaluated in the way it concretely proceeds, affecting the lives of ordinary people. He is particularly concerned with concentrated power, which tries to make itself unaccountable and robs individuals of their autonomy. Concerned with how power can harm others, he insists that when serving a just cause, power must be employed nonviolently. Always suspicious of concentrated power, Gandhi hopes to domesticate power by diffusing it, scattering it in many small parcels in order to assure that some do not hoard it and use it at the expense of others.

Does this mean that, to take Gandhi seriously, it is necessary to accept his entire theory of nonviolence, applying it to every circumstance and at any time? Many commentators have shown that Gandhi himself makes some exceptions to the use of nonviolence. Others argue that his theory does not apply to ruthless regimes, such as those of Hitler and Stalin.[61] Each person must decide how and where to apply Gandhian principles, but such an exercise cannot be a matter of convenience or interests. I hold that to take Gandhi seriously and yet to make exceptions in his theory requires a principled stand that does not change with convenience or interest and which does not contradict one's other strong moral principles.

Notes

1 For an extended discussion of the central place of harmony in Gandhi, see Anthony Parel, *Gandhi's Philosophy and the Quest for Harmony* (Cambridge, England: Cambridge University Press, 2006).
2 Those with great power seldom consider what they do as cruel or evil but as necessary and good. Hence, they take no responsibility for their

actions that spawn or perpetuate injustice, whether intended or unintended. By inventing and then applying their own standards to judge themselves, the powerful typically exempt themselves from accountability or any broader decency. This tends to feed the arrogance of the powerful who are deaf to other ways of judging and hearing.

3   Gandhi's position is taken up later by Martin Luther King who argues it is not good enough to try to persuade opponents with scientific reasoning or carry a passive faith that God will correct all injustice. People must act on behalf of their own consciences. See his *Strength to Love* (New York: Pocket Books, 1968), particularly pp. 146–8.

4   Gandhi holds that it "is necessary for workers to become self-reliant and dare to prosecute their plans if they so desire, without hankering after the backing of . . . persons supposed to be great and influential" (*Young India*, 19 May 1927).

5   Nonviolence places constraints on individuals in the ways they deal with their adversaries. Violence lessens and often obliterates these constraints. Physical violence involves injury or even death to an individual, group, or nation. From Gandhi's perspective, the use of physical force denies the essential dignity and equality of human beings. Violence says, in effect, the potential objects of violence do not know how to behave, and it is up to those with power to use force to discipline them and make them compliant. The powerful proceed believing not only that they have sufficient power to carry out their plans, but they also know what is best for everyone, including those they are prepared to injure. Too often, the powerful are able to intimidate the weak and force them into submission. Violence, he insists, robs its victims of their free choices. Moreover, Gandhi holds that it degrades those who engage in violence. Violence makes reconciliation and forgiveness difficult to achieve, fostering an environment of continued suspicion and anger with the always-potent possibility that violence will flare up again. Even though Gandhi is convinced that nonviolence is the superior way of proceeding, he holds that it is better to be violent than quietly withdraw in the face of injustice.

6   A person "cannot do right in one department in life whilst he is occupied in doing wrong in any other department. Life is one indivisible whole" (*Young India*, 27 January 1927).

7   "Truth is my God. Truth is the means of realizing Him" (*Young India*, 8 January 1925). See also *Young India*, 20 January 1927, where he writes, "I will not sacrifice Truth and Non-violence even for the deliverance of my country or religion".

8   We "will never all think alike and . . . we shall always see *Truth* in fragments and from different angles of vision. Conscience is not the same thing for all" (*Young India*, 23 September 1926).

9   See *Young India*, 22 September 1927, where he argues that all the great religions contain aspects of the truth but that each is incomplete.

10 Gandhi holds that "the true source of rights is duty. If we all discharge our duties, our rights will not be far to seek" (*Young India*, 8 January 1925).

11 Anthony Parel (ed.), *Gandhi: Hind Swaraj and Other Writings* (Cambridge, England: Cambridge University Press, 1997), p. 81.

12 *Young India*, 17 July 1924.

13 The civil disobedient person must be ready to accept punishment.

14 To be free from colonialism brings only a partial freedom for many, such as women and dacoits. For a discussion of a variety of Gandhi's campaigns, see Joan Bondurant, *Conquest of Violence* (Berkley: University of California Press, 1967).

15 For Gandhi's discussion of the need for continued training in civil disobedience in his conception of the ideal village, see his *Constructive Programme* (Ahmedabad, India: Navajivan, 1941). Also found in Gandhi's *The Collected Works of Mahatma Gandhi* (Navajivan, New Delhi: Publications Division, Ministry of Information and Broadcasting, Government of India, 1954–1998, 100 vols), vol. 75, pp. 146–66.

16 See Philip Pettit, *Republicanism: A Theory of Freedom and Government* (Oxford, England: Oxford University Press, 1997). For Pettit, nondomination "means the absence of domination in the presence of other people, not the absence of domination gained by isolation" (p. 66). Also see Iris Marion Young, *Justice and the Politics of Difference* (Princeton, NJ: Princeton University Press, 1990).

17 According to Judith Shklar, "We often choose peace over justice, to be sure, but they are not the same. To confuse them is simply to invite passive injustice. Inactive government is . . . abusive in individual cases when the weak and vulnerable are left to their fate". *The Faces of Injustice* (Cambridge, MA: Harvard University Press, 1984), p. 118.

18 There are many worthwhile conceptions of justice: religious and secular, as well as economic, political, and cultural ones. Gandhi finds that no single theory of justice is comprehensive and therefore trumps all other conceptions of justice.

19 According to Shklar, "the difference between misfortune and injustice frequently involves our willingness and our capacity to act or not to act on behalf of the victims, to blame or to absolve, to help, mitigate and compensate, or to just turn away". *The Faces of Injustice*, p. 2.

20 For an extended discussion of Gandhi's conception of power, see my 'Gandhi, Power, and Democracy', *International Journal of Gandhian Studies*, 1.1 (forthcoming).

21 In a similar vein, Judith Shklar finds that because "social distances create the climate for cruelty, then less inequality may be the remedy". *Ordinary Vices* (Cambridge, MA: Harvard University Press, 1984), p. 28.

22 Accordingly, Gandhi wants to have power dispersed. We see this in graphic detail in his discussion of his ideal village and its economy and politics which he elaborates in his *Constructive Programme*.

23 See Robert Dahl on the many locations and expressions of power in a democracy, particularly *Who Governs?* (New Haven, CT: Yale University Press, 1961).

24 See Michael Walzer, *Spheres of Justice* (New York: Basic Books, 1983). Walzer fears that those with power in one sphere believe they should have power and privileges in other spheres.

25 *Young India*, 9 February 1921. He argues that unjust governments do not deserve our support (*Young India*, 28 July 1920).

26 *Young India*, 5 January 1922. He holds that "You assist an administration most effectively by obeying its orders and decrees ... Disobedience of the laws of an evil state is, therefore, a duty" (*Young India*, 27 March 1930).

27 See Stuart Hampshire, *Justice as Conflict* (Princeton University Press, 2000). Without conflict, he argues, the old order with all of its injustices would continually repeat itself.

28 What Gandhi wants from his opponents, he also expects from his allies. He tells his supporters, "We shut the door of reason when we refuse to listen to our opponents, or having listened make fun of them. If intolerance becomes a habit, we run the risk of missing the truth" *(Harijan, 31 May 1942).*

29 He claims that "petitions must be backed up by force" (*Hind Swaraj*, p. 21). He later writes, "A petition backed by force is a petition from an equal" (*Hind Swaraj*, p. 85).

30 *Young India*, 16 February 1922.

31 See Michel Foucault, *Discipline and Punishment* (New York: Pantheon, 1977) and Young, *Justice and the Politics of Difference.*

32 See, e.g., *Hind Swaraj*, p. 89.

33 *Young India*, 1 October 1931.

34 *Young India*, 8 January 1925.

35 M. Chatterjee, *Gandhi's Religious Thought* (London: Macmillan, 1983), p. 89.

36 Satyagrahi refers to someone who practices satyagraha.

37 *Harijan*, 25 March 1939.

38 *Young India*, 19 March 1925. Gandhi holds that the voluntary suffering of the satyagrahi will, in time, move even the most calloused opponent who will acknowledge that the punishments the satyagrahi willingly accepts are not just.

39 *Young India*, 4 October 1928.

40 In earlier times, many thought their fate was decided by gods far away. One expression of modern fatalism can be found among those who hold that economic and cultural globalization is inevitable, for better or for worse. Such contemporary fatalists believe that globalization cannot be significantly altered.

41 Gandhi wants people to think for themselves early. When he talks about a solid education, he tells us that "if teachers are to stimulate the reasoning faculties of boys and girls under their care, they would continuously tax their reason and make them think for themselves" (*Young India*, 24 June 1926).

42 Gandhian sceptics refuse to accept the bromides of fatalists; sceptics ask what is being ignored in the current order of things. Because Gandhian sceptics are also expected to be hopeful, they insist they can help chart their future. They are sceptical both of the claims of legitimacy of the dominant order and the notion that the present is immovably fixed.

43 *Hind Swaraj*, p. 24

44 Gandhi recognizes that all knowledge is incomplete; that each frame or window takes in a particular view and filters out what is thought to be extraneous. However much we see, much is left unseen and consequently unattended, and Gandhi wants to call attention to this matter.

45 On Gandhi's hope, see Judith M. Brown, *Gandhi. Prisoner of Hope* (New Haven and London: Yale University Press, 1989).

46 Jurgen Moltmann, *Theology of Hope* translated by James W. Leitch (New York: Harper & Row, 1967), p. 45. He goes on to argue that "Only as long as the world and the people in it are in a fragmented and experimental state which is not yet resolved, is there any sense in earthly hopes... Hope and the kind of thinking that goes with it consequently cannot submit to the reproach of being utopian, for they do not strive after things that have 'no place', but after things that have 'no place *as yet*' but can acquire one".

47 Norberto Bobbio, *The Philosophy of Decadentism: A Study in Existentialism*, trans. David Moore (Oxford, England: Basil Blackwell, 1948), p. 11.

48 *Ibid.*, pp. 46–7, 50.

49 Norberto Bobbio, *The Age of Rights*, trans. Allan Cameron (London: Polity Press, 1996), p. 71. For both Gandhi and Bobbio, we need ideals; without them, we risk a deadening cynicism or blindly following rules sanctioned by the reigning fatalism.

50 J. Nehru captures the centrality of courage in Gandhi: "the dominant impulse in India under British rule was that of fear–pervasive, oppressing strangling fear; fear of the army, the police, the wide-spread secret service; fear of the official class, fear of laws meant to suppress and of prison; fear of the landlord's agent; fear of the moneylender; fear of unemployment and starvation, which were always on the threshold. It was against this all-pervading fear that Gandhi's quiet and determined voice was raised: 'Be not afraid'". Jawaharlal Nehru, *The Discovery of India* (London: Meridian Books, 1946), p. 303.

51 Bhikhu Parekh, *Gandhi's Political Philosophy: A Critical Examination* (Notre Dame, IN: Notre Dame University Press, 1989), p. 46.

52 Gandhi holds that "cowardice itself is violence of a subtle and therefore dangerous type and far more difficult to eradicate than the habit of physical violence". According to him, the solider risks his life but the coward risks nothing and runs away from danger (*Young India*, 18 December 1924). Earlier he writes, "I can no more preach nonviolence to a coward than I can tempt a blind man to enjoy healthy scenes. Nonviolence is the summit of bravery" (*Young India*, 29 May 1924).

53 For his part, Barry Glassner notices that fear stymies action, but without action the underlying causes of fear are not addressed. He finds that one "of the paradoxes of a culture of fear is that serious problems remain widely ignored even though they give rise to precisely the dangers that the populace most abhors". *The Culture of Fear* (New York: Basic Books, 1999), p. xviii. Shklar finds that 'acute fear' is a means of 'social control'. 'Liberalism of Fear', in *Liberalism and the Moral Life*, ed. Nancy Roenblum (Cambridge, MA: Harvard University Press, 1989, p. 27.

54 John Keane, 'Fear and Democracy' in *Violence and Politics: Global-ization's Paradox*, ed. Kenneth Worcester et al. (New York: Routledge, 2002), pp. 235, 240.

55 I discuss Gandhian courage in *Gandhi: Struggling for Autonomy* (Lanham, MD: Rowman and Littlefield, 1998), pp. 191–4.

56 R. Iyer, *The Moral and Political Thought of Mahatma Gandhi* (Oxford, England: Oxford University Press, 1973), p. 69.

57 *Hind Swaraj*, pp. 39, 41.

58 Writing some years after General Dyer orders his troops to fire into a peaceful gathering in Amritsar, killing almost four hundred people and wounding another eleven hundred, Gandhi observes, "terrorism is bad whether put up in a good cause or bad...General Dyer did what he did "for a cause he undoubtedly believed to be good". Gandhi goes on to recognize the "intensity" of the General's conviction, and concludes "pure motives can never justify impure or violent action" (*Young India*, 18 December 1924).

59 Consider the use of torture by the Bush administration in its conduct of the war with Iraq and its deleterious effects on American ideals and the standing of the United States in the international community.

60 In this regard, Gandhi could readily agree with Judith Shklar's observa-tion that the "basic units of political life are...the weak and the power-ful". In the spirit of Gandhi, she argues that a good politics would secure "freedom from the abuse of power and intimidation of the defenseless that this difference invites" ('The Liberalism of Fear', p. 27).

61 I take this up in *Gandhi: Struggling for Autonomy*. See pp. 204–14 and the citations included there.

7   Gandhi's moral economics: The sins of wealth without work and commerce without morality

THOMAS WEBER

Soon after Gandhi arrived back in India after almost two decades in South Africa, he gave a lecture titled 'Does economic progress clash with real progress?' to the Muir College Economic Society in Allahabad. In his presentation, he admitted that he knew little of economics the way his audience understood the term. However, he told the listeners that choices had to be made, as God and Mammon could not be served concurrently and because the monster of materialism was crushing society. He pleaded for an economy where there was more truth than gold, where there was more charity than self-love. He added that the United States may be the envy of other nations, and while some may say that American wealth may be obtained while its methods avoided, such an attempt is foredoomed to failure:

> This land of ours was once, we are told, the abode of the gods. It is not possible to conceive gods inhabiting a land which is made hideous by the smoke and the din of null chimneys and factories and whose roadways are traversed by rushing engines dragging numerous cars crowded with men mostly who know not what they are after, who are often absent-minded, and whose tempers do not improve by being uncomfortably packed like sardines in boxes and finding themselves in the midst of utter strangers who would oust them if they could and whom they would in their turn oust similarly. I refer to these things because they are held to be symbolical of material progress. But they add not an atom to our happiness.[1]

Five years later, Gandhi clearly pointed out that he did not "draw a sharp or any distinction between economics and ethics".[2] For him, it was clear that standard economic doctrine failed to take account of ethical considerations, and this meant that it was illusory and had little relevance in real life: "The economics that disregard moral and sentimental considerations are like wax-works that being life-like still lack the life of the living flesh. At every crucial moment, these new-fangled economic laws have broken down in practice. And nations or individuals who accept them as guiding maxims must perish".[3]

What exactly did the Mahatma mean? The better part of a century ago, he summed up the situation that formed the basis for the new economic thinking by the likes of E. F. Schumacher, an economics where *people* mattered,[4] and mattered more than merely as social entities.

THE BACKGROUND

During his South Africa years, Gandhi financed, wrote for, and eventually took over a money-losing newspaper called *Indian Opinion*. When he became aware that the paper was in even worse financial shape than feared, on the first day of October 1904, Gandhi set off from his home base to Durban, where the press was situated, to put things right. It was a twenty-four-hour train trip from Johannesburg, and when his close friend Henry Polak saw him off at the station, he gave Gandhi a book that he "was sure to like" to read on the journey.[5]

That book was John Ruskin's classic political tract, *Unto This Last*. Gandhi couldn't put it down. The book resonated with some of the deep convictions that Gandhi was gradually coming to. It caused him a sleepless night, and, there and then, he made a resolution to "change my life in accordance with the ideals of the book". Gandhi was later able to claim that the book "brought about an instantaneous and practical transformation in my life".[6] He translated (or more accurately paraphrased) the book into Gujarati under the title of *Sarvodaya* (the welfare of all), and sarvodaya was to become a central plank of Gandhi's philosophy.[7] In short, through this book, it may not be a great exaggeration to call Ruskin the father of Gandhian economic thought.

Gandhi summarized the teachings of *Unto This Last* under three truths:

1. That the good of the individual is contained in the good of all.
2. That a lawyer's work has the same value as the barber's inasmuch as all have the same right of earning their livelihood from their work.
3. That a life of labour, that is, the life of the tiller of the soil and the handicraftsman, is the life worth living.[8]

Gandhi added: "The first of these I knew. The second I had dimly realized. The third had never occurred to me. *Unto This Last* made it clear as daylight for me that the second and the third were contained in the first". The chapter in his *Autobiography* where Gandhi recounts this conversion, he titled 'The Magic Spell of a Book'. In the introduction to the English retranslation of Gandhi's paraphrase of Ruskin's tract, the Mahatma tells us that in the West, physical and economic well-being is sought in disregard of morality and that this is contrary to divine law, "as some wise men in the West have shown". Of course, here, Gandhi is referring to Ruskin who proclaimed that "men can be happy only if they obey the moral law".[9]

The thirty-five-year-old Gandhi immediately took steps to remove the printing press to a rural setting, which became known as Phoenix Settlement. Here, all laboured for the same living wage and attended the press in their spare time. In his seventies, Gandhi was to recall that the book "transformed me overnight from a lawyer and city-dweller into a rustic living away from Durban on a farm, three miles from the nearest railway station".[10]

In response to the question, asked during an interview in London with the editor of *The Spectator*, Gandhi confirmed his debt to Ruskin and added that "Tolstoy I had read much earlier. He affected the inner being".[11] Gandhi's chief biographer and secretary in later life, Pyarelal, claims that so deeply was Gandhi's thinking "impregnated with Tolstoy's that the changes that took place in his way of life and thinking in the years that followed [his reading of Tolstoy] can be correctly understood and appreciated only in the context of the master's life and philosophy".[12]

A year after he landed in South Africa, Gandhi went through a time of religious ferment, engaging in wide-ranging religious discussions and reading eclectically among the religious texts that came his way. One of these texts was Tolstoy's book on living an authentic Christian life. Gandhi confessed that "Tolstoy's *The Kingdom of God is Within You* overwhelmed me. It left an abiding impression on me. Before the independent thinking, profound morality, and the truthfulness of this book, all the books given me . . . seemed to pale into insignificance".[13] In that book, subtitled *Christianity not as a mystical doctrine but as a new understanding of life*, Tolstoy portrayed Christ as a teacher and moral example rather than as "a divine savior atoning for the sins of mankind and offering eternal life".[14] Here, Tolstoy emphasized the law of love as the moral core of Christianity and accused the majority of Christians of not acknowledging "the law of nonresistance to evil by violence", which he saw as being at the core of the religion. And these interpretations of Christian teachings by Tolstoy backed up Gandhi's growing understanding of his own Hindu faith. Further, from his reading of Tolstoy, Gandhi realized that the best way to help the poor was to get off their backs and practise "bread labour... the divine law that man must earn his bread by labouring with his own hands",[15] which was to be central to his economic and social philosophy. The book became mandatory reading for members of Phoenix Settlement. When, in 1908 and 1909, Gandhi started his regular rounds of imprisonment as part of his political campaigns, Tolstoy's book was a constant companion.

As important as Ruskin and Tolstoy were in helping Gandhi to formulate his philosophy of a morally based economics, they really only added to what he was discovering was the essence of his own religion. Gandhi believed that the whole of Hinduism could be summed up in the first verse of Isha Upanishad, one of the holy texts. Although it was the shortest of the Upanishads, Gandhi was convinced that even the holy Bhagavad Gita could be seen as merely a commentary on it, and even on that initial verse. Basically, it comes down to this: God occupies everything in the universe, thus nothing actually belongs to us. Therefore, we must surrender to God and renounce everything. Then we can reap the rewards of renunciation, that is, the enjoyment of all we need. But the word 'enjoy' has a special meaning. It is that we may not take more than is necessary for us. We should not covet what belongs to another. If we renounce everything, we become God's responsibility and we will be looked after. However, Gandhi also believed that this renunciation had to be undertaken anew each day, so that this central fact of life is not forgotten.[16] With this renunciation of worldly accumulation, the spiritual path is revealed.

ECONOMICS AS IF PEOPLE MATTERED

Early in its history, economics was referred to as the 'dismal science' because it was seen as being devoid of any moral underpinning and because it seemed to be about untold riches for some and abject poverty for others. Modern economists, of course, do not see it this way. They tend to see the market as being a value-neutral mechanism that is quite good at arranging for a wide and relatively equitable distribution of wealth. Some critics, however, point out that now that technology has enabled the production of countless goods for human consumption, it has not only made possible unlimited consumption and greed but also legitimized it. As demand grows, the problem of unfulfilled needs (at least in the affluent world) becomes one of unfulfilled wants. Economic theory, the critics argue, ignores "social wastefulness as distinguished from market wastefulness".[17] It neglects questions concerning the right to employment, the state as an institution of violence, or the corporate system as an institution of exploitation. They claim that the maximization of consumption and the continual raising of 'living standards' became the measures of success. The critics further assert that the expansion of production that led to this also leads to environmental problems, and that so-called efficiency leads to unemployment, exploitation, and international inequalities. This expansion is not only aimed at satisfying wants but also at creating ever new (material, not spiritual) ones. In short, for these critics, economic science ceased being dismal, having evolved into the art of a rat race.[18] The Gandhian economist, J. D. Sethi, for example, makes the point that it is little wonder that the beneficiaries of this system push Gandhi "from the debate and the curricula because of his emphasis on making ethical means the central core of economic theory and practice". He adds that the questions posed by the consequences of current economic thought and practice make "the study of Gandhi, his philosophy of economics and his methods" suddenly relevant and urgent.[19]

Gandhi claimed that "True economics never militates against the highest ethical standard just as all true ethics, to be worth its name, must at the same time be also good economics... True economics stands for social justice; it promotes the good of all equally, including the weakest and is indispensable for decent life".[20] As early as 1909, in the seminal source of his philosophy, the small book known as *Hind Swaraj*, Gandhi was already writing about the evils of modern civilization with its abundance of material goods, where people become factory slaves or slaves to materialism, abandoning morality and religion, where rapid railway travel spread plagues and prevented people from having a chance to get to meet and establish kindred feelings with their neighbours on long journeys, where educated lawyers further divided rather than reconciled disputing parties, and where doctors treated symptoms so that causes did not need to be tackled.[21] He remarked that the "mind is a restless bird; the more it gets the more it wants, and still it remains unsatisfied". He added that while "a man is not necessarily unhappy because he is rich, or unhappy because he is poor", "life-corroding competition" and large cities do not further health or happiness.[22]

Gandhi's notion of revitalizing village India through the spinning wheel and his attack on industrialization and mass transport struck many as anachronistic, but the logic of his arguments took on greater force after his death. Gandhi's economic ideals were not about the destruction of all factories and machinery, but a regulation of their excesses. He noted that what was required was decentralization of production and consumption, which in turn had to take place as near as possible to the source of production. Such localization would do away with the temptation to speed up production regardless of the costs and would alleviate the problems of an inappropriately structured economic system.

In his economics of locally handmade goods, the Mahatma saw the poor as being delivered from the "bonds of the rich".[23] His approach was "wholly different" from ordinary economics, which "takes no note of the human factor"'. He added that the "former wholly concerns itself with the human. The latter is frankly selfish, and the former necessarily unselfish".[24]

GANDHIAN ECONOMICS

Several decades after the publication of *Hind Swaraj*, but still several decades before E. F. Schumacher took up similar issues with his work on 'Buddhist economics', Gandhi had explained that his small-scale rural-based economic system was not based on an abhorrence of machinery per se, but on an objection to the "craze for machinery":

> The craze is for what they call labour-saving machinery. Men go on 'saving labour' till thousands are without work and thrown on the open streets to die of starvation. I want to save time and labour, not for a fraction of mankind, but for all. I want the con-centration of wealth, not in the hands of a few but in the hands of all. Today machinery merely helps a few to ride on the backs of millions. The impetus behind it all is not the philanthropy to save labour, but greed.[25]

This leads to what Gandhi termed 'parasitism':

> Man is made to obey the machine. The wealthy and middle classes become helpless and parasitic upon the working classes. And the latter become so specialized that they also become help-less. The ordinary city-dweller cannot make his own clothing or produce or prepare his own food. The cities become parasitic upon the country. Industrial nations upon agricultural nations. Those who live in temperate climates are increasingly parasitic upon tropical peoples. Governments upon the peoples they gov-ern. Armies upon civilians. People even become parasitic and passive in regard to their recreation and amusements.[26]

And, as Gandhi realized, this is unsustainable. In a now-famous saying, he told his secretary that the "Earth provides enough to satisfy every man's need but not for every man's greed".[27] From this, we can say that Gandhian economics clearly has normative, encompassing ethics as its highest principle. Diwan and Lutz point out that an integrated and holistic perspective in economics, in this case the essentials of Gandhian economics, "boils down to this simple injunction: never advocate actions or policies that lead to ('economic') material advancement at the cost of ('non-economic') social, moral, or spiritual impoverishment. Instead, the economist, as the holistic economist, should ascertain that his organizational principles and policies enable, possibly even encourage, a higher overall quality of life for all".[28] Although he favoured a life of simplicity, Gandhi certainly was not in favour of grinding pauperism (which led to moral degradation) because God looked like a loaf of bread to a hungry person.[29] For him, a high quality of life had a strong spiritual underpinning, and exploitation can never be reconciled with spiritualism.[30]

In one of his newspaper columns, Gandhi reproduces some pithy quotations sent in by a 'fair friend'.[31] These include what have become known as Gandhi's Seven Social Sins. They are: politics without principles, wealth without work, pleasure without conscience, knowledge without character, commerce without morality, science without humanity, and worship without sacrifice. These and many of Gandhi's own writings make it quite clear that the Mahatma did not compartmentalize his life. For him, economics together with politics, morality, and religion formed an indivisible whole. They were all part of a quest for the realization of the self, and therefore the basis of even politics and economics was spiritual. This should become clear as the key elements of Gandhi's economic scheme are discussed below.

BREAD LABOUR AND SWADESHI

During his celebrated Salt March to Dandi in 1930, in his speech at the village of Bhatgam after the 'Petromax incident' (where his followers bestowed unwarranted services and goods on him and his immediate group), Gandhi commented in some anger that "to live above the means befitting a poor country is to live on stolen food".[32]

Bread labour became one of the core elements of his economic philosophy. This simply means that one should earn their daily bread by the sweat of their own brow. Gandhi knew that most people did not derive pleasure from labouring and that in fact, in the case of labourers in a hierarchical system that left the dirtiest work to those at the bottom of the social structure, it could be degrading. If bread labour were compulsory, it would "breed poverty, disease and discontent" and would amount to no more than slavery, even though every person has the right to live decently. He was hoping that it would be taken up willingly, and in this way lead to contentment and health.[33] In this regard, Gandhi quotes the Gita approvingly: "one who eats without labour eats stolen food" because he sees humility inherent in labour. Of course, if one does labour merely to earn money, this is not selfless action; however, if work is done for the good of others, it becomes yajna (sacrifice). If it is done in a spirit of service, "in all humility and for self-realization" it will lead to self-realization.[34]

Gandhi wanted people, especially those living in cities, to consume locally produced rather than imported goods, and, where possible, village industry rather than factory-produced goods. He did this not merely as part of his political struggle against British domination, but also, or indeed more so, because of the ideal of neighbourliness. He summed this up well when he claimed that, "I refuse to buy from anybody anything, however nice or beautiful, if it interferes with my growth or injures those whom nature has made my first care".[35] Swadeshi (or local self-sufficiency), as Diwan and Lutz point out, "demands the sacrifice of utility for the sake of loyalty".[36]

Gandhi's ideas on swadeshi were summed up during his first major Indian struggle and repeated almost verbatim throughout the next thirty years. At a women's meeting in 1919, he was already pointing out to his audience that "swadeshi is that spirit in them which required them to serve their immediate neighbours before others and to use things produced in their neighbourhood in preference to those more remote. So doing, they served humanity to the best of their capacity. They could not serve humanity neglecting their neighbours".[37]

However, at a deeper level, swadeshi implies far more than this. A votary of swadeshi in fact tries to identify him or herself with the entirety of creation, and "seeks to be emancipated from the bondage of the physical body" by initially dedicating themselves to the service of their immediate neighbours and environment.[38]

NON-POSSESSION AND TRUSTEESHIP

Stealing generally means taking something from another without their knowledge and permission. Gandhi takes the notion a lot further. Permission or no, it is stealing if we take more than we need, even if this is done inadvertently: "We are not always aware of our needs, and most of us improperly multiply our wants, and thus unconsciously make thieves of ourselves". He continues, "Today we only desire possession of a thing; tomorrow we shall begin to adopt measures, straight if possible, crooked when thought necessary, to acquire its possession".[39] In short, in the Gandhian scheme, ownership can be seen as a species of violence. Because every person possesses an equal spark of the divine, the idea of privileges over others or rights over nature obscures the fact that there is enough for everyone without the need for exploitation.

Gandhi's insistence on nonviolence and his belief in the interconnectedness of life meant that it is our duty to protect the weak. If all of us realized this obligation, we would regard it as a sin to amass wealth. This would end inequalities of wealth. The test for the progress of a country would not be measured by the number of millionaires, but by the well-being of the masses.[40] Gandhi's emphasis on non-possession is a clear indictment on a society based on a multiplication of wants and unnecessary consumption. And now, in a time of planet-wide economic problems and environmental destabilization, perhaps it is necessary to examine ways of limiting wants and sharing what we have more equitably. Gandhi called his recommended method of working towards this ideal 'trusteeship'.

Under Gandhi's theory of trusteeship, the rich will be left in possession of their wealth, and they would use what they reasonably require for their own personal needs and act as trustees for the remainder "to be used for the society". The honesty of the trustee had to be assumed.[41] The reasoning behind Gandhi's recommendation of trusteeship was: that it corresponded with the principles of nonviolence (there was no need to confiscate wealth or property by force as would be the case with a communist alternative); that it recognized that while all had the right to equal opportunities, not everyone had the same abilities;[42] and that it could be implemented gradually – there was no need for any general revolution, it could be started by one good-hearted individual at a time: "We invite the capitalist to regard himself as a trustee for those on whom he depends for the making, the retention of, and increase of his capital".[43]

If the rich were not willing to become the guardians of the poor who were further crushed, there was always the answer of nonviolent noncooperation. After all, the rich could not accumulate wealth without the cooperation of the poor.[44] The idea was to delegitimize the gross accumulation of wealth because in the final analysis, trusteeship is a "principle of economic conscience".[45] Of course, the rich may not immediately undergo changes of the heart and become trustees, but through moral pressure and persuasion, their conversion was possible. And it was more likely to come about through such mechanisms than through various forms of violence. Gandhi added that if the capitalists refuse to act as trustees, there would be room for "legislative regulation of the ownership of wealth".[46]

The reasons for trusteeship are many. They come from Gandhi's belief in nonviolence and that the ends grow out of the means, foreclosed the use of violence, where ends justify means, and his belief in *aparigraha*, or non-possession.[47] However, even these considerations have deeper metaphysical meaning than physical peace and a fair distribution of the earth's resources. Possession implies retention for the future, and this is not possible without a readiness to defend the possessed goods. This, in turn, requires the use of force and coercion and so precludes a nonviolent way of life. Further, when someone is born, they gain access to resources that they did not create, and if these are not replenished then there is a case of the appropriation of the fruits of the labour of others and the depletion of non-renewable resources. With birth comes a debt that, if not repaid, equals theft.[48] In the words of Raghavan Iyer, "The selfish grasping for possessions of any kind not only violates the deeper purposes of our human odyssey but eventually breeds possessiveness and greed, exploitation and revenge. The best trustee may be someone who has obtained an inward moral balance, but the struggle to become a good trustee can in turn teach altruism and bring its own spiritual rewards".[49]

While trusteeship sounds like a utopian idea, there are now several large enterprises where the owners have taken on the role of trustees and turned their companies into worker-owned cooperatives. Probably the best-known example is provided by the originally English Quaker-founded Scott Bader Commonwealth, and other such companies.[50]

SARVODAYA

In chapter xiii of *Hind Swaraj*, 'What is True Civilization?', Gandhi describes civilization as

that mode of conduct which points out to man the path of duty. Performance of duty and observance of morality are convertible terms. To observe morality is to attain mastery over our mind and our passions. So doing, we know ourselves. The Gujarati equivalent for civilization means 'good conduct'.... We notice that the mind is a restless bird; the more it gets the more it wants, and still remains unsatisfied. The more we indulge our passions, the more unbridled they become. Our ancestors, therefore, set a limit to our indulgences. They saw that happiness was largely a mental condition. A man is not necessarily happy because he is rich, or unhappy because he is poor. The rich are often seen to be unhappy, the poor to be happy. Millions will always remain poor.

Gandhi goes on to laud the position of India, which did not embark on the road to amassing "luxuries and pleasures", a society that did not end up with a "system of life-corroding competition". He insisted that this was not because the Indian sages of old did not know how to invent machinery, but

> our forefathers knew that, if we set our hearts after such things, we would become slaves and lose our moral fibre. They, there-fore, after due deliberation decided that we should only do what we could with our hands and feet. They saw that our real happi-ness and health consisted in a proper use of our hands and feet. They further reasoned that large cities were a snare and a useless encumbrance and that people would not be happy in them, that there would be gangs of thieves and robbers, prostitution and vice flourishing in them and that poor men would be robbed by rich men. They were, therefore, satisfied with small villages.

Gandhi did not want to abolish everything above the bare necessities and have everyone living at a subsistence level. However, the essential needs of the poor had to be satisfied before the craving for luxuries by the more well off.[51] He made the point that there was nothing intrinsically good in returning to primitive methods of grinding grain. However, he advocated it because "there is no other way of giving employment to the millions of villagers who are living on idleness".[52] If economics is to a large degree about human – not just narrowly defined individual – welfare, then the goal had to be sarvodaya, the welfare of all. Gandhi had proclaimed that "A votary of ahimsa cannot subscribe to the utilitarian formula (of the greatest good of the greatest number). He will strive for the greatest good of all and die in the attempt to realise the ideal".[53]

Sarvodaya was to be a counter to a non-egalitarian society, but the task was not just to uplift the poor because the life of the rich was no less deprived than that of those they exploited. Through their exploitation and indulgent lives, the rich had fallen from the ethical path, the path to a fuller, more meaningful life. In fact, the rich have fallen to the degree that the poor have not risen. The rich could gain in moral stature and ethical development by renouncing their privileges and, as trustees, dedicating their surplus wealth to the good of society. If such a new outlook could take hold, "we shall cease to think of getting what we can, but shall [also] decline to receive what all cannot get. It occurs to me that it ought not to be difficult to make a successful appeal to the masses in terms of economics and a fairly successful working of such an experiment must lead to immense and unconscious results".[54]

INDUSTRIALIZATION

A quarter of a century after first organizing his thoughts on how an ideal civilization should operate in *Hind Swaraj*, Gandhi reiterated his thinking on the problems of industrialization when he insisted that "any machinery which does not deprive masses of men of the opportunity to labour, but which helps the individual and adds to his efficiency, and which a man can handle at will without being its slave", was a good thing. In fact, he would

> prize every invention of science made for the benefit of all.
> There is a difference between invention and invention. I should
> not care for the asphyxiating gases capable of killing masses
> of men at a time. The heavy machinery for work of public
> utility which cannot be undertaken by human labour has its
> inevitable place, but all that would be owned by the State and
> used entirely for the benefit of the people. I can have no consid-
> eration for machinery which is meant either to enrich the few at
> the expense of the many, or without cause to displace the useful
> labour of many.[55]

While machines could contribute towards economic progress, they were all too often controlled by only a few who employed them "regardless of the interests of the common man and that is why our condition has deteriorated today".[56] The problem was that the spread of machinery did not seem to stop at some ideal level, but led to large-scale industrialization resulting in a system that created unemployment and concentrated economic power in the hands of the few. He likened machinery to strong medicine that needed to be used with caution.

In a discussion, noted in note twenty-five, with his educationist colleague G. Ramachandran, Gandhi had talked of his objection to the craze for machinery. By way of clarification, he added:

> The supreme consideration is man. The machine should not
> tend to make atrophied the limbs of man. For instance, I would
> make intelligent exceptions. Take the case of the Singer Sewing

Machine. It is one of the few useful things ever invented, and there is a romance about the device itself. Singer saw his wife labouring over the tedious process of sewing and seaming with her own hands, and simply out of his love for her, he devised the sewing machine, in order to save her from unnecessary labour. He, however, saved not only her labour but also the labour of everyone who could purchase a sewing machine.

Of course, he saw that there would need to be factories to make sewing machines. There the remedy was that such factories had to be nationalized or state controlled with the workers in them working under

> the most attractive and ideal conditions, not for profit, but for the benefit of humanity, love taking the place of greed as the motive. It is an alteration in the conditions of labour that I want. This mad rush for wealth must cease, and the labourer must be assured, not only of a living wage, but a daily task that is not a mere drudgery. The machine will, under these conditions, be as much a help to the man working it as to the State, or the man who owns it. The present mad rush will cease, and the labourer will work (as I have said) under attractive and ideal conditions. This is but one of the exceptions I have in mind. The sewing machine had love at its back. The individual is the one supreme consideration. The saving of labour of the individual should be the object, and honest humanitarian considerations, and not greed, the motive.

As the charkha (spinning wheel) he plied and the Singer sewing machine he lauded were machines, the problem was one of freedom and control. He drew the line of utility "Just where they cease to help the individual and encroach upon his individuality".[57] Gandhi feared that machines "may finally engulf civilization". This, however, would not occur if people controlled machines, but it would "should man lose his control over the machines and allow them to control him".[58] Where people work to the rhythm of the machine, rather than the machine merely aiding them in their work, it becomes unclear who or what is using whom. And, for Gandhi, human freedom was far more important than an increase in the production of some goods that, more than likely, were not of an essential nature.

Of course, in some instances, large machines and even large-scale industries were necessary (e.g. for shipbuilding, etc.). In these cases, the factories would need to be nationalized and the workers ensured their dignity: "I am socialist enough to say that such factories should be nationalised, or state-controlled. They ought only to be working under the most attractive conditions, not for profit, but for the benefit of humanity, love taking the place of greed as the motive. It is an alteration in the condition of labour that I want".[59]

EVALUATING GANDHIAN ECONOMICS

Are Gandhi's pronouncements on economics utopian, or did he actually see them as practical ways of dealing with real-world problems? Dasgupta notes that Gandhi was laying the foundations of an economic system to strive for rather than a plan that could be easily implemented. He did not sketch some futile Utopia; instead, in keeping with his belief in focussing on the means rather than the end, Gandhi looked at economic problems from a sarvodaya point of view. This does not mean that applying Gandhian principles to economics is impractical or impossible. And, if one remembers the context in which his ideas were formulated, a far more pragmatic view of his economic doctrines surfaces.[60] While issues such as industrialization and its connection with unemployment have to be seen in terms of India's poor rural population, much of what the Mahatma had to say about the spiritualization of economics is as applicable today as ever, and possibly more so.

Gandhi's vision of an India composed of self-sufficient but interlinked rural republics with decentralized small-scale economic structures and participatory democracy was quickly dispensed within the newly independent India bent on industrialization. Nevertheless, we know from various indices of happiness[61] that our general rate of contentedness has not risen with a vast increase in economic wealth and rampant consumption. And we also know that the patterns of consumption, especially in the wealthy countries, are implicated in patterns of poverty elsewhere and in serious environmental problems. E. F. Schumacher, who popularized Gandhian economics with his slogan 'small is beautiful', explained that smallness meant reuniting small-scale production and small-scale consumption, thus minimizing transport, as transport added cost without adding anything of real value to goods. He noted that the economics of scale, which were a nineteenth-century truth, had been shown to be a twentieth-century myth.[62] He also affirmed Gandhi's dictum that "high-thinking is inconsistent with complicated material life", noting that "all real human needs were essentially simple, therefore only frivolities and extravagances like supersonic transport were invariably complex".[63] He believed that the crises of resource depletion, ecological destruction, and personal alienation suffered by the modern world could be overcome with "Gandhian work with a spirit of truth and nonviolence that inspired Gandhi".[64] Capital had to be saved so that people did not simply become minders of very expensive machines, diminished in personality development and robbed of creative spirit. And finally, noting Gandhi's vision for a rural-based India (one that was not based on an inherently violent factory civilization built on exploitation, but on a rural-minded nonviolence), he called Gandhi a nonviolent social revolutionary.[65] Given the economic and environmental state of the planet, perhaps a superficial negative appraisal of Gandhian economics is less than helpful.

ECONOMICS AND SPIRITUALITY

Gandhi's economics is normative. Unlike the materialist who is interested in goods, Gandhi is interested in liberation. To paraphrase Schumacher, the keynotes of Gandhian economics are simplicity and nonviolence, while for modern economists who measure 'standards of living' by amounts of consumption, this is difficult to understand. In modern economics, consumption is the end and purpose of economic activity; in Gandhian economics, on the other hand, ownership and consumption are merely means to an end.[66] The multiplication of wants and the desire to fulfil them do nothing to further personal growth. They add nothing to self-respect or long-term contentment,[67] and ownership is merely a clouding of the fact of impermanence.

Gandhi provides guidelines, which, if followed, would lead to a very different economic system, one that is sustainable and, rather than being an end in itself, would be a means to a greater spiritual end. Gandhi claimed that "True economics never militates against the highest ethical standard just as all true ethics, to be worth its name, must at the same time be also good economics . . . True economics stands for social justice; it promotes the good of all equally, including the weakest and is indispensable for decent life";[68] and, as noted above, he drew no distinction between economics and ethics. However, there was also far more than this to Gandhi's economic thought. As hinted at above, it was a way to further an individual's spiritual quest, a way to assist in the attainment of self-realization, nothing less.

Although Gandhi placed the individual at the centre of his moral thought, he strongly stressed that human nature predisposed us to cooperation rather than individualism. In order to fulfil their nature, individuals had to exercise their individualism for the good of all, and this includes working towards the reformation and reorientation of society to enable a greater scope for the self-realization of all individuals. Because of this relationship, the converse is also true: "I do not believe...that an individual may gain spiritually and those that surround him suffer. I believe in Advaita. I believe in the essential unity of man and for that matter all that lives. Therefore I believe that if one man gains spiritually the whole world gains with him and, if one man fails, the whole world fails to that extent".[69] This, simply put, means that we should not only do to others that which we would like them to do to us, but that what we in fact do to others we do to ourselves. If we aid those less fortunate than ourselves, the good is not only intrinsic but for Gandhi may also be instrumental, aiding us in our own quest for self-realization, which comes from a realization of underlying connectedness. An ethical economics is therefore a spiritual economics, and a pursuit of wealth and power are not necessarily incompatible with spiritual pursuits.

Gandhi's ultimate goal of self-realization naturally carried over into his economic thinking. It meant more than an identification with the mere personal ego, it required a merging with a greater Self. Where this occurred, one had achieved the purpose of life: the attainment of Truth. This could not come about through exploitation, but demanded social justice and the good of all. Towards the end of his life, Gandhi wrote:

> I will give you a talisman. Whenever you are in doubt or when the self becomes too much for you, apply the following test. Recall the face of the poorest and weakest man whom you have seen, and ask yourself if the step you contemplate is going to be of any use to him. Will he gain anything by it? Will it restore him to a control over his own life and destiny? In other words, will it lead to Swaraj for the hungry and spiritually starving millions? Then you will find your doubt and your self melting away.[70]

In short, if this line of thinking is carried over into the realm of what can narrowly be defined as economics, it means an identification with the poorest and most marginalized, in fact with all that lives – and this identification reveals the Self/Truth.

Notes

1 'Speech at Muir College Economic Society, Allahabad', 22 December 1916, *The Collected Works of Mahatma Gandhi* (New Delhi, India:

Publications Division of the Government of India, Navajivan, 1958–94, 100 vols), vol. 13, pp. 310–17. (Henceforth, *CWMG*.)

2 'The Great Sentinel', *Young India*, 13 October 1921.

3 'The Secret of It', *Young India*, 27 October 1921.

4 See especially, E. F. Schumacher, *Small Is Beautiful: A Study of Economics as if People Mattered* (London: Abacus, 1974).

5 H. S. L. Polak, 'Some South African Reminiscences', in C. Shukla (ed.), *Incidents of Gandhiji's Life* (Bombay, India: Vora, 1949), pp. 230–47.

6 M. K. Gandhi, *An Autobiography or The Story of My Experiments with Truth* (Ahmedabad, India: Navajivan, 1940), p. 220.

7 See M. K. Gandhi, *Sarvodaya (The Welfare of All)* (Ahmedabad, India: Navajivan, 1954).

8 Gandhi, *An Autobiography*, p. 221.

9 M. K. Gandhi, *Ruskin: Unto This Last A Paraphrase* (Ahmedabad, India: Navajivan, 1951), p. 1; and 'John Ruskin', (Gujarati) *Indian Opinion*, 16 May 1908.

10 To American Friends, 3 August 1942, *CWMG*, vol. 76, pp. 357–9: at p. 358.

11 Interview to Evelyn Wrench, *The Spectator*, 24 October 1931.

12 Pyarelal, *Mahatma Gandhi, volume I: The Early Phase* (Ahmedabad, India; Navajivan, 1965), p. 628. For the influence of Ruskin and Tolstoy on Gandhi, see T. Weber, *Gandhi as Disciple and Mentor* (Cambridge, England: Cambridge University Press, 2004), pp. 36–45.

13 Gandhi, *An Autobiography*, p. 99.

14 J. D. Hunt, *Gandhi and the Nonconformists: Encounters in South Africa* (New Delhi, India: Promilla, 1986), p. 42.

15 Letter to Narandas Gandhi, 14/16 September 1930, *CWMG*, vol. 44, pp. 147–50: at p. 149.

16 See 'Speech at Quilon', 16 January 1937, *CWMG*, vol. 64, pp. 257–60; and 'Speech at Haripad', 17 January 1937, *CWMG*, vol. 64, pp. 263–66; and other speeches in the following days.

17 J. D. Sethi, 'Foreword', in R. Diwan and M. Lutz (eds.), *Essays in Gandhian Economics* (New Delhi, India: Gandhi Peace Foundation, 1985), pp. xiii–iv.

18 Sethi, 'Foreword', p. xiii.

19 Ibid., pp. xxii–iii.

20 'Primary Education in Bombay', *Harijan*, 9 October 1937.

21 See M. K. Gandhi, *Hind Swaraj* (Ahmedabad, India: Navajivan, 1938), chapter VI 'Civilization', chapter IX 'The Condition of India: Railways', chapter XI 'The Condition of India: Lawyers', and chapter XII 'The Condition of India: Doctors'.

22 Gandhi, *Hind Swaraj*, chapter XIII 'What Is True Civilization'.

23 'No and Yes', *Young India*, 17 March 1927.

24 'Some Posers', *Young India*, 16 July 1931.

25 'Discussion with G. Ramachandran', *Young India*, 13 November 1924.

26 'Notes', *Young India*, 15 April 1926.

27 Quoted in Pyarelal, *Mahatma Gandhi, volume X: The Last Phase, Part-II* (Ahmedabad, India: Navajivan, 1958), p. 552.

28 Diwan and Lutz, 'Introduction', in Diwan and Lutz (eds.), *Essays in Gandhian Economics*, p. 13.

29 'Speech at Meeting of Missionaries', *Young India*, 6 August 1925.

30 'Urban v. Rural', *Young India*, 25 July 1929.

31 'Notes', *Young India*, 22 October 1925.

32 'Turning the Searchlight Inward', *Young India*, 3 April 1930. This is implied in Gandhi's interpretation of the Bhagavad Gita: see Discourse 3/12; and chapter 14 '*Yajna* or Sacrifice' in M. K. Gandhi, *From Yeravda Mandir* (Ahmedabad, India: Navajivan, 1932).

33 'Duty of Bread Labour', *Harijan*, 29 June 1935.

34 'Talks with Ashram Women', 1926, *CWMG*, vol. 32, pp. 485–95: at p. 491.

35 'Swadeshi and Nationalism', *Young India*, 12 March 1925.

36 Diwan and Lutz, 'Introduction', in Diwan and Lutz (eds.), *Essays in Gandhian Economics*, p. 14.

37 'Speech at Women's Meeting, Godhra', *Young India*, 20 August 1919.

38 Gandhi, *From Yeravda Mandir*, p. 39.

39 Ibid., pp. 14–15.

40 'Speech at Muir College Economic Society, Allahabad', 22 December 1916, *CWMG*, vol. 13, pp. 310–17.

41 'Equal Distribution', *Harijan*, 25 August 1940.

42 See 'Talk with Manu Gandhi', 15 April 1947, *CWMG*, vol. 87, p. 284.

43 'Questions and Answers: Can You Avoid Class War?', *Young India*, 26 March 1931.

44 'Equal Distribution', *Harijan*, 25 August 1940.

45 J. D. Sethi, 'Introduction', in J. D. Sethi (ed.), *Trusteeship: The Gandhian Alternative*. New Delhi, India: Gandhi Peace Foundation, 1986, p. xiii.

46 'Practical Trusteeship Formula', *Harijan*, 25 October 1952. This was drawn up during Gandhi's life by some of his lieutenants and approved by him. See K. Raghavendra Rao, 'The Moral Economy of Trusteeship', in Sethi (ed.), *Trusteeship*, p. 38.

47 For Gandhi's views on this topic, see in particular his speech at Guildhouse Church, *The Guildhouse*, 23 September 1931, *CWMG*, vol. 48, pp. 50–8.

48 R. Varma, 'Gandhi's Theory of Trusteeship: An Essay in Understanding', in Sethi (ed.), *Trusteeship*, pp. 47–8.

49 See R. Iyer, 'Gandhian Trusteeship in Theory and Practice', in Sethi (ed.), *Trusteeship*, pp. 1–16.

50 See G. Deshpande, 'Trusteeship: The Experiments in the United Kingdom' in Sethi (ed.), *Trusteeship*, pp. 225–35; and Schumacher, *Small is Beautiful*, pp. 230–7.

51 See 'Answer to Questions at Constructive Workers' Conference, Madras', *The Hindu*, 26 January 1946.

52 'Why Not Labour-Saving Devices', *Harijan*, 30 November 1934.

53 'The Greatest Good of All', *Young India*, 9 December 1926.

54 'What of the West?', *Young India*, 3 September 1925.

55 See 'A Discussion', *Harijan*, 22 June 1935.

56 'Talk with Manu Gandhi', 10 April 1947, *CWMG*, vol. 87, p. 249.

57 'Discussion with G. Ramachandran', *Young India*, 13 November 1924 and 20 November 1924.

58 'Interview to London General Press', *The Hindu*, 21 December 1931.

59 Letter to G. Ramachandran, *Young India*, 13 November 1925.

60 Ajit K. Dasgupta, *Gandhi's Economic Thought*, London: Routledge, 1996, p. 2. See also Bharatan Kumarappa's 'Editor's Note' to Gandhi, *Sarvodaya*, pp. iv–v.

61 We know, e.g., that in relatively wealthy countries there appears to be no correlation between generally rising income and increased happiness. See, e.g., Alan Thein Durning, *How Much is Enough?* (London: Earthscan, 1992), p. 39.

62 S. Hoda, 'Schumacher on Gandhi', in M. Choudhuri and R. Singh (eds.), *Mahatma Gandhi: 125 Years* (Varanasi, India: Sarva Seva Sangh/ Gandhian Institute of Studies, 1995), pp. 101–2.

63 Hoda, 'Schumacher on Gandhi', p. 44.

64 *Ibid.*, p. 99.

65 *Ibid.*, pp. 102–3. For Gandhi's influence on Schumacher, see Weber, *Gandhi as Disciple and Mentor*, pp. 218–31.

66 Schumacher, *Small is Beautiful*, pp. 47–8.

67 See 'Plain Living and High Thinking', *Harijan*, 1 February 1942.

68 'Primary Education in Bombay', *Harijan*, 9 October 1937.

69 'Not Even Half Mast', *Young India*, 4 December 1924.

70 Reproduced in D. G. Tendulkar, *Mahatma: Life of Mohandas Karamchand Gandhi* (New Delhi, India: Publications Division, Ministry of Information and Broadcasting, Government of India, 1960–3), vol. 8, between pp. 288–9.

8 Gandhi and the state

ANTHONY PAREL

The state, understood as the legitimate supreme coercive authority of the political community, is an integral part of Gandhi's political philosophy. A major goal of his political activities as a leader of the Indian nationalist movement had been the establishment of a sovereign coercive state for India. Without such a state, it would have been impossible to realize to the full his vision of *political* swaraj.

Not being a political philosopher in the formal sense, Gandhi did not write a treatise on the subject of the state. However, ideas relating to the state are found scattered in his writings. His two theoretical works, *Hind Swaraj* and *Constructive Program*, are of special importance here. The state is the focal point of *Hind Swaraj*. The work ultimately is about the sort of state that Gandhi wanted for India. The term swaraj, in the title *Hind Swaraj*, he translated as 'home rule' – a nineteenth-century term for the state that enjoyed self-government. What complicates matters for the reader is the fact that the book uses the term swaraj in a second sense, meaning 'self-rule' that the inner self enjoys or is capable of enjoying. Thus *Hind Swaraj* wants swaraj in both senses: it wants political swaraj in the sense of home rule for India and spiritual swaraj in the sense of inner 'self-rule' for Indians. The focal point of *Constructive Programme* is Non-Governmental Organizations (NGOs) of civil society. However, the general thesis of the work is that the NGOs should work in tandem with the state. The state therefore is taken for granted here.

Gandhi's vocabulary (both English and Gujarati) for the state underwent several changes between 1909 and 1947. In 1909, *Hind Swaraj*, as noted, used the term 'home rule' for the state. In 1920, he called the state "a parliament chosen by the people with the fullest power over finance, the police, the military, the navy, the courts and the educational institutions".[1] This passage makes it clear that the state envisaged had full legislative, judicial, and executive coercive power to carry out its several tasks. In 1921, in the Preface to a new edition of *Hind Swaraj*, he called the state a "parliamentary swaraj in accordance with the wishes of

the people of India".[2] The main point here is that the state that he envisaged for India had to reflect and be responsive to the wishes of all the
sections of India's heterogeneous population. In 1931, the term *purna
swaraj*, meaning 'complete independence', was adopted.[3] The emphasis here is on full sovereignty. Finally, in November 1947, immediately
after India actually attained complete independence, he used the term
surajya, 'the good state', to refer to the state that he hoped India would
develop in the future.[4]

What is common to all these terms is the notion that the raison d'etre
of the state, as the supreme coercive power of the political community, is
the securing of the political, economic, and cultural welfare of all Indians
without partiality towards their caste, tribe, religion, language, or region.
Gandhi's state, as supreme coercive power, treats, or is supposed to treat,
every Indian equally and justly. Its primary task is to defend and promote
the fundamental human rights of its citizens, to protect the nation from
external threat, and to preserve internal peace and order. All this requires
that the state be active through its several institutions. However, all its
activities have to occur within the limits of the principles of universal
justice, equality, and individual liberty set out in its constitution. The
point to grasp is that Gandhi's vision of a transformed Indian society can
come into being only with the active involvement of such a state. He
wanted the new Indian state to be a successful state, not a failed one. He
wanted Indians to be virtuous citizens, enjoying spiritual swaraj or self-
mastery. But spiritual swaraj alone was not enough. Without the active
presence of the *good state*, spiritual swaraj by itself could not produce
the material and moral well-being of Indians. It was as simple as that.

A distinction that Gandhi draws in regard to the state indicates how
deeply he had reflected on the subject. The distinction in question is that
between the state that he wanted for India and the state that he did not
want for India. There was in other words an ongoing inner debate in his
mind regarding two opposing views of the state. Indeed, this distinction
serves as the best analytical tool available for the present discussion.
After elaborating on what the distinction means, I shall discuss some of
the issues that his notion of the state raises for political philosophy in
general and for modern Indian political philosophy in particular.

I. THE STATE THAT GANDHI DID NOT WANT

The aggressive state. Gandhi identified a number of traits that he
did not want his *surajya* to have. To begin with, he did not want modern
India to be an aggressive state. An aggressive state tends to be hegemonic

in its relations to other states. And depending on the basis of its aggression, it could be oppressive towards its own people. Thus, for example, a state based on ethnic nationalism of the sort that exponents of Hindutva profess could be aggressive towards its minorities. The same is true of a state based on religion. In *Hind Swaraj*, Gandhi was afraid that some Indian nationalists were dreaming of making independent India an aggressive state. Chapter IV entitled "What is Swaraj?" exposes this delusion. Some Indian nationalists wanted India to be like the Great Britain or the Japan of the day. "As is Japan, so must India be", they seemed to say. Alternatively, they wanted India to be an imperial state like Great Britain. Swaraj for them meant only the transfer of state power from British hands to Indian hands. It did not mean or require any change in their conception of the state power that they were seeking to inherit. They wanted, says Gandhi mockingly, "English rule without the Englishman", "the tiger's nature, but not the tiger". He was afraid that their concept of the state would make "India English". And when that happened, India would be called "Englistan" not Hindustan. "This", concludes Gandhi, "is not the swaraj that I want".[5]

Gandhi's criticism of the aggressive state raises the question of the root of aggression in the modern state. In addition to economic motives, aggression in the modern state is connected to exclusive nationalism also. Gandhi had his own conception of a non-aggressive, inclusive nationalism, that is, nationalism that embraced people of different races, religions, and ethnic affiliation. I have called it *civic nationalism*, that is, nationalism based ultimately on the sanctity of the individual and his or her rights and duties.[6] A state based on civic nationalism is not, indeed cannot be, aggressive. But nationalism based on race, ethnicity, or religion is invariably aggressive. In *Hind Swaraj*, Gandhi attacks aggressive nationalism and indirectly the aggressive state based on it. His reference to the early twentieth-century imperial Great Britain and imperial Japan becomes significant in the context of the aggressive nationalism behind imperialism.

Gandhi's criticism of the aggressive state raises the broader issue of the nature of the power of the modern state. Unless self-restrained, the modern state has a tendency to overreach itself, and to seek to increase its power over its citizens in the guise of doing them good. It may lay claim to superior political ideology that it wants to impose upon the citizens. Gandhi looked upon this tendency "with the greatest fear, because although while apparently doing good by minimizing exploitation, it does the greatest harm to mankind by destroying individuality, which lies at the root of all progress".[7] That is to say, the modern state with its tendency to overreach itself can become a threat to individual swaraj. This is especially true if the state is driven by revolutionary ideologies of one kind or another. Thus "if the state suppressed capitalism by violence, it would be caught in the coils of violence itself".[8] The same was true if the state was driven by religious ideology.

The state as a soulless machine. The second point that Gandhi found objectionable in the modern state was its lack of understanding of the significance of the spiritual soul for political conduct. He upheld the view that human beings were body–soul composites and that the soul was an active centre of individual freedom and self-determination. This view definitely influenced his political thought and his conception of the state. He found the modern state allowing no room for 'soul force', arrogating as it did to itself the monopoly of 'body force' or 'brute force' (these are his terms). The brand of coercion exercised by the modern state in his view had its source, if not its justification, in the modern alienation of the body from the soul. He expressed his concerns in this matter in the following words: "The state represents violence in a concentrated and organized form. The individual has a soul, but as the state is a soulless machine, it can never be weaned from violence to which it owes its very existence".[9]

The history of the alienation of the soul from the modern state goes back to Machiavelli. He boasted how some Florentines loved their 'city' more than they did their souls. Because the state was thought to have no obligation to take into account the spiritual values of its citizens, Machiavelli believed that it could pursue its ends in open disregard of the ends of the soul. The thinker who systematized the animus against the soul was, of course, Thomas Hobbes. The famous Part I, "Of Man", of his *Leviathan* gives us the profile of the modern political man, minus the soul. This profile has room for the body – the senses, imagination, speech, instrumental reason, the passions, and the struggle for power – but not for the soul. Not surprisingly, Hobbes's political man finds himself in the state of the war of all against all. An escape from this terrible condition is possible only through the fearful coercive power of the sovereign state. The moral basis of the Hobbesian state, it is important to note, is either consent or conquest. Yes, conquest: Hobbes explicitly allows for a state founded on conquest.[10]

Reference to Hobbes is relevant to the present discussion. For, as Eric Stokes has rightly pointed out, the colonial state in India "approached most nearly Hobbes's ideal of the Leviathan".[11] The colonial state, established in India by conquest, had found its moral justification in Hobbes's philosophy. This explains why even someone of the intellectual stature of James Fitzjames Stephen could assert without a shadow of doubt that every political theory whatever was a doctrine of or about force, and that the British were morally right in introducing into India "peace compelled by force".[12]

It is not too much then to suggest that Gandhi puts together what Hobbes has cut asunder. He introduced into the modern Indian political discourse the idea of soul force that can and should operate side by side with body force. He can no longer accept that body force is the sole basis of the sovereign state. The introduction of soul force is tantamount to a repudiation of the moral legitimacy of government by conquest. As far as he was concerned, the new Indian state should be neither a soulless machine nor violence in a concentrated form. Its foundations should be large enough to accommodate the interests of both body force and soul force.

'*Reason of state*'. The theory of 'reason of state' (*raison d'état*) has given the modern state a bad name. It holds that the state, being an indispensable institution for human well-being, can make the claim that its interests are morally superior to any other human interest. As such, the state may subordinate all values, including ethical and spiritual values, to its interests. In practice, this is taken to mean that the end of the state can justify the means that it deems expedient. We are very close here to the view that the interests of the state belong to the realm of necessity and therefore that they lie outside the categories of good and evil. The state thus gets a free hand in taking ethically dubious, even evil means.

Historically, this doctrine had been identified with Machiavellism.[13] Scholars have not been slow in seeing its incompatibility with Gandhi's philosophy.[14] *Hind Swaraj* explicitly rejects 'national interest' (*prajano swartha*) – another name of 'reason of state' – as a sufficient ethical basis for state conduct. The argument is set in the context of his broader discussion of the relationship of means and the end. His position of course is that all human action, especially political action, should ensure the goodness not only of the end but also of the means. The end, in other words, cannot justify the means. Applied to the colonial situation in India, the means that Indians take should be good independently of the goodness of national independence. Accordingly, Indians would not be justified in using brute force against the British, just because the British used brute force in gaining their end. "Your belief that there is no connection between the means and the end is a great mistake", he informs his interlocutor in *Hind Swaraj*".[15] "In using brute force against the English, you consult entirely your own, that is, the national interest".[16]

Gandhi is not denying the importance of national interest to state conduct. What he is denying is that it should be the sole consideration in decision making. This is consistent with his position that the state, though necessary, is not sufficient for human well-being. In addition to the state and its end, there are dharma and moksha, with their equally necessary ends. They, too, contribute to human well-being. An adequate theory of the state therefore should be mindful of the contributions that ethics and spirituality make. Good statecraft and good statesmanship should pursue national interest only in the wider context of ethics and spirituality.

There is more to Gandhi's objection to 'reason of state' than his stand on the issue of ends and means. There is also the notion that the state should not have total control over the individual. The spheres dharma and moksha, though related to the sphere of artha (the state's sphere), really lies outside the reach of the coercive state. The power of the state over the individual therefore cannot be total, even when the state is based on consent. There are spheres in the individual's life that are closed off to the state. Consent does not give the state the right to enter these spheres. Obedience is owed to the state only when it acts ethically. This of course is the great insight underlying the practice of satyagraha, which stands in stark opposition to the theory of 'reason of state'. "That we should obey laws whether good or bad is a new-fangled notion".[17] "Man-made laws are not necessarily binding...If man will only realize that it is unmanly to obey laws that are unjust, no man's tyranny will enslave him. This is the key to self-rule or home rule".[18] Satyagraha, among others things, is a stern reminder that the parliament does not have the moral authority to legislate on matters that infringe on universally valid ethical matters.

Religion-based state. The question that has engaged South Asia for the past hundred years is whether religion should be the basis of the modern state. Put differently, whether the coercive power of the state should be used to serve the interests of a particular religion. A deeply religious man, Gandhi was firmly opposed to the theory that religion should be the basis of the state. This would seem paradoxical only to those who underestimate the extent of his political modernity. He was challenged on this by M. A. Jinnah, a non-observant Shia Muslim, and by V. D. Savarkar, an atheist Brahmin. Jinnah, feeling the pressure from some Indian Muslims who wanted to create a Muslim homeland in South Asia, led the movement that resulted in the creation of a religion-based state – Pakistan. It now faces the danger of being morphed into a militant Sharia-based Islamic state. Savarkar, in his turn, started a political movement whose goal was the establishment of a state that would promote the interests of the ideology of Hindutva (Hinduness).

Gandhi's opposition to a religion-based state was grounded in his conception of the respective ends of religion and state. The ultimate end of religion was the pursuit and the final attainment of spiritual liberation or moksha, while that of the state was the attainment of material well-being in the spheres of economics and politics (artha). The proper means available to religion and state were also quite different. A virtuous life freely pursued was the means to spiritual liberation, whereas the application of legitimate coercion was the ultimate means necessary for the attainment of material well-being. The coercive means available to the state, in Gandhi's view, could not contribute anything justifiable to the attainment of spiritual liberation. The latter was simply outside the state's competence.

Practical reasoning reinforced this abstract reasoning. South Asia was a multi-religious region, and the state, if it had any pretensions to being just, could not possibly favour one religion over another. In other words, in a multi-religious country, the state could be just only if it was neutral towards every religion. The religious pluralism of society and the religious neutrality of the state had to go hand in hand.

Gandhi found further support for his position in his theory of civic nationalism, as already noted. The nation for him was not a *homogeneous organic community*, but a *pluralistic political community*. In Europe and elsewhere, nationalism, based on religion, race, or language, favoured a homogeneous organic community rather than a pluralistic political community. Gandhi unequivocally rejected the idea that religion should be the basis of the Indian nation. Going further, he claimed that the Indian nation was religiously pluralistic:

> India cannot cease to be one nation because people belonging
> to different religions live in it. The introduction of foreigners
> does not necessarily destroy that nation, they merge in it. A
> country is one nation only when such a condition obtains in it.
> That country must have a faculty of assimilation. India has ever
> been such a country. In reality, there are as many religions as
> there are individuals, but those who are conscious of the spirit
> of nationality do not interfere with one another's religion. If
> they do, they are not fit to be considered a nation. If the Hin-
> dus believe that India should be peopled only by Hindus, they
> are living in dreamland. The Mohamedans also live in a dream-
> land if they believe that there should be only Mohamedans. The

Hindus, the Mohamedans, the Parsees and the Christians who have made India their country are fellow country men, and they will have to live in unity if only for their own interest. In no part of the world are one nationality and one religion synonymous terms, nor has it ever been so in India.[19]

Given the sentiments expressed above, the state in India had to be neutral towards all religions. Gandhi favoured the secular state, that is, the state that was neutral but not hostile to religions. "The state would undoubtedly be secular. Everyone living in it should be entitled to profess his religion without let or hindrance, so long as the citizens obeyed the common law of the land".[20] "Secular welfare", not religion, was the specific responsibility of the state.[21]

Here, it is important to point out that he did not endorse the modern Western type of secular state, insofar as the latter meant or required denial of spiritual transcendence. There is therefore a philosophical difference between Gandhi's notion of the secular state and the modern Western notion. The difference lies in his conception of the relationship between secularity and spirituality. He did not see them as being antithetical. This was because of his philosophical framework derived from the philosophy of the 'four great aims of life' (the *purusharthas*). According to this philosophy, there are four great aims of life – dharma, artha, kama, and moksha – each distinct from the other and each having its own legitimate ends, but all four belonging to the same larger kingdom of ends. The state belonged to the secular sphere of artha. As part of artha, a *purushartha*, it represented a positive human value. Dharma and moksha represented equally valid ethical and spiritual values. The secret of the good life was to strive towards bringing about a working harmony between material pursuits and spiritual pursuits, between the state on the one hand and ethics and spirituality on the other. The task before the new Indian state therefore was to reject the philosophical foundation of modern secularism, and adopt instead the Indian philosophical foundation, as explained.

2. THE STATE THAT GANDHI DID WANT

The state as the protector of rights. So far, we have considered Gandhi's negative ideas about the state. To complete an assessment of Gandhi as an activist and thinker, however, a consideration of his positive ideas also is necessary. To begin with, he regarded the state as the indispensable means of protecting the fundamental rights of citizens.

Two of his shorter writings are of special importance here: the 'Declaration of Independence (*Purna Swaraj*)' (1930) and the 'Resolution on Fundamental Rights and Economic Changes' (1931). He was the sole author of the first, and the co-author (with Jawaharlal Nehru) of the second.

The Declaration is the closest that he came to explaining why Indians should have a sovereign state. They should have one because, first, it is their inalienable collective right to have one. Second, without the sovereign state, it would be impossible for them to enjoy their individual rights to freedom and material well-being. Rights, though inalienable, are not self-executing in a well-ordered society. To execute them rightly and make them effectual, the mediation of the state is needed. The colonial state had deprived Indians of their rights; it therefore had to go. The opening lines of the Declaration read as follows: "We believe that it is the inalienable right of the Indian people, as of any other people, to have freedom and to enjoy the fruits of their toil and have the necessities of life, so that they may have full opportunities for growth. We believe also that if any government deprives a people of these rights and oppress them the people have the further right to alter or abolish it".[22]

The 'Resolution on Fundamental Rights and Economic Changes' is an elaboration of the main idea of the Declaration. Also, it gives a short preview of what a sovereign Indian state would do to bring about the social and political transformation of India.[23] The philosophy of human rights provides the framework of the Resolution. For a quarter of a century, Gandhi had been fighting the state, both in South Africa and India, against its abuses of human rights. Satyagraha, let us not forget, was a method, albeit a nonviolent method, of "securing rights by personal suffering".[24] He now takes the side of the state, no doubt the *good* state, reminding it that it is its existential duty to protect human rights. As he stated in the speech introducing the Resolution to the annual meeting of the Indian National Congress, it was meant especially for the benefit of "the poor, inarticulate Indian". Its main object was to indicate "the broad features of swaraj" and "what we propose to do as soon as we come to power". In particular, it wanted to eradicate the many historic injustices of Indian society affecting women, the poor, the Untouchables (dalits), and the religious minorities.

The first article lists nine items under fundamental rights. They include: the freedom of association, speech, conscience, religion; the right to private property; the right to bear arms; the rights of the religious minorities; equality of all citizens without regard to gender, caste, or religious differences; and equal access to public office, public roads, wells, and schools. The second article proclaims "Religious neutrality on the part of the state". The remaining eighteen articles are concerned with such rights as those affecting adult suffrage, free primary education, a living wage, and maternity leave.

The state is not only the protector but also the enforcer by coercive means of human rights. Gandhi has a warning for the well-known violators of human rights in India, the zamindars (landlords) and the maharajas (princely rulers). The new Indian state "does not seek to destroy them", he tells them "but is determined to destroy all wrong and injustice. Let them make an endeavour", he adds, "to understand the grievances of their tenants and introduce adequate measures of relief before legislation overtakes them".[25]

The state that Gandhi envisaged though coercive was not a dictatorship. It had to exercise its power within the limits of natural justice. Certainly, it was not the sort of dictatorship contemporaneously Stalin was running and Mao was hoping to run and Antonio Gramsci in Italy called "The Modern Prince".[26] Gandhi's state would be the instrument of the whole community, and not that of any particular class, however privileged.

On economic changes, too, Gandhi had given much thought, at least since 1904 when he read for the first time Ruskin's economic writings, notably *Unto This Last* and *The Political Economy of Art*. He read more works on nineteenth-century capitalism, ten of which were listed in the Appendix I of *Hind Swaraj*. Gandhi was critical of capitalism. Unlike Karl Marx, however, he was a friendly critic who wanted to reform not destroy capitalism. He rejected forthwith the notion of *homo economicus* for the reason that it had no place for soul force. His pamphlet, *Sarvodaya* (1908), based on Ruskin, argued that a just economic system should regard the dignity of free labour as its foundation and the welfare of the worst-off of society its special responsibility. The state's role was not so much to create wealth as to create conditions of justice necessary for the creation of wealth. In India, this meant the destruction of all forms of discrimination based on religion, gender, caste, or tribe. Under no circumstance did he want economic power and political power to coalesce in the hands of the state. One solution to the problem of extreme economic disparity was the practice of the moral virtue of trusteeship, according to which the wealthy would voluntarily transfer their extra wealth into a trust for social use. However, should this virtue not materialize, the state was permitted to intervene "with the minimum exercise of violence".[27]

According to the Resolution, political freedom and economic freedom of the poor had to go together.[28] It did not spell out the details of how this would be made possible, except to say that the state would have the power to control 'key industries' and own mineral resources.[29] On the question of the extent of the state's intervention in economic activities, Gandhi did not always agree with Nehru. As he wrote in *Sarvodaya*, India had to have industries, "but of the right kind",[30] by which he meant small-scale industries started locally, especially in rural areas, by the villagers themselves, producing such necessities of life as food, clothing (including his famous khadi), comfortable dwellings, means of cheap transportation, medicine, articles of sanitation, and the like. It was his conviction that the state, no matter how well intentioned, could not, on its own, lift the poor out of poverty unless the poor, *on their own, willed* to get out of it. While admitting that humans tended to live by habit, he held that it was better for them "to live by the exercise of will".[31] India's poor, numbed for so long by belief in fate and oppressed by social hierarchy, had to develop an *effective will* to emancipate themselves. Disciplined voluntary work was one way of creating such a will. Simultaneously the state should intervene and remove the impediments that stand in their way, especially impediments originating in discrimination based on religious, gender, caste, or tribal differences. The will to change, manifested through disciplined work, had to be the *logical* starting point, however. He made this point forcefully in his famous debate with the great poet Tagore (on the place of manual work and the spinning wheel in the battle against Indian poverty): "The hungry millions ask for one poem – invigorating food. They cannot be given it. They must earn it. And they can earn only by the sweat of their brow".[32] In the end, the state should be the enforcer of rights, and the individual, protected by the state, and moved by a disciplined will, be the actual creator of wealth and agent of economic changes.

State as the guardian of order and security. Already in his lifetime, his theory of nonviolence and satyagraha had virtually eclipsed everything else in Gandhi's political philosophy. Not he but some of his interpreters were mainly responsible for this. He was perceived (or rather depicted) variously as a pacifist, a utopian, and even a philosophical anarchist. Critics saw in satyagraha the moral equivalent of, if not a substitute for, war and a panacea for violence.[33] All this tended to ignore, if not conceal, an important aspect of his political philosophy, that is to say, its support for the legitimate use of coercion by the state for maintaining internal order and external security. His moral idealism did not require the sacrifice of political realism. In fact, he tried to combine the two. He had no difficulty in accepting that the state should have "the capacity to regulate national life through national representatives".[34] Even in a nonviolent society, a police force would be necessary.[35] It was not a mystery to him why "ordinarily, government was impossible without the use of force".[36] He did not object to the fact that the state had the right to enforce laws while they were on the statute.[37] It was impossible for a state nonviolently to resist forces of disorder within a country.[38]

Gandhi did not want the states to be 'absolutely independent', and warring one against another. He favoured a world order based on a 'federation of friendly and interdependent states'.[39] At the same time, he recognized the right of the states to defend themselves by military means. The right is only to defensive not aggressive war. Leaving aside the issue of his participation in the ambulance corps in both the Boer and Zulu wars, there is the question of his active recruitment for the Indian Army during World War I. The two *Bulletins* that he wrote in 1918 (critics almost never refer to these) in connection with this are of not only historical but also theoretical interest. The first *Bulletin* gives the reason why Gujaratis should join the army. They should do so to acquire 'fitness for swaraj'. They can acquire it if they develop skills necessary for national self-defence. "We can never be respected as equals of the Englishman, so long as our safety depends upon our protection by British arms and we are afraid of their police force and soldiery. We must, therefore, learn to bear arms and gain the power to protect ourselves from any aggression. *It is, therefore, our duty to join the army if we want to learn that art very quickly*".[40]

The second *Bulletin* went further. It connected India's inability to defend itself by linking it to the long-standing influence of India's ascetic culture. "It is only in India among all the countries of the world where you can meet with the sight of eight men raiding a population of 1000 and coolly looking and robbing the thousand without having to put up with a fight". The Indian intelligentsia had a great deal to do with this state of affairs. In the name of dharma, Gandhi wrote, they 'put on shelf' the duties of artha. As a result, Indians lost "the power to fight altogether and with it their bravery". And unless 'this pseudo-philosophy' was uprooted from the Indian soil, there was not going to be any real peace in the country. Joining the army would be one way of eradicating this cultural deficiency.[41]

Gandhi faced severe criticism for his support of the Indian Army. He stood his ground, however. Writing to C. F. Andrews, one of his closest friends now turned critic, he explained how "under exceptional circumstances war may have to be resorted to as a necessary evil". If the motive of self-defence was right, "it may be turned to the profit of mankind". A practitioner of nonviolence therefore "may not stand aside and look on with indifference, but must make the choice and actively co-operate or actively resist". Courage exhibited in a defensive war is as much a virtue as courage exhibited in satyagraha. Both required the overcoming of the fear of death. He saw no incompatibility between the practice of ahimsa and the exercise of self-defence. It seemed to him that 'full development of body force' was a sine qua non of full development of soul force. A deep spiritual life and good citizenship that required soldierly courage could and should go together. His interpretation of the theory of the *purusharthas* ('the great aims of life') allowed for a positive interaction between the pursuits of dharma, artha, and moksha.[42]

Gandhi's weightiest contribution in support of the state's right to self-defence by military means came in his speech at the second Round Table Conference in London (1931). This was an official conference on a future constitution for India – the only such conference he ever attended. The significance of his statement therefore may not be underestimated. "I think that a nation that has no control over her own defence forces and over her external policy is hardly a responsible nation. Defence, its Army, is to a nation the very essence of its existence, and if a nation's defence is controlled by an outside agency, no matter how friendly it is, then that nation is certainly not responsibly governed... Hence I am here very respectfully to claim complete control over the Army, over the Defence forces and over External Affairs... I would wait till eternity if I cannot get control over Defence. I refuse to deceive myself that I am going to embark upon responsible government although I cannot control my defence... That is my fundamental position".[43]

Gandhi's moral idealism, informed by political realism, hoped for a world order without war. The horrors of World War II and the introduction of nuclear weapons further strengthened this hope and forced him to rethink the right of states to self-defence by military means. He proposed progressive disarmament and the creation of nonviolent civilian defence organizations. For all that, however, he did not renounce the inherent right of states to defend themselves when attacked. One is not surprised that India's intervention in Kashmir in 1947 had his tacit approval.[44]

The good state (surajya). Towards the end of his life, Gandhi seemed no longer to be satisfied with mere political swaraj. He wanted "to transform swaraj into *surajya* [the good state]".[45] This no doubt marks a shift in his thinking. The *surajya* would be the coercive state that worked in tandem with the non-coercive agencies of civil society – popularly known today as Non-Governmental Organizations (NGOs). The insight here is that a nonviolent social order can be brought into being only if the coercive state and the non-coercive NGOs worked together.

This is the idea underlying *Constructive Programme* (1941), his last major political theory tract. It is not arguing for an alternative to the coercive state, as some mistakenly think.[46] What it is arguing for is that if India is to become less violent and more peaceful and prosperous, it should have a coercive state that accepts, both in principle and in practice, the need for the 'constructive work' carried out by a multitude of non-coercive organizations. That is to say, in addition to the *state*, voluntary organizations of *civil society* should also get involved in India's social reconstruction.

Constructive Programme[47] identified eighteen areas of Indian society where the NGOs and the state could work together. They included the areas of inter-religious relations, of discrimination against the so-called Untouchables, women, aboriginal tribes, of rural sanitation, small-scale industries including khadi, and adult education. The state, as the protector of human rights, and the guardian of internal order and external security, had its specific role to play even in these areas. At the same time, there was a good deal that the NGOs could do better than the state could. Gandhi's reasoning went something like this: "I admit that there are certain things which cannot be done without political power, but there are numerous other things which do not at all depend on political power. That is why a thinker like Thoreau said that 'that government is best which governs the least'. This means that when people come into possession of political power, a nation that runs its affairs smoothly and effectively without much state interference is truly democratic. Where such condition is absent, the form of government is democratic in name [only]".[48]

Only in societies that valued democracy, civil liberty, and freedom of association could the ideas of *Constructive Programme* be implemented. They could not be implemented for example in theocracies and dictatorships. Gandhi assumed that Indian society was advanced enough to have a vibrant civil society. He further assumed that the Indian NGOs would be sufficiently well organized and well motivated to carry out nonviolently the task of social reconstruction. Perhaps he overestimated their actual effectiveness, especially since the modern welfare state was intruding more and more into the strictly private sphere. However that might be, his point was that the creation of a nonviolent social order depended on a coercive state that was willing and able to increase the role of the NGOs.[49] He did not see that the modern welfare state could carry on the work of sustainable development all by itself.

Decentralization of political power was also an important aspect of *surajya*. It was to be achieved by both the village councils (panchayats) and the NGOs. But they were to play their roles differently: the village councils being creations of the state was part of the coercive order, whereas NGOs being voluntary and nonviolent belonged to the noncoercive sector.

In *Constructive Programme*, Gandhi took the unusual step of reviewing the place of satyagraha in *surajya*. This, too, marks a new development in his political thinking. Hitherto civil disobedience had occupied the centre stage of Gandhian politics. It was negative politics or resistance politics that looked upon the state as the adversary. The constructive work of NGOs seemed to occupy the periphery, if it occupied any place at all. All this changed in *Constructive Programme*. The work of the NGOs is now being presented as at least as important as that of satyagraha. The state is their friend, not enemy. *Constructive Programme*, in other words, redefined the relationship between civil disobedience and constructive work. Civil disobedience without constructive program, it states, is "mere bravado and worse than useless", or like "a paralyzed hand attempting to lift a spoon".[50]

Gandhi felt that while the attainment of sovereign statehood was the end of the nationalist movement, it was only the beginning of a new movement of national reconstruction. Because of this, the need for constructive work increased, he felt, "many times more". "If India is to live and live well there is no alternative to the constructive program".[51] Independent India, in other words, had to evolve into *surajya*.

CONCLUSION

Gandhi's thoughts on the state help us to have a balanced picture of his stature as a political thinker. For one thing, we can put to rest the assertion that his concept of a nonviolent society is incompatible with the coercive state.[52] As we have seen, he regarded the coercive state as a necessary means to bring about a nonviolent social order. The nonviolent social order of his conception was not one that had to be completely free of violence or indeed coercive institutions. What it sought to achieve was not the complete elimination of violence or coercion but a gradual reduction of their intensity and extent. He was quite clear about his acceptance of the reality of violence and coercion in human affairs. Perfect nonviolence was possible only in the disembodied existence. "All life in the flesh exists by some himsa [violence]...The world is bound in a chain of destruction. In other words himsa is an inherent necessity of life in the body...None, while in the flesh, can thus be entirely free from himsa because one never completely renounces the will to live".⁵³ "No doubt, destruction in some form or other of some life is inevitable. Life lives upon life".⁵⁴ And so on. Given such a social anthropology, a pacifist interpretation of Gandhi's social order is not tenable. Only a legitimate coercive state can bring about and maintain the sort of nonviolent social order that Gandhi had in mind.

We can now identify Gandhi's position concerning the duties of the good coercive state. Its primary duty is to protect and extend human rights. The greatest impediment to the attainment of a nonviolent social order is the absence of an effective human-rights enforcement mechanism. Every instance of social violence involves an infringement of human rights. Whenever human rights are self-enforced, social violence necessarily follows. The just coercive state is the only institution that can both enforce human rights and prevent their abuses. Gandhi, more than others in the modern world, understood this truth. That is why he supported both satyagraha *and* the good state.

The maintenance of internal order and external security is the state's other duty. Internal disorder inevitably results in social violence. If unchecked, it can lead to civil war. Similarly, a state that is unable to defend itself from external attacks cannot contribute to peace; it only encourages aggression on the part of strong states.

Gandhi's position on the relationship of the state to the economic order conducive to a nonviolent society was principled but flexible. The principle was that the state should play a subsidiary, not a predominant, role in the economic life of society. However, flexibility was required in the application of this principle to concrete circumstances, such as the failure of the wealthy to live by the moral principle of trusteeship. The state could then legitimately intervene through legislation.

At the beginning of his career, he was opposed to heavy industries that threatened to wipe out village industries. Towards the end of his career (by 1940), however, he was reconciled to their co-existence. But his opposition to planned industrialization never changed. "Hitherto the industrialization has been so planned as to destroy the villages and village crafts. In the state of the future, it [industrialization] will subserve the villages and their crafts. I do not share the socialist belief that centralization of the necessaries of life will conduce to the common welfare when the centralized industries are planned and owned by the state. The socialistic conception of the West was born in an environment reeking with violence...I hold that the coming to power of the proletariat through violence is bound to fail. What is gained by violence must be lost before superior violence".[55] Briefly, an economic order resting on the principle of class war can no more conduce to a nonviolent society than can one based on laissez faire.

Finally, it is implicit in Gandhi's political philosophy that civic virtues without the cooperation of the state cannot create a nonviolent social order. Virtues of course are necessary but not sufficient. Gandhi accepted this, notwithstanding the fact that his personal life was governed by Truth, nonviolence, and other virtues. If the policies of a state do not reflect the values of his system of virtues, the social order could hardly become nonviolent. The people of Myanmar, for example, may well be virtuous; but if the state of Myanmar is repressive, their virtues count for little politically. Likewise, the virtues of the Dalai Lama, the ruler of Tibet, are not sufficient by themselves if the people of Tibet are to enjoy their autonomy. The point is that virtue and state power have to work in tandem if the social order is to become nonviolent. Just as the secular state by itself cannot create a nonviolent social order, neither can virtue by itself. This profound Truth underpins Gandhi's political philosophy.

Notes

1 M. K. Gandhi, *The Collected Works of Mahatma Gandhi* (New Delhi, India: Publications Division, Ministry of Information and Broadcasting, Government of India, Navajivan, 1958–94, 100 vols), vol. 19, p. 80. (Henceforth, *CWMG*.)

2 *Ibid.*, p. 278.

3 *Ibid.*, vol. 45, pp. 263–4.

4 *Ibid.*, vol. 90, p. 24.

5 M. K. Gandhi, *Hind Swaraj and Other Writings*, ed. A. J. Parel (Cambridge, England: Cambridge University Press, 2009), p. 27. (Henceforth, *HS*.)

6 See A. J. Parel, *Gandhi's Philosophy and the Quest for Harmony* (Cambridge, England: Cambridge University Press, 2006), pp. 31–51.

7 *CWMG*, vol. 59, p. 319.

8 *Ibid.*, p. 318.

9 *Ibid.*

10 See *Hobbes' Leviathan*, ed. W. G. Pogson Smith (Oxford, England: Clarendon Press, 1952), part 2, p. 132.

11 Eric Stokes, *The English Utilitarians and India* (Oxford, England: Clarendon Press, 1959), p. 321.

12 James Fitzjames Stephen, 'Foundations of the Government of India', *The Nineteenth Century*, 1883, cited in *HS*, p. xxxii.

13 See Friedrich Meinecke, *Machiavellism: The Doctrine of Raison D'Etat and Its Place in Modern History*, trans. W. Stark (New Haven, CT: Yale University Press, 1957).

14 See Simone Panter-Brick, *Gandhi Against Machiavellism: Non-Violence in Politics* (London: Asia Publishing House, 1966).
15 *HS*, p. 79.
16 *Ibid.*, p. 84.
17 *Ibid.*, p. 89.
18 *Ibid.*, p. 90.
19 *Ibid.*, pp. 50–1.
20 Cited in Bharatan Kumarappa (ed.), *M. K. Gandhi: Sarvodaya* (Ahmedabad, India: Navajivan, 1948), p. 78.
21 Cited in N. K. Bose (ed.), *Selections from Gandhi* (Ahmedabad, India: Navajivan, 1957), p. 257.
22 *CWMG*, vol. 42, pp. 384–5, and also pp. 382–3.
23 For the text of the 'Resolution' and Gandhi's speech explaining its details, see *CWMG*, vol. 45, pp. 371–4.
24 *HS*, p. 88.
25 *CWMG*, vol. 45, p. 373.
26 See Antonio Gramsci, *The Modern Prince and Other Writings* (New York: International Publishers, 1970). The Dictatorship of the Communist Party according to Gramsci is the modern equivalent of Machiavelli's prince.
27 *CWMG*, vol. 59, p. 319.
28 *Ibid.*, vol. 45, p. 370.
29 *Ibid.*, p. 371.
30 *Ibid.*, vol. 8, p. 374.
31 *Ibid.*, vol. 59, p. 319.
32 *Ibid.*, vol. 21, p. 291.
33 See, e.g., H. J. N. Horsburgh, *Non-Violence and Aggression: A Study of Gandhi's Moral Equivalent of War* (London: Oxford University Press, 1968), and Joan V. Bondurant, *Conquest of Violence: The Gandhian Philosophy of Conflict* (Berkeley: University of California Press, rev. ed., 1967), Krishnalal Shridharani, *War Without Violence* (New York: Harcourt, 1939), Gene Sharp, *Gandhi as a Political Strategist* (Boston: Porter Sargent, 1979), and Dennis Dalton, *Mahatma Gandhi: Nonviolent Power in Action* (New York: Columbia University Press, 1993).
34 Raghavan Iyer, *The Moral and Political Writings of Mahatma Gandhi*, 3 vols. (Oxford, England: Clarendon Press, 1986), vol. I, p. 399.
35 *Ibid.*, vol. II, p. 436.
36 *CWMG*, vol. 90, p. 511.
37 Iyer, *Moral and Political Writings*, II, p. 453.
38 *Ibid.*, p. 448.
39 *CWMG*, vol. 25, p. 482.
40 Mahadev Desai (ed.), *Day-to-Day With Gandhi* (Varanasi, India: Sarva Seva Sangh Prakashan, 1958), vol. II, pp. 349–54, at 349. Italics Gandhi's.
41 *Ibid.*, pp. 353–9, at p. 357.
42 For the full text of Gandhi's important letter of 6-7-1918 to C. F. Andrews, see *ibid.*, pp. 172–8.
43 For the full text of Gandhi's speech, see *CWMG*, vol. 48, pp. 304–9.
44 *Ibid.*, vol. 90, p. 511.

45 *Ibid.*, p. 24.

46 E.g., by Sharp in *Gandhi as a Political Strategist*, p. 80.

47 For the full text of *Constructive Programme: Its Meaning and Place,* see *CWMG,* vol. 75, pp. 146–66.

48 *Ibid.*, vol. 62, p. 92.

49 On an optimistic account of the constructive work that NGOs are doing in India, see R. Sooryamoorthy and K. D. Gangrade, *NGOs in India: A Cross-Sectional Study* (Westport, CT: Greenwood Press, 2001).

50 *CWMG,* vol. 75, pp. 165–6.

51 *Ibid.*, vol. 90, pp. 24, 295.

52 See Raghavan Iyer, *The Moral and Political Thought of Mahatma Gandhi* (Santa Barbara, CA: Concord Grove Press, 1983), pp. 252–60; Bhikhu Parekh, *Gandhi's Political Philosophy* (Notre Dame, IN: University of Notre Dame Press, 1989), pp. 110–14.

53 *CWMG,* vol. 37, p. 314.

54 *Ibid.*, vol. 34, p. 130.

55 *Ibid.*, vol. 71, p. 130.

9 Gandhi and social relations

TANIKA SARKAR

Much of recent scholarship on Gandhi is propelled by three urgent contemporary concerns. First, the growth of Hindu communalism, making secular historians turn to histories of tolerance and hence to Gandhi, a Hindu martyr to Hindu communalism. Second, post-colonial scholars, anxious about what is authentic and what is derivative in Indian modernity, search for moderns like Gandhi who were firmly anchored in Indian tradition. Finally, discontents with modern developmental paradigms renew the significance of Gandhi, a forceful critic of industrialism. For all three, Gandhi offers a resolution for the ills of modernity. All, moreover, identify *an* essential Gandhi, seeking him in his moral discourses rather than in his political and social work: discourses founded on an unwavering certainty about Truth. There is a strong tendency for icon making at work, rather than historical reassessment. The present chapter, in contrast, regards Gandhi's political thinking and moral-ethical ideas as interactive, carrying profound social implications. Gandhi, moreover, never made absolute Truth claims.[1] Perhaps the most interesting aspect of his life was his capacity for changing himself, his openness to experiences, his 'experiments with Truth'.[2] His life would, at any given moment, constitute a shifting and open totality: imbibing contradictory elements and transforming its praxis continuously.

QUESTIONS OF CLASS AND POVERTY

The problem of poverty was crucial to Gandhi: "To a people, famishing and idle, the only acceptable form in which God can dare appear is work and promise of food as wages".[3] He was certain that poverty emerged with industrial modernity. Machine-based production of an infinite number of objects breeds infinite greed, causing poverty. His diagnosis does not address the problem of class power under capitalism, or the structural features of its system of production and property. Poverty appears as the moral failing of the poor.

He sought to resolve the problem of power with the trusteeship principle. Wealth is created, he said, by "exploiting the masses". Owners should, therefore, regard their property as a trust, held for the poor. They are entitled to their profits – renamed as 'commission' – because "Those who are capable wish to acquire more . . . it is natural". The poor, by implication, are less able. Once again, poverty becomes a failing of the poor.[4]

Trusteeship can be better understood in terms of a sixteenth-century Hindi religious text, very dear to Gandhi's heart, Tulsidas's *Ramcharit-manas*, whose concept of *Ramarajya* provided the pattern for his ideal swaraj. "We call a state *Ramarajya* when . . . the relationship between the two is as good as that between a father and a son . . . The people are not as wise as he (the ruler) is". Significantly, Gandhi exalted such a monarchy as superior to democracy: "It is because we have forgotten this that we talk of democracy or the government of the people".[5]

Mutual love transfigured but did not alter the fundamental form of social relationships in *Ramarajya*: among castes, between men and women, rulers and ruled. Gandhi's trusteeship meant a similar persistence of social hierarchies but now rebuilt on different meanings.

Gandhi's practical resolution to the problem of inequality was to short-circuit a social process by personal example: to be self-sufficient in all forms of labour that are necessary for the reproduction of daily life. He hoped to live without exploitation. What Gandhi and his associates did was a matter of personal conviction and choice. The poor, however, are forced to live a life of non-possession. The self-chosen poverty of the great leader did not question the brutal lacks in their lives. It morally privileged and aestheticized them.

On his return to India, Gandhi led two peasant movements, the first nationalist leader to do so. At Champaran in Bihar, peasants rebelled against European indigo planters. Kheda in Gujarat saw a no-revenue movement among a broad section of substantial landholding Patidars, though on an issue that was vital to a larger spectrum of the rural poor, suffering from the wartime rise in prices. Kheda and Champaran taught him how to bring social opposites together: merchants, middle classes, peasants, local politicians. Such cross-class mobilization required certain conditions, an issue that would unify disparate classes against European capitalists or the state and, equally, would avoid conflict among Indian classes and castes.[6] A very different situation unfolded during the agrarian depression of 1929–34 – the years of civil disobedience. Tenants were unable to pay rent to landlords or interest to moneylenders, and there were large-scale evictions of cultivators from their land. Gandhi did not advise anti-rent movements, nor did he appeal to landlords and moneylenders to desist from collecting their dues – always unfair, but particularly so at that time. In the United Provinces, a socialistic Jawaharlal Nehru insisted on a Congress movement for rent refusal. Gandhi justified it as a local emergency. He gave an ambiguous reply when he was asked if the Congress would scrap the debt burden of poor peasants when it came to power.[7] When Bengali sharecroppers in Midnapore demanded a larger crop share, local Gandhians turned away from them.[8]

Gandhian solutions for poverty – the homespun, village schools, sanitation – did not help the poor peasant facing dispossession. Nor did the rich behave as trustees, protecting the vulnerable in times of distress. As the moral economy of trusteeship failed to materialize, Gandhi reprimanded the peasant who rose up against the landlord, rather than the landlord who failed to discharge his paternal responsibilities. A number of peasant struggles, therefore, occurred outside the capacious Congress umbrella under Communist, Muslim League, or Praja Samiti leadership. So Gandhi knew – and none better – how to speak *to* the peasant. But he did not always speak *for* the peasant.

At the same time, Gandhi was the first Indian leader who solicited peasant entry into the political nation, enlarging its remit to constitute some of the largest mass movements in the history of the world. Whatever its limits, the entry of the peasant-satyagrahi into nation making did create the basis for an unprecedented democratization of Indian polity.

Since Gandhi is widely remembered as a man of the peasantry, it is interesting to recall what a very urban person he actually was: living out important phases of his life in Rajkot, London, and Johannesburg, and moving among great Indian cities. He went to villages when he needed to mobilize for Congress movements. He once tried to develop rural welfare projects in Bihar. Kasturba told local women that they should bathe regularly. They replied that they could not, as they lacked a second garment to change into afterwards. The reply struck Gandhi with the force of a revelation, as he understood, for the first time, how deep peasant vulnerability went.[9] The actual work of village welfare was done by Gandhians who lived among the peasants. Gandhi himself lived in ashrams that were simulated rural communities, but ones that were free of the social contradictions that actual villages faced.

His faith in trusteeship was painfully corroded in the dark days of 1946 when he travelled in Bengal villages trying to stop the tide of communal violence. At the very end of his life, he recognized that Hindu landlords had never been trustees to their Muslim tenants but had exploited them shamelessly. Too late, he began to rethink property relations, admitting that hereditary ownership was unfair. Too late, too, he traced Muslim rural communalism to agrarian class contradictions, and admitted that rent strikes by cultivators against landlords would be perfectly justified.[10] Had his Congress acted on such an understanding earlier, Muslim League propaganda, promising Pakistan with class equity, would probably not have been so successful among Bengali Muslim peasants.

At the end of his life, he recalled his attraction towards socialist ideas – class revolution without violence – which he had, apparently, acquired in South Africa.[11] He reaffirmed his faith in these ideals, rather than in his own model of trusteeship: "There can be no *Ramarajya* in the present state of iniquitous inequalities".[12]

Gandhi saw cities as dens of vice, making no distinction between the urban rich and the urban poor. Though many workers joined nationalist agitations, sometimes even disrupting their own class agitations to do so – as did workers of Sholapur or carters in Calcutta in 1930 when Gandhi was arrested – he did not encourage Gandhians to build up working-class bases. However, he did once lead a workers' strike, and that, too, against an Indian cotton textile mill owner, of the Sarabhai family of Ahmedabad, in 1918. He formed a docile Textile Labour Association, which abjured the strike weapon and accepted the trusteeship ideal.[13] Otherwise, he forbade strikes. "We seek not to destroy capital or capitalists, but to regulate the relations between capital and labour. We want to harness capital to our side". Rowlatt satyagraha demonstrations in 1919 were scheduled for a Sunday, a day of non-work. His abrupt withdrawal of the first phase of civil disobedience has been attributed to the pressures that business houses brought to bear on him, fearing losses in business.[14] The fear of the former and the accommodation of the latter kind of pressure are revealing.

Gandhi strove to save the uneducated from contempt and refused the intellectual any special grounds for power and privilege. But the inversion of social values did not produce actual social levelling. On the contrary, he insisted on the status quo. "The peasant... observes the rules of morality. But he cannot write his own name. What do you propose to do by giving him a knowledge of letters?... Do you want to make him discontented with... his lot?".[15]

On the other hand, even if elites have received 'false education', they are not to give it up. "We are so much beset by the disease of civilization, that we cannot altogether do without English education. Those who have received it may take good use of it wherever necessary".[16] So, no unlearning for the already educated. Instead, their privilege is now translated as a burden.

His reflections on good governance are interesting. "That which you consider to be the Mother of Parliaments is like a sterile woman and a prostitute". The British Parliament is a prostitute because it sways before many political opinions, and it is sterile as it produces no good effects. The stigmatizing of sex, work, and female sterility apart, he criticizes plurality and changeability of opinions, which are basic to all democracies.[17]

THE QUESTION OF ADIVASIS

Ramachandra Guha pertinently argues that Gandhi's powerful rural focus precluded an understanding of areas of 'wildness'.[18] The wild domains were the hill tracts and the forests of India, habitations of adivasi tribal people. Often perceived to be living outside the parameters of caste and sedentary agriculture – elements so dear to Gandhi's heart – they had a curious location within Gandhi's social thinking and nationalist politics.

In South Africa, Gandhi at times confused Indian tribals with criminals: maybe an unconscious extension of the colonial administrative term of designated 'criminal tribes' to tribes in general. He spoke in the same breath of Bhils and 'Assamese', along with criminalized thugs.[19] 'Assamese' probably meant the hill tribes of the North East, tarred with the brush of criminality on account of being tribes.

Gandhian movements in India coincided with times of adivasi activism. Many insurgents either approached the Congress for help or found in rumours about Gandhian leadership an echo of their own strivings. They often joined Congress movements, but sometimes with transgressive interpretations of Congress messages, producing homemade liquor to boycott foreign drinks. They were reprimanded. Several adivasi leaders were self-styled Gandhis, as was Jitu Santal, who led Santal sharecroppers in Bengal. The Bengal Congress did not support his programme.[20]

Congress movements were very successful among adivasis who accepted Gandhi's social reform; in the Bardoli *Taluka* in Gujarat, for instance. Wherever the Congress succeeded in capturing adivasi bases, it imposed a puritanical discipline of non-alcoholism, modest dress codes, and vegetarianism. In his insistence on a regime of 'Sanskritized' practices, Gandhi – himself a devout Vaishnavite – perhaps continued an older, pre-colonial tradition of Vaishnavite proselytization. That had involved the avoidance of blood sacrifices, meat, and drinks, also faith in a saviour deity and in morally inspiring sainthood. These were precisely the messages with which Gandhian reformers approached adivasis.

Congress mobilization of adivasis was strictly conditional on their conformity to Gandhi's political discipline. Gonds of the Gudem Rampa region on the borders of Andhra Pradesh and Orissa began an armed revolt against local traders, moneylenders, contractors, and lawyers – the very categories that constituted the local base of Congress workers. They were led by a high-caste leader, Alluri Sita Rama Raju, who had turned into an ascetic in 1922–4. The local Congress bitterly opposed the movement.[21] Apart from some philanthropic and reform work, the Gandhian Congress did not focus much on the needs and problems of adivasis, even as it sought to mobilize them for nationalist movements. It did not tolerate their autonomous political forms and techniques of struggle at all.

THE QUESTION OF CASTE

"The Gandhis belong to the Bania caste and seem to have been originally grocers".[22] His autobiography begins by suggesting a ritual mediocrity in caste status. In his early life, Gandhi showed a remarkable irreverence for caste orthodoxy. He got into trouble with his Modh Bania caste council when he defied it to go abroad. He was outcasted, and he refused to perform penance.

Defiance sharpened in South Africa where he worked closely with low-caste coolies and invited Untouchable colleagues to live on his farms. He forced 'unclean' work on himself and on his family, and he accepted Untouchables in his social and domestic circles on equal terms. He made his family and associates break pollution taboos and engage in labour that was considered very profoundly polluted: shoe-making, leatherwork, cleaning of toilets. In fact, cleaning toilets – work profoundly polluting to caste Hindus – persisted all his life. In Durban, an Untouchable Christian clerk stayed in his house as a guest. When he commanded his wife to clean his chamber pot and she refused, Gandhi, in a fit of rage, almost turned her out of the house.[23] While engaged in plague relief work at Rajkot in 1896, he candidly observed that the latrines of caste Hindus were indescribably filthy, while those of Untouchables were a pleasant surprise, being spotlessly clean.[24]

From his South African days, he learnt to couple Untouchability with racism. A barber had refused to shave him there, fearing he would lose his white clients. Gandhi understood. "We do not allow our own barbers to serve our untouchable brothers".[25] He repeated this after the Jalianwalla Bagh massacres. "Has not Nemesis overtaken us for the crime of untouchability?...Have we not practiced Dyerism and O'Dwyerism on our own kith and kin?...In fact, there is no charge that the 'pariah' cannot fling in our own faces which we do not fling in the face of Englishmen".[26] Racism and Untouchability are made equivalents, the inhumanity of one matching the other.

He said that he had abhorred Untouchability since his 'years of discretion'.[27] However, he never explains what led to this abhorrence, so remarkable for a person born into an extremely orthodox family. *Hind Swaraj* says nothing about Untouchability, even though Gandhi violated pollution norms most radically at the time of its composition. The violations are described, instead, in his autobiography, written about two decades later. Even here, his opposition appears as an unaccounted given.

Defiance continued in India. At Tagore's Shantiniketan school, he taught students to clean latrines. At annual Congress sessions, where caste segregation appalled him, he did it again.[28] He told a sadhu that he would no longer wear the sacred thread: "that right can come only after Hinduism has purged itself of untouchability".[29] He began to pay for his defiance. When an Untouchable family joined his ashram at Ahmedabad, there were rumours of a citywide social boycott. Gandhi resolved to relocate the ashram at Untouchable quarters.[30] He redefined the Brahmin as impure, in need of self-purification because of his sinful adherence to purity pollution taboos. He inverted the conventional meanings of pure–impure, of sin and penance.

The problem, however, proved more intractable, and Gandhi was simultaneously besieged by two contrary forces: orthodox Sanatanists and a radical Untouchable politics, critical not just of upper castes but of the Gandhian Congress. For quite some time, he was more eager to persuade Sanatanists whom he saw as friendly adversaries, even claiming he was one of them. He held that Untouchability could be abolished by moral reasoning, that good Hindus knew that while caste divisions were a part of their faith, Untouchability was not. Untouchabilty, moreover, had to be fought by upper castes alone and not by the victims of the system. He, therefore, initially had little time or patience for Untouchable politics.

Compromises began to appear as he sought to persuade the Sanatani orthodoxy. Pollution taboos had not been tolerated at all in his South African farms. In Indian ashrams, however, non-observance was voluntary. From 1918, he began to distinguish between varna and jati.[31] The former was supposedly the rational and liberal core of the faith. It contained no contempt for any caste or labour forms but, at the same time, enjoined hereditary labour divisions. The latter was extraneous, complicating the elegant simplicity of the fourfold varna structure. Untouchability was beyond both, no part of faith but its horrible perversion.

The distinctions did not pacify either group, both of which became increasingly strident from the mid-1920s. In 1924, Gandhi sought to appropriate and redirect the Vaikom satyagraha, which had been started by low-caste Ezhavas for temple entry in the Hindu princely state of Travancore. He told the Brahmin authorities that low castes were already penalized by the gods for misdeeds in their past births; man should not add to their sufferings. The plea fully endorsed the theological justification of caste. The compromise settlement that he negotiated was criticized, and Ezhavas accused him of sabotaging their movement.[32]

Sometimes he endorsed Brahmin claims to purity. In 1931, he described the four varnas thus: Brahmins were 'imparters of knowledge', Kshatriyas were 'defenders of the defenceless', and the two others were traders and farmers/labourers.[33] The first two varnas were given exalted descriptions, the second two – Vaisyas and Shudras – had none. He said in 1933, "I have to believe that of all the classes in the world, the Brahmins will show the largest percentage of those who have given up their all in search of . . . Truth".[34] And, again, "A true Brahmin is one who possesses the attributes of a Kshatriya, a Vaishya and a Shudra and has, in addition, learning . . . Shudras are not, of course, wholly devoid of learning but service is their chief characteristic".[35] Brahmans alone are authorized to impart the highest form of knowledge or *brahmagyan*.[36] Or, "Regarding a Brahmana and a bhangi (scavenger) as equals does not mean that you will not accord to a true Brahmana the reverence that is due to him".[37]

Varnadharma – the fourfold scriptural division of Hindu society – 'emanated from the law of Nature or God'. It was, therefore, immutable, non-negotiable. It was, also, sternly hereditary, and no one possessed the right to change his occupation.[38] Dharma is obedience to one's calling, he said, adding a distinctly Protestant flavour to caste-divided labour forms. Changing ancestral profession leads to social confusion and to dereliction of the divine mandate. It does not allow for Untouchability but neither does it allow intercaste marriage or intercaste dining.[39] In fact, the more he defended caste as non-hierarchical, the more urgent it became to salvage it from the harshness of Untouchability, in order to claim that it was equitable and benign.

He tried to improve the lot of Untouchables in small, concrete ways, primarily by removing the stigma that their work and name carried. He renamed them Harijans or children of God. "I regard Harijans as a fitting name because the caste Hindus cannot be properly considered God's children but the untouchables certainly can".[40] The renaming did not please radical Untouchables who later came to prefer the term dalit or oppressed, a word that proclaimed their real state rather than mystify it.[41] He tried to render Untouchables physically cleaner, suggesting that they avoid eating leftover food and carrion, which are filthy habits and are also considered sinful by holy scripture. They should desist from handling carcasses of animals and should bathe frequently. Gandhi advised households, whose latrines they cleaned, to provide them with a separate sets of garments for their work. He asked municipalities to give them handcarts so that they do not carry night soil on their head. He advised about cleaning latrines with dry earth and told volunteers to teach them to clean hide more effectively. All this flowed from the belief that it was their handling of physical filth that lay at the root of ritual taboos. Once their bodies were cleaned, the stigma would vanish.

His advice fell on deaf upper-caste ears, which refused to accept his inversion of the origins of caste, from ritual injunctions to the nature of work. It was often spurned by Untouchables as well. Untouchable children at Aundh state told him that if they did not consume leftover food or carrion, they would starve, that they did not have enough water to bathe in, that they did not want to visit temples. Reform, clearly, ran into obstacles that he had not foreseen.[42]

He tried to explore if scripture could be bent to provide loopholes for their ritual acceptability. A. S. Altekar had told him in 1932 that Hindus would never accept that Untouchability was extraneous to religion. Gandhi replied that he knew that the Smritis did mention it and, also, possibly, the Vedas. However, he asked the scholar to translate the strictures in a way so that pollution would appear as a consequence of 'external practice' and not of birth. By attaching impurity taboos to 'impure' work, he sought to render them a temporary and not a permanent inherited condition, removable by penance rather than a fixed stain.[43]

The new politics of Untouchables, however, severely disturbed his definitions. Though he saw caste and Untouchability as a religious problem, their political aspects came to haunt him, as Untouchable leaders negotiated with the state about separate electorates, spurning their Hindu identity, and as they became relentlessly critical of Congress moderation. Gandhi's debates with Ambedkar began to assume the proportions of an epic confrontation, as the latter's mobilization of vast numbers of Untouchables and his threat to defect from the Hindu fold dangerously narrowed down the space for manouevre.[44] Ambedkar over-threw Gandhi's distinction between *varnadharma* and Untouchability, insisting that the two are integrally connected. He demanded an annihi-lation of caste.

The encounter was based on mutual criticism, as well as mutual appreciation. Ambedkar criticized Gandhi's emphasis on temple entry and his relative inattention to the socio-economic and political marginal-ization of Untouchables. But he also said that Gandhi first brought the issue of Untouchability to the forefront of national politics. Gandhi's responses were more complex.

Initially, Gandhi took Ambedkar to be an upper-caste person. Ambedkar's educational achievements and social confidence marked him out from the abject Untouchable that Gandhi had in mind when he talked of Harijans. He referred to his achievements patronizingly: "He has received a liberal education . . . He has more than the talents of an average educated Indian . . . His exterior is clean . . . ", though his interior is a mystery.[45] He insisted that Untouchables did not need Ambedkar as they had the Congress to lead them. At the second Round Table Con-ference in 1931, he went further: "I, myself, in my own person, claim to speak for the whole of untouchables".[46] The contentious issue of rep-resentation articulates his core ideas about the valid remit of Untouch-able politics. They should seek to transform their condition neither by legal redress nor by political autonomy. The burden of transformation must lie with upper-caste penitence, which would lead to social change. The burden, however, was also a privilege. If it underlined upper-caste guilt, it also vested political activism solely in them, re-rendering the Untouchable as passive victim, incapable of effective action. Rejuve-nated by penance, upper castes would rightfully reclaim trusteeship. It was a return to hierarchy on a higher plane.

Gandhi saw the temple entry issue as a religious entitlement that Untouchables, being Hindus, ought to possess. Ambedkar defined it as a matter of civic rights, of reclaiming public spaces. Above all, their dif-ference involved the nature of Untouchable politics. In the mid-1920s, Ambedkar organized a series of satyagrahas at Mahad, over the use of roads and tanks adjacent to temples. It was a challenge to Gandhi's assur-ance that Untouchability could be conquered by upper-caste penance and capacity for self-reform. The Congress maintained an uncomfort-able silence, even though the movements were peaceful, self-designated satyagrahas, but the naming was a covert tribute to Gandhi. When some Untouchables forced their way into the Parvati temple at Poona, Gandhi sent right-wing Congressmen, Jamnalal Bajaj and Pandit Malaviya, to investigate the incident. He condemned it on the basis of their reports. Mahadev Desai, Gandhi's secretary, once overheard him say that if Untouchables were given separate electorates, they would join hands with Muslim hooligans and kill caste Hindus.[47]

In 1932, Gandhi went on a fast unto death against the 'Communal Award', by the Secretary of State for India, which, in the absence of any agreement between the different communities, granted Ambedkar's demand for separate electorates. He succeeded only with costly electoral concessions. Chastened, he hurried into conspicuous welfare work for Harijans as an alternative to Ambedkar's combative militancy, opening up some wells, school tanks, and roads for Untouchables. The Harijan Sevak Sangh was founded in 1934. It replaced an earlier venture, the Anti-Untouchability League, whose name had a more militant ring to it. Initially, Ambedkar was inducted as a member, but when he fell out with right-wing Congressmen, it was he who had to leave. Reform happened under severe limits.

Ambedkar's work, however resented at first, did eventually thrust a very painful engagement with the problem of caste on Gandhi, especially as neither Sanatanis nor the bulk of the upper castes showed signs of penitence. Since Hindu scripture acknowledged Untouchability norms, it put his faith – more precious to him than his own life – in a state of crisis. In May 1933, he went on a second fast – this time, against Untouchability. He wrote to Nehru, "There is nothing so bad in all the world as untouchability . . . My life would be a burden to me if Hinduism failed me. But then, I cannot tolerate it with untouchability".[48] He said that it was better for Untouchables to fight against high-caste Savarnas than to live as 'wretched slaves': validating, implicitly, Ambedkar's alternative.[49] More significantly, he said, "If this kind of untouchability were an integral part of Sanatan Dharma that religion has no use for me".[50]

Gandhi was beginning to change: at least, he was learning more relentless introspection. D. R. Nagaraj has suggested that his stance sometimes shifted under interlocution. He wrote that though he did not visit temples much as they prohibited the entry of Untouchables, they did sustain millions and "no faith has done without a habitation".[51] When Rabindranath Tagore retorted that God was never enclosed in temples but only in human hearts, Gandhi gave up his defence. Similarly, his exchanges with B. R. Ambedkar gradually changed his ideas about how to engage with Untouchability.[52] However, it is evident from the weekly newspaper, *Harijan*, that there was no linear progress or a single decisive moment of shift in Gandhi's position. There was, instead, a co-existence of different tonalities, which pushed against one another.

Some of them sharpened over time as a result of the dialogue, but some remained constant: the defence of varna, for instance.

It was only at the very end of his life that Gandhi was prepared to accept a legal-constitutional prohibition of Untouchability: an admission that upper-caste self-reform would not happen. Earlier, he would endorse intra-caste marriage at the most. Now he advised upper-caste girls to marry Untouchable men,[53] disobeying the taboo of *pratiloma* or hypogamous marriages, so loathsome to Hindu orthodoxy. He was fast giving up the fundamentals of caste distinction. Ashis Nandy has argued that it was this that made him so dangerous to his adversaries in the Hindu Right, along with his defence of Indian Muslims. His assassin, Nathuram Godse, was an orthodox Brahmin from the purest of Brahmin categories.[54]

It is evident, once again, that shortly before his death, his deep faith in the potential of trusteeship as a foundation of a just social order had crumbled, leaving behind a radically altered worldview that he did not have time to articulate systematically.

QUESTIONS OF GENDER, SEXUALITY, AND THE BODY

For Gandhi, an ideal gender equation was based on separate but equal spheres of work, the woman inhabiting the domestic interior, the man active in the public world: "I do not envisage the wife as a rule following an avocation independently of her husband. The care of the children and the upkeep of the household are quite enough to fully engage all her energy".[55] Neither should be socially devalued or legally disabled.[56] There was, in this conception of equality, something akin to his approach to caste.

Given his idealization of a split and gendered world, it is ironical that Gandhi's politics filled public places with women – coming from all social and age brackets, and taking their place in all political work. Earlier nationalists had revered the memory of patriotic heroines of royal lineage. Political activism among women contemporaries, however, was unthinkable. By delinking the National Social Conference from the Congress, earlier nationalist leaders had sealed off gender reform projects from nationalist activism. The swadeshi movements of the early twentieth century had marked a slight shift. By asking women to boycott British goods, they created an active female support base, but one that was still confined to the home. Except for a brief moment in Bengal in the early 1930s, revolutionary terrorists used women as providers of logistical help, not as comrades in arms.

Gandhian movements changed this. Peasant women, upper-caste middle-class women, upper-class Muslim women, tribal women came together in nationalist demonstrations, picketed foreign-goods shops, organized social boycotts of loyalists and public burning of foreign cloth, filled up prisons, became local level 'dictators' during civil disobedience when their men were arrested. No aspect of Gandhian politics was sexually segregated. In the process, a remarkable tumbling of social spaces occurred, bringing women of disparate and distanced milieus into closest proximity, even intimacy. It was a learning process, as they came to recognize not only their own political capabilities, but also those of women far above or below them in social rank.[57]

This owed much to the self-representation of Gandhian movements. Led by a man who was seen more as a saint than as a politician, and using a vocabulary of religious sacrifice, his nonviolent activism recast politics – something still new and transgressive for most women – as worship, something that women were expected to do. Some of the specific modes of political work were, indeed, home based: boycott of foreign articles for domestic use, for instance. They rewrote the nation as family and recast the woman's work for the former as a corollary of her work in the latter. The emphasis on salt meant more to women who used it daily for cooking. The spinning wheel could be used at home, and began to generate small incomes for impoverished women. The movement against drinking struck a chord in many female hearts as it was predominantly a male habit, responsible for domestic violence and bankruptcy. Social boycott of loyalists was a political weapon that women could deploy successfully against errant kin groups, neighbours, and family members.[58]

Gender boundaries crumbled further as men were nudged towards work that women were meant to do. The spinning wheel was compulsory for both, as was a reorientation of domestic consumption. Both were trained to face aggression without retaliation, which was the way 'virtuous' women traditionally behaved in the face of domestic tyranny. Gandhi never tired of pointing out that their acquired habits of deference, acceptance, and patience made women ideal patriots, born satyagrahis. Their presence purified the unruly world of politics as they embodied 'sacrifice and suffering' more than men did.[59]

This conjoining of female patriotism with female virtue was paradoxical. It eased the Indian woman into the public domain, into transgressive activities and spaces; it made her a valued political subject. "The ideal satyagrahi is the twentieth century Sati", said Gandhi, thereby casting the widow immolation rite as a heroic act of female commitment.[60] In equal measure, it rendered suffering and self-sacrifice privileged female qualities, it re-anchored her in them. Her politics was purchased with a fresh invention of the wheel.

Gandhi at first resisted the entry of women in public spaces, forbidding them to join the Rowlatt satyagrahas, as well as the later Salt March to Dandi in 1930. Women made their own way into them, forcing a change upon Gandhi's gender politics. In 1930, they were leading local Congress units; in 1942, Aruna Asaf Ali organized militant mass movements and underground activities. In 1946, Gandhi – a man who considered rape to be a fate worse than death – took young and unprotected Hindu women with him to Noakhali, a district ravaged by Muslim communal violence, predominantly directed at Hindu women. He asked the nationalist wife of an ICS officer to leave home and work in Noakhali villages. Her absence reoriented her household as the husband had now to care for the children.[61]

So women remade Gandhi, just as Gandhi made them into new subjects. As their participation widened, so did the boundaries between the political and the social become increasingly porous. Women in prisons were obliged to eschew dietary and caste taboos; women in movements mingled and worked freely with men, with women of other castes and classes. Since the Congress believed that placing them at the front of nationalist processions and picket lines would minimize police attacks, they often led these. When independence came, there was little objection to universal adult franchise; already, the politics of Gandhian nationalism had effectively enfranchised women. Nor did things stay entirely in place at home, despite Gandhi's perspective. When activist women returned home, they were transformed human beings, prepared to renegotiate domesticity on new terms.[62]

Some women, however, were outcasted from his politics. Gandhi was particularly harsh about unchaste women, demanding more moral purity from women as he believed that they were naturally superior to men: their lapses, therefore, were an offence against their nature. He reprimanded Congress workers at Barisal when they allowed local prostitutes to join their work.[63] His conviction led him to strange conclusions. During the communal holocaust at Noakhali in 1946, he pronounced that women could always save themselves from rape if they were truly virtuous. If somehow they failed to do so, they should commit suicide or kill their assailants. Modern women had become loose in their morals, he said, they behaved like 'Juliet' and solicited lovers. They had brought about their own downfall.[64] There was, thus, great violence in his approach towards 'blemished' women.

At the same time, he advised families of women abducted in the turmoil of partition to take them back, and asked volunteers to marry them and reintegrate them into society.[65] Perhaps he feared the social and moral anarchy that would prevail if large numbers of unanchored women were let loose on society: or, perhaps, he thought that if the families had failed to protect them, they should pay the price. The response was a strange amalgam of cruelty, compassion, and pragmatism.

Gandhi approved of certain changes in domesticity: female education, at least literacy, abolition of child marriage, and remarriage of child widows. Though these projects recall earlier liberal reform ventures, his reasons were different. Earlier reformers had thought that the changes would lead to female self-realization. For Gandhi, on the other hand, child marriage awakened premature sexual desires that became virulent later. Widowhood was a sacred vocation, providing the celibate widow with a moral surplus: it had to be willed and not imposed on children, too young to know its worth.[66] His notion of gender equality meant an undifferentiated regime of self-restraint. He was convinced that male lust was pervasive, aggressive, and overwhelming, thus reducing women to subjected, domesticated instruments for male self-gratification. He traced women's subordination to male desire. By abdicating mutual desire – at least, after the basic procreative tasks were fulfilled – married couples would experience mutual friendship, which was the basis of true gender equality.[67]

Scholars vary in their interpretation of Gandhi's stance on gender. Madhu Kishwar has claimed that Gandhi, as social reformer, was far ahead of the nineteenth-century liberals, as he brought many more openings to women. Sujata Patel, however, argues that nineteenth-century liberal gender reform amounted to dangerous transgressions of male privilege in their own times. In Gandhi's time, things had altered much already, and the changes that he wrought were no longer so radical. In some ways, he was actually regressive.[68]

The idea of satyagraha first came to him in South Africa after he had vowed to live a celibate conjugal life.[69] Thereafter, he equated political virtue with sexual abstinence, conjoining the political and the moral and insisting that his ashram inmates – the core satyagrahis – had to be as chaste as he was. He imposed a regime of severe continence: even married couples should renounce sexual relationships. Disciplining of sexual activity meant more than absolute prohibition. It required unceasing policing of desire by the ashram authorities, above all, by Gandhi himself. He insisted on a complete transparency in interactions between men and women. They must not write to each other nor meet in privacy and they must report to him about their state of mind. He intercepted letters, read them out to other inmates if he found them suspicious, demanded a total and fierce surveillance of relationships. Women with dubious pasts – like 'N', a woman of European origin, apparently with a 'lewd Bohemian' past – were especially kept away from others, and those who tried to form close friendships with her were publicly chastised. Even biological events were scrutinized. He was worried about 'N's' "decrease in the monthly flow". It indicated that she "was not yet free from the sex emotion, and unless you are entirely free from it in thought, word and deed, irregularity or scarcity in your monthly condition must be regarded as a sign of some internal derangement".[70] Missives to errant associates were publicized in the pages of his journals as a novel mode of public shaming.[71] Altogether, they should be empty selves, hollowed out of real substance, existing for collective moral action. 'N' was chastised when she worried about her dying son, her maternalism branded as self-centred: since the entire ashram was her family, why should the fate of the biological child matter especially, particularly as Gandhi himself had regarded the possible deaths of his wife and sons with equanimity.[72] He urged the ashramites not to pursue personal inclinations. Their education had to be basic, not geared to a satisfaction of curiosity, stimulation of questioning, imagination or intellectual urges, but to practical self-sufficiency, simple arithmetic and literacy and, above all, moral virtues.[73] Their sense of the self had to be pared down to evacuate all forms of interiority, even individuality.[74]

His own life was his basic text, a source of moral reflections and lessons for himself and others. His father was probably a man of carnal appetites, he thought, since he had had four wives. Nonetheless, Gandhi was devoted to him. His mother was remarkably committed to ritual fasts and mortifications, which he admired. He tried to appropriate her qualities. He loved to perform menial services for his father, as his mother would. He learnt to fast as often as she did. Later, he would be a mother to all his associates, nursing them in illness, preparing and prescribing their diet, tending to their daily welfare.[75] In his autobiography, he says how he much wanted to be needed by his parents. He does not say if he needed them. A school friend was his dark alter ego, introducing Gandhi to brothels, meat, drinks, and smoking. Gandhi overcame the temptations. Later, too, he visited brothels a few times but came out unscathed. He admired an English girl in London, but he kept his distance from her. Temptations were a perpetual necessity. They tested his integrity only triumphantly to affirm it.

His most troubled and absorbing relationship was with his wife. Kasturba was thirteen when they were married and so was he. At thirteen, Indian girls learnt to acquire a mature poise, while boys remained awkward, filled with troubling, unruly adolescent desires. Gandhi thus found himself at a disadvantage, the more so as the young wife was physically more courageous and also strong willed. Just as his attraction grew, so did his desire to strip her of independence, to tame her. He formed an obsessive jealousy about her movements; he wanted to extract total submission, to render her his chattel. Friendship and regard came later, only after physical passion had been renounced.[76]

> But these were lessons that came much later. When the relationship first commenced, he rejoiced in it: "And, oh, that first night!...no coaching is really necessary in such matters as instincts learned in past lives resurface to direct..."[77]

Three incidents awakened and finally confirmed his revulsion to sexual desire. When his father lay dying, he forced himself on his pregnant wife in the next room, failing to go to him in his last moments. Later, the child born of that sexual act died just a few days old. He laid the burden of the double deaths at the door of his intemperate lust. He never again felt comfortable about his sexuality. In South Africa, he once had to assist at his wife's childbirth, and the whole process drained him of the urge for procreation. During the Zulu War, when he served with the ambulance corps in South Africa, he found his love for his family a drag upon his more important commitments. He then decided to renounce desire altogether and eventually succeeded, after a few stumblings. We do not know how Kasturba felt about this, but she never tempted him. He did not ask for her consent before he took the final vow of celibacy in 1906.[78]

When he became celibate, a friendship and a comradeship grew between them. He compared his feelings for her with his love for the Hindu faith: both moved him more than other faiths and women, despite their many flaws.[79] It still was not an equal relationship. He praised her for her obedience. She was uneducated and no intellectual equal, he said, so obedience was natural and necessary.[80] He seldom explained his commands to her and was brutal when she disobeyed, even though he regretted his violent anger afterwards. He threatened to turn her out of his house when she refused to clean the chamber pot of an Untouchable. He was haunted ever after by his memories of her humiliation: "even today, I can recall the picture of her chiding me...pearl drops streaming down her cheeks".[81]

With his sons, his authority was uncomplicated and total. There are no descriptions of love or play with his children, nor of their infant ways. Instead, we read of a stern father, overriding his son's desire for a literary and English education, treating another with medicine of his own devising, which brought him close to death's door.[82]

If his surveillance of his own sexuality was relatively simplified with the injunction of total abstinence, disciplining of his body, especially through the control of food and healing techniques, was far more of an absorbing and enduring preoccupation. He advised others about diet and medicine at enormous length. Each time he refused medicine that included ingredients he felt were forbidden on religious grounds and faced death, it was a major triumph of will, an affirmation of his moral power, his claim to leadership. The regimes could never stabilize, requiring, instead, unending attention and vigilance, as he improvised fresh privations and new modes of diet and medicine. The innovations provided the core of his care of the self.[83] He tried hard to minimize his food consumption, aiming at an uncooked, unspiced, unsalted diet of fruit and nuts, trying to eliminate from food of all excess that makes it desirable. To his regret, failing health forced him to return to salt and to goats' milk eventually. He compensated by going on frequent fasts. Fasts were kept for a variety of purposes. He observed most of the holy fasts on the Vaishnava ritual calendar. He also undertook them as penance, for moral persuasion and for pressure on wrongdoers. The body, like the inner self, had to be pared down to the bones, brought, practically, to its vanishing point. His approach towards a body with needs was unforgiving.

The last two or three years of his life introduced new compulsions and purposes to his habitual fasts and sexual self-probing. He now undertook dangerous fasts unto death to reform an entire nation that had gone mad with communal frenzy. This time, however, fasts were mixed up with total despair and a profound sense of personal failure and guilt.[84] I have referred to his revision of many cardinal strategies, even values, in his last years. The revision was not so much a linear accumulation of insights and wisdom over the years as a violent breakdown of convictions and confidence under the catastrophic advent of Indian independence with partition. He suspected that his quest for the former had unleashed a process that made the latter possible. The trauma made him review his own understandings and prescriptions and, very possibly, he found them wanting. He abandoned hope in swaraj with *Ramarajya*, in the potential of trusteeship, in upper-caste penance. More strikingly, he began to rely on the resources of modernity that he had previously spurned: socialism, nonviolent class struggle, legal-constitutional prohibitions of Untouchability, abandonment of caste laws. He even accepted B. R. Ambedkar as Law Minister in the new government of independent India. They went against the grain of what he had so far stood for.

Since *Hind Swaraj* was written, he had regarded communalism as an Indian failing, not something imposed by British cunning. But independence came with a communal violence, never before seen in Indian history. The mutual slaughter anguished him more than the break-up of the country. He had no words left for his people on the eve of freedom: "I have run dry of messages".[85]

Calamities always made him doubt himself. Now, more than ever, he needed to probe his resolve and capacity for chastity. Moreover, his isolation was growing. The man who had swayed millions with his urgings to face danger and death, who had ruled over the Congress unilaterally, making and unmaking movements and strategies, found himself left behind as his disciples wrangled over the spoils of freedom. Even his closest disciples in the ashrams began to drift away. There were no resources left for the last struggle. He could only throw his frail, aged, failing body into the fray, even to the point of death. Its absolute purity, supremely tried and tested, was, therefore, essential. His body was now both a weapon and a possible trap. He had to rise above even the faintest suspicion of unchastity, to recover the strength of a true satyagrahi. The 'Mahatma's finest hour'[86] was, therefore, a bleak and dark one, marked by bizarre and cruel experiments: with his grand-niece, Manu Gandhi, with whom he slept naked at Sodepur, with his doctor, Sushila Naiyar, who had to bathe and massage his naked body, as he searched frantically for signs of weakness, as he implored his companions to look closely for them. He spoke of his moral impregnability, claiming that he was a mother to Manu. He also confessed his possible moral vulnerability when he looked for symptoms of weakness. Even his closest associates found these experiments disgusting. They said Manu was turning into a neurotic. Gujarati newspapers exchanged scurrilous gossip, and the ashram at Sodepur buzzed with horrified speculation.[87] Fasts and sexual tests became his last experiment with Truth. They made his body a site of self-inflicted ordeals, an instrument of torture that was turned against itself. Perhaps, as Ashis Nandy argues, in these last tragic days, he wanted its extinction as passionately as did his would-be assassin.

Gandhi's understanding of India's social problems and in turn his politics of the social, then, encompassed hugely diverse and seemingly disconnected fields that were, nonetheless, intricately interwoven. It was a politics that never fully stabilized nor became a seamless Truth, finally and fully grasped: each aspect dialectically carried seeds of self-transcendence and self-cancellation.

Notes

1 Akeel Bilgrami takes Sumit Sarkar to task for suggesting that Gandhi's nonviolence flowed from his conviction that all versions of Truth are provisional: given that, no one can use force to impose one's own version. S. Sarkar, *Modern India* (Delhi and London: MacMillan 1983). For Bilgrami, this may hold for Western philosophers like John Stuart Mill, whereas Gandhi's truth was absolute and certain. Bilgrami, 'Gandhi's Integrity: The Philosophy Behind the Politics', *Post Colonial Studies*, 5.1 (2002). He also suggests here that Gandhi's philosophy was always fully formed and entirely coherent and unchanging and constituted the core of his being.

2 "Far be it from me to claim any degree of perfection for these experiments... I am far from claiming any finality or infallibility for my conclusions". *An Autobiography or The Story of My Experiments with Truth* (Ahmedabad, India: Navjivan Trust, 1927), Introduction.

3 Gandhi's response to Tagore, *Young India*, 13 October 1921; Sabyasachi Bhattacharya (ed.), *The Mahatma and the Poet: Letters and Debates between Gandhi and Tagore, 1915–1941* (New Delhi, India: National Book Trust), p. 88.

4 Interview to Charles Petrasch, London, 29 October 1931. *CWMG*, vol. 48, pp. 241–2.

5 Speech at Morvi, 24 January 1928. *Ibid.*, vol. 35, pp. 489–91.

6 On Champaran and Kheda, see Jacques Pouchepadass, *Chapmaran and Gandhi: Planters, Peasants and Gandhian Politics* (Delhi, India: Oxford University Press, 2000); David Hardiman, *Peasant Nationalists of Gujarat: Kheda District, 1917–1934* (Delhi, India: Oxford University Press, 1981).

7 Interview to Charles Petrasch, London, 29 October 1931. *CWMG*, vol. 48, pp. 242–3.

8 Hiteshranjan Sanyal, *Swarajer Pathe* (Calcutta, India: Papyrus, 1976), p. 271.

9 Gandhi, *An Autobiography*, p. 388.

10 Nirmal Kumar Bose, *My Days with Gandhi* (New Delhi, India: Orient Longman, 1974 edition), pp. 23–4.

11 *Ibid.*

12 *Harijan*, 1 June 1947. *CWMG*, vol. 97, pp. 273–4.

13 Jan Breman, *The Making and Unmaking of an Industrial Working Class: Sliding Down the Labour Hierarchy in Ahmedabad, India* (Delhi, India: Oxford University Press, 2004), chapter 2.

14 Sarkar, *Modern India*, chapter 6.

15 *Hind Swaraj* in Anthony Parel (ed.), *Gandhi: Hind Swaraj and Other Writings* (Cambridge, England: Cambridge University Press, 1997; reprint New Delhi, India: Foundation Books, 1997), p. 101.

16 *Ibid.*, p. 104.
17 *Ibid.*, pp. 30–3.
18 R. Guha, 'Mahatma Gandhi and the Environmental Movement', in Ramashray Roy (ed.), *Gandhi and the Present Global Crisis* (Shimla, India: Institute of Advances Studies, 1996), pp. 113–39.
19 *Hind Swaraj*, 1909; included in Parel (ed.), *Gandhi: Hind Swaraj and Other Writings*, p. 45.
20 Tanika Sarkar, 'Tribals in Colonial Bengal: Jitu Santal's Rebellion in Malda', in *Rebels, Wives, Saints: Designing Selves and Nations in Colonial Times* (Delhi, India: Permanent Black, 2009).
21 David Arnold, 'Rebellious Hillmen: The Gudem Rampa Risings 1839–1924', in R. Guha (ed.), *Subaltern Studies* (Delhi, India: Oxford University Press, 1982), vol. 1.
22 Gandhi, *An Autobiography*, p. 3.
23 *Ibid.*, p. 255.
24 *Ibid.*, p. 156.
25 *Ibid.*, p. 193.
26 *Young India*, 19 January 1921; cited in V. Geetha (ed.), *Soul Force: Gandhi's Writings on Peace* (Chennai, India: Tara Publishing, 2004), pp. 253–4.
27 *Young India*, 7 February 1927.
28 Gandhi, *An Autobiography*, pp. 206, 357.
29 *Ibid.*, p. 361.
30 *Ibid.*, p. 365.
31 D. Hardiman, *Gandhi in His Time and Ours* (Delhi, India: Permanent Black, 2003), p. 101.
32 Nicholas Dirks, *Castes of Mind: Colonialism and the Making of Modern India* (Delhi, India: Permanent Black, 2001), p. 258.
33 'A Caste and Communal Question', *Young India*, 4 June 1931.
34 *Harijan*, 25 March 1933.
35 *Harijansevak*, 12 May 1933.
36 *Harijanbandhu*, 19 March 1933.
37 *Young India*, 7 February 1927.
38 *Harijanbandhu*, 19 April 1933.
39 *Ibid.*, 19 March 1933.
40 *Harijan*, 11 March 1933.
41 *Ibid.*, 11 March 1933.
42 Material from March–April 1933. *CWMG*, vols. 54 and 55.
43 Letter to Altekar, 9 December 1932. *Ibid.*, vol. 52, p. 157.
44 On this, see Gail Omvedt, *Dalits and The Democratic Revolution: Dr. Ambedkar and the Dalit Movement in Colonial India* (Delhi, India: Sage, 1994); Christophe Jaffrelot, *Dr. Ambedkar and Untouchability* (Delhi, India: Permanent Black, 2004); M. S. S. Pandian, *Brahman and Non Brahman: Genealogies of the Tamil Political Dissent* (Delhi, India: Permanent Black, 2007).
45 *Harijan*, 11 March 1933.
46 Hardiman, *Gandhi in His Time and* Ours, p. 131.
47 *Ibid.*, p. 131.

48 Letter to Nehru, 2 May 1933. *CWMG*, vol. 55, p. 96.
49 *Harijanbandhu*, 23 April 1933.
50 *Harijanbandhu*, 19 March 1933.
51 *Harijan*, 11 March 1933.
52 D. R. Nagaraj, *The Flaming Feet: A Study of the Dalit Movement* (Bangalore, India: South Forum Press, 1993), pp. 1–30.
53 Hardiman, *Gandhi in His Time and Ours*, p. 134.
54 Ashis Nandy, 'The Final Encounter: The Politics of the Assassination of Gandhi', in *At the Edge of Psychology: Essays in Politics and Culture* (Delhi, India: Oxford University Press, 1980).
55 *Harijan*, 12 October 1934.
56 *Young India*, 17 October 1929.
57 On this, see Geraldine Forbes, *Women in Modern India, The New Cambridge History of India*, 1V.2 (Cambridge, England: Cambridge University Press, 1996), chapter 5; Radha Kumar, *The History of Doing: An Illustrated Account of Movements for Women's Rights and Feminism in India, 1800–1990* (Delhi, India: Kali for Women, 1993), chapters 3 and 4.
58 See my 'Politics and Women in Bengal: The Condition and Meaning of Participation', in J. Krishnamurty (ed.), *Women in Colonial India: Essays on Survival, Work and the State* (Delhi, India: Oxford University Press, 1989).
59 M. K. Gandhi, *Hindu Dharma* (Ahmedabad, India: Navajivan, 1950), p. 382.
60 Pyarelal, *Mahatma Gandhi: The Last Phase* (Ahmedabad, India: Navjivan, 1956), p. 306.
61 Ashoka Gupta, *Noakhalir Durjoger Dine* (Calcutta, India: Dey's, 1999).
62 My interview with Sudha Mukhopadhya, a widow, who recalled her "intervention in history" in the Quit India movement with pride and said, "Maybe, the women returned to the same homes. But they were not the same women who had left home to join politics". Calcutta, 30 May 1988.
63 Madhu Kishwar, 'Gandhi on Women', *Economic and Political Weekly*, XX.40, 5 October and 12 October 1985.
64 Pyarelal, *Mahatma Gandhi: The Last Phase*, pp. 305–11.
65 *Ibid.*, p. 311.
66 M. K. Gandhi, *Women and Social Justice* (Ahmedabad, India: Navjivan, 1954).
67 Gandhi, *An Autobiography*, p. 256.
68 Kishwar, 'Gandhi on Women', 1985; Sujata Patel, 'Construction and Reconstruction of Women in Gandhi', *Economic and Political Weekly*, 20 February 1988.
69 Gandhi, *An Autobiography*, pp. 191–2.
70 Letter to N, *Harijansevak*, 19 May 1933. *CWMG*, vol. 55, pp. 209–10.
71 See *Harijanbandhu* and *Harijan*, April, May, 1933.
72 *CWMG*, vol. 55, p. 246.
73 Gandhi, *An Autobiography*, pp. 184–5, 307.

74 Ajay Skaria evades these aspects of ashram life, which he describes as a site of "neighbourliness". 'Gandhi's Politics: Liberation and the Question of the Ashram' in Saurabh Dube (ed.), *Enchantments of Modernity: Empire, Nation, Globalisation*, Critical Asian Studies Series (London: Routledge, 2009).

75 E. H. Erikson has noted his wish to be more motherly and womanly than women themselves could be. *Gandhi's Truth: On the Origins of Militant Nonviolence* (New York: Norton, 1969), p. 111.

76 Gandhi, *An Autobiography*, p. 190.

77 *Ibid.*, p. 10.

78 For Gandhi's concerns with his sexuality, see his account of his early life in his autobiography.

79 *Young India*, 6 October 1921.

80 Gandhi, *An Autobiography*, p. 256.

81 *Ibid.*, p. 255.

82 *Ibid.*, pp. 83–4, 184.

83 Foucault's ideas about the care of the self, which requires constancy of attention rather than a resolution of problems, are highly instructive for understanding Gandhi. 'The Ethics of the Concern for Self as a Practice of Freedom' in Paul Rabinow (ed.), *Michel Foucault: Ethics: Essential Works of Foucault, 1954–1984* (London: Penguin, 1994).

84 For a somewhat different view of his last years, see Judith M. Brown, *Gandhi. Prisoner of Hope* (Delhi, India: Oxford University Press, 1990).

85 Bose, *My Days with Gandhi*, p. 177.

86 Sarkar, *Modern India*, p. 147.

87 Bose, *My Days with Gandhi*, pp. 3–176.

Part III

The contemporary Gandhi

10 Literary and visual portrayals of Gandhi

HARISH TRIVEDI

Since shortly after he entered Indian public life on return from South Africa in 1915, Gandhi has permeated Indian literature and the arts; he is to be found everywhere, from office walls to public spaces to collective memory either personal or transmitted. He has been represented to enduring effect by a variety of foreign writers and artists as well, from points of view that serve to illuminate him differently and often with a striking supplementarity.[1] Several surveys in print and now increasingly on variously websites indicate the sheer richness of materials of which the account that follows is a necessarily small and partial selection.[2]

POETRY

The regard in which Gandhi was held not only by the common man in India but also by many of its eminent literary figures found spontaneous expression as the news spread that he had been assassinated on 30 January 1948. Over the next 108 days (a number sacred in Hindu belief), Harivansh Rai Bachchan (1907–2003), probably the most popular Hindi poet of the twentieth century, wrote 204 poems paying tribute to Gandhi, the first one of which began "Today our Bapu has passed on/Today our flag is lowered in shame" and concluded "Today he has died and become immutable/Today he has died and become immortal".[3] These poems were collected the same year in two volumes under the emblematically Gandhian titles, *Khadi ke Phool* (Khadi Flowers) and *Soot ki Mala* (A Garland of Homespun Thread). Bachchan, then a lecturer in English at the University of Allahabad, was no Gandhian; his early poetic inspiration was Omar Khayyam and he proceeded in the 1950s to write a doctoral thesis at Cambridge on W. B. Yeats. Writing poetry, he said in the preface to one of these Gandhi volumes, had been a compulsion in his life, and he had "probably never felt this compulsion more acutely than at the time of Bapuji's sacrifice".[4]

Another major Hindi poet, Bhavaniprasad Mishra (1913–85), wrote thirteen poems in thirteen days (the period of the ritual Hindu mourning) following Gandhi's assassination while observing a fast for the entire duration. As this austere act may indicate, he had been a confirmed Gandhian ever since he had a glimpse of Gandhi at a railway station in 1930, and he went to jail for three years for answering Gandhi's call to participate in the Quit India movement of 1942. Later, he worked on editing Gandhi's collected works in Hindi, edited the journal *Gandhi Marg* (The Gandhian Way), and on Gandhi's birth centenary in 1969 published *Gandhi Panchashati* (Five Hundred Poems on Gandhi), all his own, dating from 1930. Of these, the first three hundred poems are directly about Gandhi, while the remaining two hundred are relevant reflections of a poet who led a Gandhian life and was steeped in a Gandhian sensibility; Mishra has indeed been described as "the Gandhi of poetry".[5]

Mishra was only one of the innumerable Indian writers of at least three generations who not only wrote about Gandhi but whose lives were personally impacted and influenced by Gandhi in all kinds of transformative ways. In 1969, to mark Gandhi's birth centenary, Mishra co-edited *Mrityunjayi* (The Immortal), an anthology comprising one poem each on Gandhi by eighty-six Indian poets from sixteen languages including Sanskrit and English, each transcribed in Devanagari and translated into Hindi.[6] Another such birth-centenary anthology, *Gandhi-Shatadal* (1969; A Hundred Poems on Gandhi), of one poem each by 101 poets from fourteen Indian languages, was edited by Sohanlal Dwivedi, whose own poem in the volume is one of the best known of all. Titled 'Yugavatar' (An Epoch Incarnated), it begins: (Wherever his two feet walked, there walked a million others/ Whatever he looked upon, a million eyes gazed on".[7] Several other poems in this anthology, too, describe Gandhi as an epoch-making man, as in the title 'Yugadevata' (God of the Epoch), many address him simply as 'Mahatma' (great soul) or 'Bapu' (father), and one is titled 'The Naked Fakir', in an ironic reference to Churchill's description of Gandhi in 1930 (see note forty-two).[8]

The aesthetic effect of these poems, most of which have already been translated once into Hindi, is difficult to convey in English, especially of a sonorous and highly allusive line such as *Tum sanmay chinmay tanmay tum, mrinmay tum kab thay O Akaam?*,[9] which acclaims Gandhi's transcendent spirituality through a culturally embedded and allusively resonant upanishadic vocabulary, to say nothing of the cadence and the alliteration. It is easier to abstract from them the many mythical and historical comparisons and the poets' sense of Gandhi's enduring significance. Meghram Pathak calls Gandhi a Yudhishthir (the moral hero of the *Mahabharata*) in his sense of justice and a Buddha in compassion. Mallagi Jayatirtha says his heart was as holy as the river Ganga and his deeds as firm as the Himalaya. For Umashankar Joshi, the three bullets that took his life were indeed the three flaming fingers of the god of sacred and sacrificial fire. For Bharatidasan, Gandhi's teachings were the 'sweet essence of the Vedas'. Subramania Bharati compares him to the Hanuman who in the *Ramayana* found and brought a reviving medicine and to the Krishna who lifted a mountain on his little finger to shield a whole village from cataclysmic rain and thunder. C. Narayana Reddy acclaims Gandhi's birthday as the birthday of Rama and of Rahim (Allah the compassionate). G. Sankara Kurup compares him and his philosophy of nonviolence in an elaborate simile with the moon and its soft and soothing radiance. Vallathol Narayana Menon finds in Gandhi the great sacrifice of Christ, the preservation of dharma by Krishna, the equanimity of the Buddha, the genius of the philosopher Sankaracharya, and the resolve of the Prophet Mohammad. And Shivamangal Singh 'Suman' says that to see Gandhi in flesh and blood as an ordinary mortal was proof enough for believing that Rama and Krishna, too, had similarly walked on this earth, and to hear Gandhi speak was to renew one's faith in the teachings of the Buddha and Christ.[10]

It may be doubted whether any historical and fully documented human being of our age or any other was ever acclaimed in such superhuman and indeed divine terms, especially in his own lifetime, and indeed from a relatively early stage of his life. Makhanlal Chaturvedi (1888–1967), a committed Gandhian, published in 1917 a poem entitled 'Satyagrahi', asserting the supremacy of Gandhi's chosen method of resolutely nonviolent and peaceful political action over all the 'brute force' of the world and over even 'Jagadishwar' (Lords of the Universe). Among his numerous other Gandhian poems are 'Jallianwala ki Vedi' (1920; The Altar of Jallianwala), 'Adalat men Satyagrahi Qaidi ke nate Bayan' (A Statement in a Court of Law by a Satyagrahi Prisoner), which he in fact delivered in a court on 5 July 1921, and 'Qaidi aur Kokila' (The Prisoner and the Singing-Bird), which is possibly among the finest prison poems ever written.[11]

Besides such lifelong Gandhians (and Chaturvedi died, as he had said he wanted to, on the same date that Gandhi had, 30 January), there were numerous other writers who came under the spell of Gandhi but then, as time passed, moved on to respond to other modes of thought and action as well. Sumitranandan Pant (1900–77) had, at Gandhi's call during his non-cooperation movement in 1921, quit the University of Allahabad where he was a student, published *Gramya* (1940; Village

Poems) inspired by Gandhi's statement that India resided in its villages, and written several poems on Gandhi including his own series of tributes at Gandhi's assassination,[12] while he was also discovering successively other sources of influence as varied as Rabindranath Tagore, Marxism, and the revolutionary-mystical patriot Sri Aurobindo.

More remarkable is the case of Akbar Ilahabadi (1846–1921), a humorous poet in Urdu who was a whole generation older than Gandhi, served the British Raj loyally as a judge and was rewarded with the title Khan Bahadur, but remained a trenchant satirist of what has come to be called colonial modernity. His poems on Gandhi, posthumously collected under the title *Gandhinama* (1948), testify to Gandhi's wide and almost irresistible appeal.

> If Akbar weren't already an odalisque of the Government
> You'd have found him too among the *gopis* of Gandhi,

he wrote, his transgressive and even seditious sentiment wittily underlined by his use of the Hindu image of the *gopis*, that is, female companions of the god Krishna whose attachment to him has become a byword for Bhakti or loving devotion. Akbar also offers perhaps the pithiest account of Gandhi's ability to mobilize the simple common man:

> *Buddhu Mian bhi aajkal Gandhi ke saath hain.*
> *Ik mushte-khaq hain magar andhi ke sath hain.*

> Mr Simpleton too is now with Gandhi.
> A mere handful of dust, he rides a storm.

Akbar here used the obvious Hindi/Urdu rhyme of Gandhi/*andhi* (storm, whirlwind) to better effect than other poets, and through his use of the Muslim honorific 'Mian', he implied that Gandhi had supporters among the Muslims equally.[13]

FICTION

It is in the genre of the novel that, in a well-known postcolonial formulation, the nation is narrated. Gandhi is depicted as a 'real-life' character in several Indian novels, but these are exceeded in number and often quality, too, by novels that have not Gandhi himself as the hero but instead some local Gandhian figure who acts according to Gandhi's principles and ideals. Among the earliest such narratives is *Premashram* (1921; The Abode of Love) by Premchand (1880–1936), generally acclaimed as the greatest novelist in both Urdu and Hindi. It depicts a peasant movement in the Hindi-speaking heartland of India in which both the violent and the nonviolent modes of resistance are put forward, with no happy resolution, as the movement ends in a pious compromise as reflected in the title. "While the pull of one [violence] draws him [Premchand] to the Russian revolution, the other [nonviolence] attracts him to Gandhi".[14] Another greater novel by Premchand, *Rangabhumi* (1925; The Stage/Playground), which remained his own favourite, shows no such ambivalence. The hero here is a blind and devout beggar who takes on the might of the British Raj and is at the end of this epic narrative shot to death by the British district officer. A statue of him erected by his supporters shows him in a Gandhi-like posture holding a long walking stick in one hand with the other hand extended forward, "as if some divine supplicant were asking the gods to grant the boon of the welfare of the world".[15]

Another major Hindi novelist, Phanishwarnath Renu (1921–77), caught in his *Maila Anchal* (1954; A Backward District) the postcolonial phase of expedient political reversal in which the landed aristocracy, who had always collaborated with the British, promptly metamorphose themselves into the new leaders of the Congress Party, while a dedicated old Gandhian who has participated in several nationalist movements, spent time in jail, has met Gandhi, and treasures the letters he has received from him, decides, on the first anniversary of Gandhi's death to lay down his own life in a vain attempt to stop corruption rather than live on and face further disillusionment in independent India.[16] In some other novels, Gandhi and his message are counterpointed with other contestatory political ideologies in the kind of dialogic manner that has been identified as a generic characteristic of the novel. Bhagwati Charan Varma (1903–80) in his *Terhe Merhe Raste* (1946; Zig-Zag Ways) depicts a father who is a big landlord and whose survival thus depends on keeping on the right side of the British, with three sons of whom the eldest is a prominent Congress leader and goes to jail in the Salt Movement of 1930–1, the middle one returns from Germany as a convert to Communism, while the youngest gets caught up in the activities of a so-called terrorist group working towards an armed revolution against the British. The author stages a vigorous engagement in which all the ideologues seem to be fairly and even-handedly treated, but that did not stop a committed Communist novelist, Rangeya Raghav (1923–62) from writing a novel in rejoinder, *Seedha Sada Rasta* (1951; The Straight and Simple Path), in which the followers of Gandhi are given summary treatment.[17]

Pervasive traces of Gandhi's personal and political impact are also found in two epic novels by Yashpal (1903–76), who had started out as a follower of Gandhi but then became an active leader of the bomb-throwing Hindustan Republican Socialist Party, was ambushed by the police and jailed, and on release became a staunch Communist. His *Jhootha Sach* (1960; The False Truth) is simply the greatest novel yet written about partition and its aftermath, and *Teri Meri Uski Baat* (1973; Yours, Mine and His Story) is an epic of the evolving political scenario in India in the 1930s leading up to the Quit India movement of 1942, during which the heroine eventually embraces Communism while the hero remains a Congress-Socialist. Yashpal had already published in 1942 a tract titled *Gandhivad ki Shav-Pariksha* (Gandhism: A Post-mortem) but in his later novels, his artistic instincts do seem to keep his ideological predilections on a loose leash.[18] A recent Hindi novel offers over its one thousand pages an elaborate and meticulously researched construction of Gandhi's early political life in South Africa working among and for the *girmitiyas*, that is, the Indian population there, many of whom descended from indentured labourers.[19] (This formative phase of his career, not widely known in India, is also the theme of an unrelated film, *The Making of the Mahatma*, directed by Shyam Benegal.)

As far as Indian fiction in English is concerned, a Gandhi novel was written by each one of its three founding fathers. In the climactic scene of Mulk Raj Anand's *Untouchable* (1935), a young scavenger named Bakha goes to hear Gandhi address a public meeting. What Gandhi says, to the effect that the problem of Untouchability should be resolved thorough 'love' and 'peaceful persuasion',[20] is represented in direct speech over five pages, and it leaves Bakha deeply moved, but then, on his way home, he happens to overhear a young and radical poet offer a more modern solution to the problem, 'the flush system', which Bakha prefers.[21] *Waiting for the Mahatma* (1955) by R. K. Narayan (1906–2001) portrays Gandhi as staying for several days in the small town of Malgudi without any lasting impact,[22] but then the novel veers away to narrate a fitful love story involving its feckless hero and devotedly Gandhian heroine. The surprise here is not that the novel is an artistic failure but that the resolutely apolitical Narayan, going clearly against his grain, should have felt obliged to write a Gandhi novel at all.

In contrast, *Kanthapura* (1938), the first novel by Raja Rao (1908–2006), towers above all other Gandhi novels in English and perhaps in any language. It describes with fine inwardness the initially resistant but then euphorically transformative process through which Gandhi's message reaches the simple tradition-bound inhabitants of a small and remote village through a surrogate figure, the young Moorthy who is called 'our Gandhi'. The villagers are all swept off their feet and inspired to break down caste divisions, to picket toddy shops, and to oppose the exploitation at Mr Skeffington's coffee estate. The women play a larger and more dynamic role than the men, and they all act with resolute nonviolence, of course. But when they are brutally beaten back and even obliged to flee their village, Moorthy, too, begins to speak of following Nehru instead who is an 'equal-distributionist'.[23] Gandhi is acclaimed as an incarnation of God who has descended, like Krishna before, to protect and restore the true dharma, but then, a city loyalist says that Queen Victoria, too, after the Mutiny, had proved to be 'a saviour' of Hinduism![24] The portrayal of Gandhi here is one of the most celebratory in all fiction – the novel reverberates with *Mahatma Gandhi ki Jai!* (Victory to Mahtama Gandhi) – but it is not one-sided and therefore the more credible.

Of the novels about India written by Westerners, *A Passage to India* (1924) by E. M. Forster is entirely and conspicuously silent on Gandhi. His more prolific and politically engaged contemporary Edward Thompson (1886–1946) in his play *Atonement* (1924) presented Gandhi under thin disguise as 'Mahatma Ranade', listing him in the 'Dramatis Personae' as 'Leader of the Non-co-operation Party in India',[25] and in his novels *An Indian Day* (1927) and *A Farewell to India* (1931) had his British protagonists repeatedly debate Gandhi and his impact on contemporary India and the health of the Raj. As Thompson reported, Gandhi himself chided him for giving his last-named novel that terminal title, remarking humorously: "How do you think that you are ever going to say farewell to India? You are India's prisoner".[26] Though *The Raj Quartet* by Paul Scott (1920–78) features a Muslim as its most prominent Indian leader, it begins with the long-serving missionary Edwina Crane feeling so shocked by Gandhi's 'seditious' call to the British to 'Quit India' that in protest, she takes down a portrait of Gandhi from a wall in her house, which leaves another painting, entitled 'The Jewel in the Crown' and depicting Queen Victoria in her glory as the Empress of India, hanging there all by itself.[27]

A once-controversial but now largely forgotten Western novel on Gandhi is *Nine Hours to Rama* (1962; film 1963) by Stanley Wolpert, an American historian. It depicts the nine hours spent by Gandhi's assassin Nathuram Godse immediately prior to his shooting Gandhi dead at 5.17 PM on 30 January 1948, with the focus mainly on Godse and, in extensive flashbacks, on his mentors and associates in the conspiracy. 'Natu' (so referred to throughout the novel in an inexplicable misspelling) is shown dodging the police in Delhi and visiting first a prostitute and then Rani, his love interest, with whom he goes to bed immediately before he proceeds to shoot Gandhi. Gandhi himself is shown as disenchanted with the developments in the country after independence and partition and, with his creed of nonviolence, shrugging off the security arrangements for him that the police wish to enforce.[28] This largely inconsequential, superficial, and somewhat sleazy novel was banned by the Government of India, as was the Marathi play *Mee Nathuram Godse Boltoye* (1998; I am Nathuram Godse Speaking) by Pradeep Dalvi by the government of Maharashtra, the state that Godse came from, while it continued to be performed in other parts of India in Gujarati and Hindi. (All this while, two books by Godse himself about his action and beliefs were available in print.)

FILMS

A film about the assassination of Gandhi, *Hey Ram* (2000), written and directed by Kamal Hassan with himself in the lead and with a multi-star cast from both commercial and art cinema, depicts a fictional character who also wants to assassinate Gandhi but is pre-empted by Godse and then has a change of heart and becomes a Gandhian. It won several national awards and was the official Indian entry for the best foreign language film category of the Oscar awards. As reflected in this film, the historical fact of the assassination of Gandhi when represented in art has often taken on a symbolic dimension, which relates to the legacy of Gandhi and the erosion or continuance of Gandhian values and ideals in Indian public life; it is in this larger sense that Gandhi is said either to have died or he lives on. Another powerful Hindi film on Gandhi that exploits this symbolic aspect is *Maine Gandhi ko Nahin Mara* (2005; I Did Not Kill Gandhi, directed by Jahnu Barua), which is about a retired professor of Hindi who, fifty years after Gandhi's assassination, becomes so obsessed by a sense of guilt at the devaluation of Gandhi in the public sphere that he begins to hallucinate that he himself stands accused of having killed Gandhi. To cure his mental condition as diagnosed by a medical expert, a mock trial is staged where he can plead his innocence, affirming, "I am a devotee of Gandhi. I never tell a lie", and is honourably acquitted.

Another film that initially adopts a view apparently hostile to Gandhi is *Gandhi My Father* (2007, directed by Feroze Abbas Khan, with Gandhi played by Darshan Jariwala); it focuses on his 'rogue', rebellious, and recalcitrant eldest son Harilal and Gandhi's bittersweet relationship with him. At the end of the film, Gandhi says with a rueful smile that "the greatest defeat of his life" was his failure to communicate with two persons: "the first, my friend from Kathiawar [the region in Gujarat he himself came from], Mohammad Ali Jinnah, and the second, my own son, Harilal".

But the two films on Gandhi that have had the biggest popular impact and won many honours must be Richard Attenborough's *Gandhi* (1982) in English (released in India also in a dubbed Hindi version), and a Hindi film *Lage Raho Munnabhai* (2006). *Gandhi* won eight Academy awards, while *Lage Raho Munnabhai* won four National film awards in India. What is more, unlike any of the other films we have mentioned, both these films were great box-office hits as well, *Gandhi* internationally though not really in India, and *Lage Raho Munnabhai*, of course, only in India though it did good business, as all successful Hindi films now do, among the worldwide Indian diaspora.

The two films could not be more different from each other, separated as they are by a quarter of a century in time and also by the fact that Hollywood and Bollywood stand poles apart in their respective aesthetics. At nearly double the length of an average Hollywood movie, *Gandhi* makes the space to depict most of the major events of its protagonist's political life in what is still a fast-moving and tightly edited narrative. It begins with the climactic and emotive moment of Gandhi's assassination and funeral, and then goes back, not to his childhood or (what might have been more difficult to resist for a British director) his student years in London, but to South Africa in 1893 and to the catalytic moment when he is thrown out of a train at Pietermaritzburg on racist grounds. After Gandhi comes back to India in 1915, the two scenes in his early career that are done with a distinct overtone of what may be called brute realism are the merciless beating up by the police of wave after wave of unflinching nonviolent Gandhian satyagrahis at Dharsana, and the notorious massacre ordered by General Dyer at the Jallianwala Bagh, an episode that is placed right in the middle of the film. They set the tone and define the issues: as shown in this film, it is a battle between might and right and between physically stronger brute violence and morally superior nonviolence.

It is a part of the film's aesthetic design that Gandhi himself is absent from both these scenes. It is not only his physical presence but also his moral and spiritual influence that pervade the film. Some commentators have seen the film as being distinctly reverent, and it is true that, unlike, for example, the play and the films that have Godse or Harilal in focus, it does not interrogate Gandhi, though it does show him as not always successful in what he seeks to do. Nor does it seek to explore his psychology as, reportedly, an earlier screenplay written in 1973 by Robert

Bolt entitled 'Gandhiji' had sought to do, which was sent to the director Joseph Losey; apparently, an even earlier 'treatment' of the subject by Emeric Pressburger was considered around the year 1960 by David Lean, who had Alec Guinness in mind for the lead role.[29] Attenborough himself had been interested in making a film on Gandhi since about the same time and had already met Prime Minister Nehru and Indira Gandhi in this connection in 1963, when Nehru had said to him: "Whatever you do, do not deify him – that is what we have done in India – and he was too great a man to be deified".[30]

Attenborough does not deify Gandhi, but Gandhi does emerge from his film as a very great man. This is testified by the responses it evoked, especially from some quarters where Gandhi's historical greatness and achievement are not likely to meet with ready approbation. A leader in *The Sunday Telegraph* (London) roundly rebuked Attenborough for "turning the film into a piece of straight political propaganda for India, at the expense of his own country's imperial past which is grossly traduced",[31] and the Government of Pakistan came forward to encourage and fund a similar film on Mohammad Ali Jinnah, who too was felt to have been traduced by Attenborough. This film, *Jinnah* (1998), 'developed' and produced by an eminent Pakistani scholar of Islam, Akbar Ahmed, and directed by Jamal Dehalvi, achieved nothing like the international success of *Gandhi* and became controversial in Pakistan, too, for casting Christopher Lee, who had earlier played Dracula, as Jinnah.[32] But perhaps the sharpest critical voice against the film was raised by Salman Rushdie, who described it as "inadequate as biography, appalling as history, and often laughably crude as a film".[33] As it happened, Rushdie had the same year defended *Midnight's Children* against a plethora of errors and distortions, including his hero Saleem getting wrong the 'date' of Gandhi's assassination (as well as the year, it may be added, by a wide margin)[34] by arguing that his 'novel' had been read in the wrong way, as "the history ... which it was never meant to be" – an artistic privilege he had not thought of granting Attenborough when he called his film "appalling as history", and so forth.

In contrast, the Gandhi depicted in the Hindi blockbuster *Lage Raho Munnabhai* (i.e. 'Carry On, Munnabhai', as the film was a sort of sequel to an earlier film, *Munnabhai M.B.B.S.*) could hardly be debated to be historically accurate or not, if only because what we are shown is Gandhi's spirit or apparition that is visible only to the hero. In this comic romance, which pays little heed to realism of representation, the hero is a shady semi-literate rogue and unscrupulous knife-carrying wheeler-dealer, and the heroine a radio phone-in anchor whom he falls in love with just by listening to her. To get near her, he decides to participate in a quiz she is hosting on Gandhi on his birthday, 2 October, and as he does not know the first thing about Gandhi (having seen him only on banknotes and imagining that if he won us freedom he must have been in the army), he kidnaps and then impersonates a professor of history to be able to win the quiz. Later, to keep up his credibility with the heroine, he actually visits the 'Mahatma Gandhi Granthalaya' (the Mahatma Gandhi Library) to bone up on Gandhi, and after he has spent three sleepless nights in the quest, Gandhi himself appears to him. "Hey, the guy's stepped out of the books!"

Gandhi now teaches him to apologize to those to whom he has caused offence, to treat even his rivals with respect and love, and to resolve conflicts by practising satyagraha – some of which Munnabhai to some extent attempts to practise. His half-hearted efforts to give up his old ways and to reform along Gandhian lines are treated in the film in terms of broad comedy and even farce, but they are yet meant to redound to the credit of the kind of basically incorrigible but good-hearted character that Munnabhai is. A characteristic example of this is his coining of the term *Gandhigiri* – as the counterpart of *dadagiri*, which is a pejorative term that means 'bullying, loutish behaviour'.[35] Here, the positive word 'dada', meaning 'elder brother', is turned into something negative by the suffix 'giri', which means any low-class professional and profitable practice, to signify altogether something like 'Big-Brotherism' or indeed gangsterism. The offending part of the word is thus not *dada* but *giri*, and adding it to Gandhi's name would similarly imply practising Gandhian principles not because they are noble principles but rather in a calculating and professional manner so as to derive advantage or benefit from them. The film does at one point attempt to highlight this semantic crux when, during the radio programme, Munnabhai says, with his usual street-idiom swagger, ... *apun Gandhigiri men number one hai* (I am number one in *gandhigiri*), and the heroine tries to redeem the situation by saying: *You mean, aap Gandhivadi ho, right?* (You mean to say you are a follower of Gandhism, don't you?).

Such elaborate exposition of the term *Gandhigiri* may seem uncalled for except that the film succeeded in making it a buzzword even among people who had never seen the film, so that it looks likely to take its place as a usurper alongside 'Gandhian' and 'Gandhism' (or, in Hindi and many other Indian languages, *Gandhivad* and *Gandhivadi*). This seems to have been made possible in part because many persons even among the Hindi speakers in India (a large proportion of whom are still illiterate) are perhaps not quite able to distinguish sufficiently between these two terms, indicating respectively good and proper Gandhism and a roguishly appropriated and even somewhat perverted Gandhism. Though *Gandhigiri* in the latter sense is unreservedly valorized in the film, it must strike traditional Gandhians as a travesty of Gandhian values, as well as of proper usage in Hindi, a language Gandhi had begun projecting as the national language of India as early as 1918.

It may be relevant to note one more aspect of representations of Gandhi on film. Given the innumerable photographs, sound recordings, and even the extensive documentary film footage that we have available of Gandhi, especially from the 1930s onwards, it should have been a great challenge for any actor, however gifted, to impersonate Gandhi convincingly in a film. Nevertheless, a fair number of them seem to have done just that. Ben Kingsley won the Oscar for the best actor in Attenborough's film and is probably the wide world's idea of just what Gandhi looked, walked, and talked like, except that for Indian viewers (despite his hybrid Anglo-Indian origins and his start in life with the name Krishna Bhanji), he never in the film could sit convincingly on the floor with his legs folded together to one side like Gandhi (or indeed Nehru or Patel) and could not walk or smile like Gandhi either. What is more remarkable, two fairly unheard of Indian actors, Darshan Zariwala and Dilip Prabhavalkar, also won awards in India for their enactment of the Gandhi persona in the films *Gandhi My Father* and *Lage Raho Munnabhai* respectively, in their supporting roles. Does this signify that almost any actor (and Kingsley, too, was unheard of before *Gandhi*) can come along and persuasively enact Gandhi or, alternatively, that one does not really have to look like Gandhi or walk or talk like Gandhi but rather only to sound like Gandhi to carry conviction – that in Gandhi's case, it is the message and the substance that count and not appearance and mannerisms?

PHOTOGRAPHS AND THE LOINCLOTH

To turn from films to photographs is to turn from the dynamic, indeed kine(ma)tic, to the still and static. And yet, it is also to turn from the imaginative and fictional to the real and historical. Gandhi was, according to the post-colonial critic and historian Robert Young, one of the most photographed men of the twentieth century, except that, given the ideological bias against Gandhi in post-colonial discourse generally,[36] this is meant as anything but a compliment.

Gandhi's physical image in the tens of thousands of photographs of him that were taken not only evolves necessarily from childhood to youth to old age but it is along the way radically transformed. He moves on from wearing a Parsi cap and a long jacket in his first couple of photos from 1876 and 1883 to wearing Western clothes as a student in London and then as an attorney in South Africa. On 18 December 1913, he decides to begin wearing an 'indentured labourer's dress',[37] that is, a white kurta and a dhoti wrapped in the South Indian way, and this is the dress in which he is photographed on return to India in 1915. After launching, in August 1921, a campaign for the boycott and burning of foreign cloth, Gandhi begins, on 21 September, to dress like one of the poor masses of India, with the torso bare and a dhoti going down not to the ankles (as it normally does) but only to the knees, and often he wears only a *langoti*, a loincloth – the bare minimum (if that's the phrase) that one could wear in public. He never alters or compromises this dress beyond wrapping the upper half of his body in cold weather in a white woollen chadar or shawl, and this is how he turns up at Buckingham Palace in 1931 at a tea party for the Round Table Conference delegates. Reputedly, when asked by a press reporter if he had enough on to meet the King-Emperor, Gandhi replies, in an anti-imperial thrust: "I'm sure the King-Emperor will have enough on for both of us".

Gandhi's own recollections and comments on his sartorial progress are of significance. When he arrived in England as a student in September 1888, he disembarked at Southampton wearing a white flannel suit and found in a moment of colonial cringe that he was "the only person wearing such clothes".[38] Shortly afterwards in London, he spent an extravagant amount of money on a hat, a suit, and ties so that he may "look the thing",[39] as he recounts in a chapter of his autobiography ironically entitled 'Playing the English Gentleman' in English translation but 'Jaisa Des Vaisa Bhes' in Hindi, which would in an idiomatic equivalent be 'Dress in Rome as Romans Do'.[40]

Gandhi's decision later to dress as an indentured labourer in South Africa or as a common peasant in India would thus seem to be not only an act towards identifying with those he sought to represent, but also in part a reaction against such craven aping of the colonial masters by him previously. In contrast, in a sceptical post-colonial view of the matter, Robert Young has described Gandhi as "a master of sartorial semantics, which he wielded more effectively than sabre or rifle", characterized his loincloth comically as "the not quite full monty", and (following Emma Tarlo's discussion) argued that the effect of this performance or 'spectacle' depended on the fact that "it was always out of place" and that it underlined "the difference between how he was dressed and who he was".[41] This charge of strategic theatricality and even hypocrisy does not even countenance the possibility that Gandhi may have been simply practising what he preached, and not performing or enacting a role but in fact embodying his principles.

CARTOONS, PAINTINGS, STATUES

If Gandhi looked out of place in his attire anywhere, it was, as glimpsed above, to superior British eyes in London in 1931 where he had gone to take part in the second Round Table Conference. Shortly before the Gandhi–Irwin pact, which had persuaded Gandhi to go to London, was signed on 5 March 1931, Winston Churchill had famously fumed at "the alarming and also nauseating sight" of Gandhi, "posing as a fakir of the type well known in the East, striding half-naked up the steps of the Viceregal palace",[42] thus recognizing (from his own years in India) and at the same time deriding the austere spirituality that lay behind Gandhi's appearance. This remark inspired a delightful cartoon by 'Reynolds' in *The Morning Post* (London) under the title 'Change of Garb' in which Gandhi stands in the left half in tails, bow-tie, striped trousers, and a top hat with a cane in one hand, a brief-case in the other, and a cigar stuck in his mouth, while in the right half stands Churchill, big and bare with just a little piece of cloth tied round his waist, looking sheepish and opening a brolly held below the waist to alleviate his shame.[43] Another cartoon morphs Gandhi's face onto a similar formal attire, with the caption saying: "this American camera-trick shows him as he will not appear" before His Majesty the King.[44]

Among other cartoons in this selection from the Indian and foreign press (including publications from South Africa, the United States, Germany, and even New Zealand) and dating from 1907 to 1948 is one by David Low showing Viceroy Willingdon in 1933 going on a counter-fast to the one announced by Gandhi and lying in a canopied bed in his full regalia with doctors anxiously hovering around while the bare-bodied Gandhi sits in another corner busily spinning his wheel with a goat in attendance. Another anonymous cartoon shows Gandhi trying desperately to flag down a train speeding at full steam before the two lines of the track diverge disastrously, with one going to Pakistan and the other to India.[45] A caricaturist who has achieved wide circulation in India is Ranga, with his trademark manner of showing Gandhi from behind in broad and bold outline; one of these drawings conflating the figure of Gandhi with the map of India has appeared on an Indian postage stamp.[46]

Of the paintings and woodcuts, perhaps the most famous is the one by Nandalal Bose, with Gandhi seen in profile marching with a tall walking stick planted at an angle before the front foot and parallel with it; the woodcut was made to mark the Salt March to Dandi and is now so ubiquitous as to be iconic. A series of six woodcuts by Dhiren Gandhi, done while observing Gandhi on a three-week fast in February 1943, includes one showing him emaciated to the bare skeleton, in a deep allusion to a famous ancient sculpture of the Buddha from the second century AD, now in the Lahore Museum, variously called the Fasting/Starving/Skeletal Buddha. Of the notable paintings of Gandhi, perhaps the most remarkable, for an uncanny non-artistic reason, is the one by Feliks Topolski (1907–89), a Polish-born British artist, which shows Gandhi, bathed in a blood-red light and leaning on two young women, calmly slumping to the ground – except that this was painted in 1946, as if in precise premonition of Gandhi's assassination two years later. It was later reworked as one part of a large four-panel painting titled 'The East 1948', which Jawaharlal Nehru acquired on a visit to London in 1949 and which now fills a wall in the Rashtrapati Bhavan in New Delhi.[47]

Of all the forms of visual representation, statues are probably the most substantial and publicly accessible and the most enduring. Gandhi is often shown walking or striding in his full-length statues, including the one in the city centre at Pietermaritzburg where his political career began when he was thrown out of a train on a cold winter night in June 1893 – and where there are now as many as three plaques at the railway station, including one by the railway company, as well as a portrait of Gandhi hanging in the waiting room where he had spent that freezing night. Sometimes, he is shown leading a group of men and women in a march, as in the Martyrs' Memorial (popularly called the 'Gyarah Murti', i.e. Eleven Statues) by Debi Prasad Roy Chaudhuri, located on a curving road just off the Presidential Estate in New Delhi, and also in another massive sculpture in black marble 'in the cubistic style' (as the plaque says) by Advait Gadanayak, which shows Gandhi with twelve associates on his Salt March; this dominates the front garden of the National Gandhi Museum in New Delhi.

The large and arresting sculpture of Gandhi by the Polish émigré sculptor Fredda Brilliant, installed in Tavistock Square in central London in 1968 to herald his birth centenary, shows him sitting cross-legged with a shawl draped over his right shoulder, his loincloth visible only from the sides because in front he has his left hand placed on his ankles folded together, and his brow deeply and triply furrowed with a somewhat abstracted expression on his face. The equally monumental bust in the grounds of the Parliament House in New Delhi is rather more serenely contemplative; it is by Ram Sutar (1925–) whose statues and busts of Gandhi, commissioned by the Government of India or other national and international institutions, stand in about fifty other cities and countries of the world many of which the sculptor himself has never visited.[48]

The posthumous Gandhi who appears as a spirit in *Lage Raho Munnabhai* says at one point in that film:

> Go and knock down all the statues of mine all over the country. Take down my portraits from every wall. Take my name off all the buildings, roads and cross-roads named after me. If you wish to find a place for me at all, just keep me in your hearts.

Such a wish seems perfectly apt in the case of Gandhi who knew that in India, an inveterately idolatrous country, to iconize and idolize anyone could easily be a way of bracketing him off from relevance and reality.

As it happens, in the best of the literary representations of Gandhi such as Premchand's *Rangabhumi* and Raja Rao's *Kanthapura*, there is an obliqueness of representation, and the burden of disseminating his principles and ideals is borne not by Gandhi himself but by a surrogate local figure, 'our Gandhi', who seems to be an avatar of Gandhi, just as Gandhi himself was sometimes seen as an avatar of divinity. This also bears testimony to the range of his vast impact and influence, working, through refraction, well beyond the orbit of his physical presence, even though he travelled enormous distances all over India throughout his life to spread his message.

In contrast, the appeal of Gandhi's visual portrayals lies in precisely the fact that they must embody his corporeality in immediate and directly recognizable terms. An advantage of this is that Gandhi, who was not only a thinker but even more a doer, can be represented in action, as for example himself marching ahead and visibly leading others. In some other photographs and sculptures, he is seen, on the other hand, as looking deep within himself, and thus contemplatively and even spiritually withdrawn from the viewer and the world. In many such cases, in both literature and the visual media, it is precisely when he seems absent that he is the most powerfully present, and just when he is there in a much too realistic sense that his representation becomes an empty shell. For several years through the 1960s and the 1970s, it was suggested by many that a statue of Gandhi should fill the spot left vacant by the removal of a standing statue of George V at the India Gate in Delhi, an architectural high point of the new capital that the British built for themselves between 1911 and 1931 and which was meant to serve as such for a thousand years. But the spot beneath the high canopy remains empty, for it was successfully argued by others that Gandhi was anything but a successor to the imperial masters and opposed to all their pomp.

A GANDHI SONG

There is one memorable instance in which the written and the visual come together to pay a tribute to Gandhi, which must be one of the most widely known and cherished in India. This is a song in the Hindi film *Jagriti* (1955; Awakening), portrayed in the film as composed and sung by a crippled schoolboy on crutches on the occasion of the Gandhi Jayanti (Gandhi's birth anniversary) in the school hall before a bust of Gandhi, with the whole school present and joining in as a chorus for the refrain. This simple song has been played and sung in numerous real schools and other public places throughout the last half century – and not only on successive Gandhi Jayantis each year – in an enduring instance of life imitating art. Written by the lyricist Pradip (who contributed two other patriotic songs to the same film), this abiding film song, celebrating in the medium of the masses a man of the masses, represents perhaps the definitive image of Gandhi that has circulated and persisted among a vast segment of the people of India over the last two or three generations, notwithstanding all the artistic, scholarly, and theoretical sophistication and complexity that informs other images of and discourses on Gandhi. Indeed, this may be described as the subalterns' Gandhi – though it certainly is not the Gandhi of the subaltern historians or post-colonial critics.

As evident in three selected stanzas from this song, given below in a literal translation (with the middle stanza illustrating the rhyme scheme), it consistently employs military imagery to underline ironically Gandhi's method of nonviolence, perhaps his most striking and greatest achievement, while it also vividly highlights his unprecedented success in mobilizing the masses.

> You gave us freedom without wielding a shield or a sword.
> O Saint of Sabarmati,[49] what a miracle you wrought!
> Gandhi, your torch burnt bright through every storm.
>
> You gave us freedom without wielding a shield or a sword.
> O Saint of Sabarmati, what a miracle you wrought.
> . . .
> Whenever your bugle sounded, the youth came marching up.

Workers came marching up and peasants marching up.
Hindus and Mussalmans, Sikhs, Pathans came marching up.
A hundred million souls behind your step came marching up.
Leaving his bed of roses came running Jawaharlal.
O Saint of Sabarmati, what a miracle you wrought!

Nonviolence in your heart, on your body a loin cloth,
You moved around the masses wielding the baton of Truth.
To look at, you were but a little man.
But even the Himalayas bowed before you.

Bapu, you were a man without an equal in the world.
O Saint of Sabarmati, what a miracle you wrought! . . .

Notes

1   I am grateful to my old friends Gopal Gandhi and Ramachandra Guha
    for their helpful suggestions, and to Dr Varsha Das, Director, and Mr
    S. K. Bhatnagar, Librarian, of the National Gandhi Museum at Rajghat,
    New Delhi, for their gracious assistance. Unless otherwise stated, all
    the translations in this chapter are mine.

2   For literary portrayals, see, for example, the entries on 'Gandhian Liter-
    ature' in fifteen different Indian languages, from Assamese and Bengali
    to Tamil and Telugu including English and Sanskrit, in Amaresh Datta
    (ed.), *Encyclopaedia of Indian Literature* (New Delhi, India: Sahitya
    Akademi, 1988; rpt. 1996), vol. II, pp. 1347–63, and H. M. Naik (ed.),
    Gandhiji in Indian Literature (Mysore, India: Institute of Kannada Stud-
    ies, University of Mysore, 1971). For photographs, see *Mahatma Gandhi*
    (New Delhi, India: The Publications Division, Government of India,
    1954), and Peter Ruhe (ed.), *Gandhi* (London: Phaidon Press, 2001); see
    also various websites.

3   Harivansh Rai Bachchan, *Bachchan Rachanvali* [in Hindi: The Col-
    lected Works of Bachchan], ed. Ajit Kumar (New Delhi, India: Rajkamal
    Prakashan, 1983), vol. I, pp. 501, 503.

4   *Ibid.*, p. 447.

5   Bhavaniprasad Mishra, *Bhavaniprasad Mishra Rachanavali* [in Hindi:
    The Collected Works of Bhavaniprasad Mishra], ed. Vijay Bahadur Singh
    (New Delhi, India: Anamika, 2002), vol. 1, *passim.*, and blurb on the
    back cover.

6   Bhavaniprasad Mishra and Prabhakar Machwe (eds.), *Mrityunjayi* [in
    Hindi: The Immortal] (Delhi, India: Shabdakar, for the Central Hindi
    Directorate, 1969).

7   Sohanlal Dwivedi (ed.), *Gandhi-Shatadal* [in Hindi: A Hundred Poems
    on Gandhi] (New Delhi, India: Publications Division of the Government
    of India, 1969; rpt. 1994), p. 64.

8   *Ibid.*, pp. 66, 67, and *passim.*

9 Balkrishna Sharma Navin, in Mishra and Machwe (eds.), *Mrityunjayi*, p. 317. This line acclaims Gandhi's transcendent spirituality and even divinity through evoking vocabulary first employed in the Upanishads (c. fifth century BC) with regard to the atman, the individual soul, and *paramatman*, the great soul or God.

10 In Mishra and Machwe (eds.), *Mrityunjayi*, pp. 59, 95, 126, 155, 166, 193, 226–7, 283, and 325 respectively.

11 Makhanlal Chaturvedi, *Makhanlal Chaturvedi Rachanavali* [in Hindi: Collected Works of Makhanlal Chaturvedi] (Delhi, India: Vani Prakashan, 1995), vol. VI, pp. 50, 68–9, 71–3, 137–41.

12 Sumitranandan Pant, *Sumitranadan Pant Granthavali* [in Hindi: The Collected Works of Sumitranandan Pant], vol. II. (New Delhi, India: Rajkamal Prakashan, 1979), vol. II, pp. 24–6, 29–33, 127–78.

13 For a fuller discussion of Akbar's poetry, see Shamsur Rahman Faruqi, 'The Power Politics of Culture: Akbar Ilahabadi and the Changing Order of Things'. Accessible at www.columbia.edu/itc/mealac/pritchett/ oofwp/srf/srf_akbar_ilahabadi.pdf. My translation of the two verses quoted here differs from Faruqi's.

14 Amrit Rai, *Premchand: A Life*, trans. Harish Trivedi (New Delhi, India: People's Publishing House, 1982), p. 139.

15 Premchand, *Rangabhumi*, in *Premchand Rachanavali* [in Hindi: The Collected Works of Premchand] (1925; rpt. Delhi, India: Janavani Prakashan, 1996), vol. III, p. 474, and vol. VI, *passim*.

16 Phanishwarnath Renu, *Maila Anchal* [in Hindi: A Backward District] (New Delhi, India: Rajkamal, 1954; rpt. 1990).

17 Harish Trivedi, 'Nationalist Politics in Hindi Fiction: Liberal Zig-Zag vs. the Straight and Simple Left', in V. R. Mehta and Thomas Pantham (eds.), *Political Ideas in Modern India: Thematic Explorations* (New Delhi, India: Sage, 2006), pp. 138–52.

18 For an authoritative account of Yashpal's life and works, see Madhuresh, *Yashpal* [in Hindi] (Panchkula, India: Aadhar Prakashan, 2006).

19 Giriraj Kishore, *The Girmitiya Saga*, trans. Prajapati Sah (New Delhi, India: Niyogi Books, 2010), p. 1026.

20 Mulk Raj Anand, *Untouchable* (1935; rpt. New Delhi, India: Orient Paperbacks, 1970), p. 164.

21 *Ibid.*, p. 171.

22 R. K. Narayan, *Waiting for the Mahatma* (1955; rpt. Mysore, India: Indian Thought Publications, 1991), pp. 24–74.

23 Raja Rao, *Kanthapura* (1938; rpt. New Delhi, India: Orient Paperbacks, 1996), p. 183.

24 *Ibid.*, p. 92.

25 Edward Thompson, *Atonement: A Play of Modern India* (London: Ernest Benn, 1924).

26 Quoted and discussed in Harish Trivedi, '*Passage* or *Farewell?*: Politics of the Raj in E. M. Forster and Edward Thompson', in Harish Trivedi (ed.), *Colonial Transactions: English Literature and India* (Manchester, England: Manchester University Press, 1995), pp. 139–73. See also Mary

Lago, *'India's Prisoner': A Biography of Edward John Thompson 1886–1946* (Columbia: University of Missouri Press, 2001).

27 Paul Scott, *The Raj Quartet* (London: Guild, 1985), pp. 2, 16–19.

28 Stanley A. Wolpert, *Nine Hours to Rama* (London: Hamish Hamilton, 1962).

29 Joseph Chapman 'The Raj Revival: *Gandhi* (1982)', in Joseph Chapman and Nicholas J. Cull (co-authors), *Projecting Empire: Imperialism and Popular Cinema* (London: I. P. Tauris, 1982), pp. 189–90.

30 *Ibid.*, pp. 190–1.

31 *Ibid.*, p. 195.

32 http://news.bbc.co.uk/2/low/south_asia/180736.stm.

33 Salman Rushdie, 'Attenborough's Gandhi', in his *Imaginary Homelands: Essays and Criticism 1981–1991* (London: Granta/New Delhi, Penguin Books India, 1991), pp. 102–6.

34 Salman Rushdie, '"Errata" or "Unreliable Narration in *Midnight's Children"'*, in Rushdie (ed.), *Imaginary Homelands*, pp. 22–5.

35 R. S. McGregor, *The Oxford Hindi–English Dictionary* (Delhi, India: Oxford University Press, 1997), p. 489.

36 Harish Trivedi, 'Revolutionary Non/Violence: Gandhi, Marx and Postcolonial Discourse', in Gangeya Mukherjee (ed.), *Learning Non-Violence* (Shimla, India: Indian Institute of Advanced Study, forthcoming).

37 See 'Chronology of Mahatma Gandhi', at *www.mkgandhi-sarvodaya .org/chrono/chrnology_main.htm*

38 M. K. Gandhi, *An Autobiography or The Story of My Experiments with Truth*, trans. Mahadev Desai (Ahmedabad, India: Navjivan, 1927; rpt. 2002), pp. 41–2.

39 *Ibid.*, p. 47.

40 *Ibid.*

41 Robert J. C. Young, *Postcolonialism: An Historical Introduction* (Oxford, England: Blackwell, 2001), pp. 327–8.

42 Winston Churchill, report of a speech given on 23 February 1930 to the Council of the West Essex Unionist Association, under the title 'Mr Churchill on India', *The Times* (London), 24 February 1930. http:// en.wikiquote.org/wiki/Winston_Churchill

43 Durga Das (ed.), *Gandhi in Cartoons* (Ahmedabad, India: Navajivan, 1970; rpt. 2007), p. 103.

44 *Ibid.*, p. 105.

45 *Ibid.*, pp. 131, 132.

46 Ranga, *Bapu* [in Hindi]/*Gandhi*, p. 13.

47 Ranga, *Gandhi* (Delhi, India: Chitra Kala Sangam, 1996), p. 13.

48 Personal conversation, 10 February 2010.

49 Sabarmati is the name of the ashram in Ahmedabad where Gandhi lived from 1915 to 1930.

11 Gandhi in independent India

ANTHONY PAREL

The attainment of independence was no ordinary turning point in Indian history. It marked, according to Nehru's celebrated 'Tryst with Destiny' speech of 15 August 1947, the end of an age and the beginning of a new one. Gandhi, more than any other Indian, had contributed to this transition. His contributions were made during the pre-independent period (he lived only for six months into independence). They had their sources in his struggle against colonial rule and in his deeply cherished aspirations for the future of his country.

There are two ways of looking at Gandhi's contributions to independent India. One is to look at them as *norms* by which to evaluate India's fortunes over the last six decades. The other is to use the fortunes of independent India *to test* the empirical viability of his contributions. Both approaches are relevant to the present discussion.

Of the numerous contributions that he has made to India, the following are the more significant. First, there is his idea of India as an inclusive nation – *ek-praja* ('one-nation') as he called it. Second, there is his scheme of building a nonviolent social order in a country rent for centuries by violence originating in caste, gender, and religious differences. Third, there is his approach to solving the problem of India's chronic poverty and his doubts about the suitability of the nineteenth-century type of industrialization. Fourth, there is his contribution as a writer and thinker, which calls into question the habit of those Indian intellectuals who rely on non-Indian philosophical frameworks for thinking about India. He sets a good example to them by contributing to the creation of the modern Indian political canon, one that does justice to the needs of modern India and to the valid claims of ancient India. Finally, there is his redefinition of the relationship of secular values to spiritual values, which he hoped the civilization of independent India would accept.

Indians are by no means unanimous in their appreciation of Gandhi's contributions. Some like the Indian Marxists and Maoists disregard them totally. Others like the dalits, following the philosophy of B. R. Ambed-kar (1891–1956), are opposed to him on specific issues, such as the way to solve the caste problem. Almost all other ideological groups in India invoke his name in order to give themselves respectability. This is true even of the Hindutva (Hinduness) ideologues, who in principle question the validity of an inclusive India.

On the other side, there are numerous Gandhi organizations scattered throughout India, engaged in different kinds of voluntary work. Notable among them are the Gandhi Peace Foundation in Delhi and the Gandhi Bhavans (Houses) on University campuses. The followers of famous Gandhians, Vinoba Bhave (1895–1982) and Jayprakash Narayan (1902–79), play a prominent role in peace activities. Still others like the followers of Jawaharlal Nehru (1889–1964) are trying their best to implement Gandhi's ideas within the framework of the state, sometimes departing from one or other of his economic policies.

Indian intellectuals are divided in their estimate of Gandhi's status as a thinker. Some believe that he is not a political thinker at all but only a political strategist. The academics who adopt a Marxian framework of thought, including those who follow the so-called subaltern approach to Indian history, see him as a representative of Indian bourgeois thought. Others embrace his key ideas but not his intellectual framework. They interpret him with the aid of their own more or less worn-out Western liberal intellectual framework, and present him as just another Indian thinker who did the usual 'political thought in India', rather than original 'Indian political thought'. We shall keep this roster of opinions in mind as the discussion proceeds.

AN INCLUSIVE INDIA

Independent India is a nation with a difference. The difference is that it is multilingual, multi-religious, and multi-ethnic – features that are not normally associated with the concept of nation, especially in the West. The thinker who is mainly responsible for producing a theory of nationalism appropriate for India is Gandhi. To begin with, he used an Indian term *praja* (and its variant, *ek-praja*, one-nation) to convey the modern non-Indian concept of nation. The Indian term suited Gandhi's purposes admirably, for it connoted neutrality towards religion, language, or ethnicity. A Raja for example can have as his *praja* people belonging to different religions, languages, and ethnicity, all enjoying equal status. Similarly, peoples belonging to different religions, languages, and ethnicity could now be equal citizens of a modern Indian nation. What, according to Gandhi, makes India a nation is territory, history, a diffused tradition of mutual tolerance, re-enforced, since the first half of the twentieth century, by the idea of human rights and common citizenship. The *primary* unit of such a nation is the individual citizen considered as a bearer of fundamental rights and a subject capable of swaraj, that is, self-determination and self-development. While the individual is the primary unit of his 'nation', India's religious, linguistic, and ethnic groups are its *subsidiary* units. This enables him to make room for the linguistic rights and the religious rights of minorities. Finally, he sees the state as the enforcer of these rights and an effective mediator of the disputes that might arise between them.

Gandhi did not participate in the deliberations of the Constituent Assembly that drew up the Constitution of India. This notwithstanding, the idea of India that underlies the Constitution is virtually Gandhian. In this sense, his philosophy of nationalism is the intellectual glue that holds independent India together. It also supplies an ethical norm by which to evaluate independent India's handling of issues related to national unity; and in the last six decades, it had to handle a number of such issues.

We begin with the fact of India's linguistic diversity and the way it has been accommodated. During the first four decades following independence, the map of India was redrawn several times along linguistic lines. Andhra Pradesh was created in 1953, Kerala in 1956, Gujarat and Maharashtra in 1960, Nagaland in 1963, Punjab and Haryana in 1966, Manipur, Meghalaya, and Tripura in 1972, and Arunachal and Mizoram in 1987. These political surgeries, though painful, in the end contributed to the health of the Indian body politic.

The idea of dividing India along linguistic lines did not come as a total surprise, for Gandhi had prepared the way for such a division. He did so in 1920 in connection with the new Constitution of the Indian National Congress that he was drafting. He wanted "the redistribution of India for the purposes of the Congress on a linguistic basis".[1] The Congress accepted his proposal. Thanks to this, during the next three decades, India got a chance to accustom itself to the idea of linguistic diversity within an overarching sense of nationhood. The redrawing of the linguistic map by independent India has not led to Balkanization, however, as some had feared.

Independent India has retained English, alongside Hindi, as a language for all-India communication. Sarvepalli Gopal, the historian, has rightly described English "as the only non-regional language in India. It is a link language in a more than administrative sense, in that it counters blinkered provincialism".[2] The retention of English in independent India is fully in keeping with Gandhi's spirit of accommodation. During the pre-independence period, he had proposed Hindi written in both Devanagari and Persian scripts for all-India communication. At the same time, he was fully cognizant of the need to retain English. "If Hindi could take the place of English I for one would be happy. But we realize full well the importance of the English language. We need the knowledge of English for the study of science and of modern literature, for contact with the rest of the world, for trade and commerce, for keeping in touch with officials and various other things. We have to learn English whether we wish or not".[3] The context of these remarks is particularly relevant to the present discussion: they were made in his *presidential address* to the 1935 annual session of the Hindi Sahitya Sammelan (Hindi Literature Conference).

It should be emphasized that, according to Gandhi, what binds a nation like India together is not so much this or that language as the willingness of Indians to respect each other's individual rights and group rights, and the ability of the country to diffuse material prosperity equitably. However natural the ability of the mother tongue may be to form a basic language community – and Gandhi readily recognizes that it has such ability – that ability by itself does not bring with it the sense of civic justice. But the latter can, and does, come with civic nationalism. The civic nation (which is distinct from the language community) therefore does not have to be unilingual. As long as the values of civic justice and economic justice are operative in a multilingual India, it can maintain its unity despite its linguistic diversity. This insight, originating in Gandhi, still guides the behaviour of multilingual India. There is no gain saying, however, that India, because it is a multilingual nation, has to pay serious attention to human rights and regional economic well-being.

Religious diversity poses more problems for independent India than does linguistic diversity. In addition to the idea of the Indian nation state, a majority of Indians has accepted Gandhi's idea that religion ought not to be the basis of Indian nationality, and that therefore India should develop as a multi-religious nation. However, a significant minority – including some Hindus, Sikhs, and Muslims – still challenge his inclusive vision of India. What is common to them is also their readiness to use violence, including terrorist violence, against their opponents. Gandhi's assassination (1948), inspired by the ideology of Hinduness, was of course the most horrible of these acts of violence. It was followed by periodic attacks on religious minorities – on the Sikhs in Delhi in 1984, on a historic mosque in Ayodhya in 1991, on the Muslims in Mumbai in 1993, and in Ahmedabad in 2003, and on the Christians in Orissa in 2008. Hindu radicals were also involved in the persistent harassment of the celebrated Indian painter, M. F. Husain, who for personal safety had to flee India in 2006 and seek asylum in Qatar.

The main complaint of Hindu radicals is that non-Hindus, particularly Muslims and Christians, lacking Hinduness, are not sufficiently Indian. They therefore deserve to be marginalized or at least kept under Hindu domination. Only in this way, they believe, can they make independent India Indian, strong and united.

A very small minority within the Sikh community wants to create a nation-state called Khalistan (the land of the pure) out of the state of Punjab. Led for a short period by the charismatic Sant Jarnail Singh Bhindranwale (1947–84), they believe that the practice of pure Sikhism is possible only in a Sikh nation-state. Ironically, the desire for Khalistan is felt more strongly by sections of the Sikh diaspora living outside India than by those within India itself.

Muslim separatism, active in Kashmir, is a leftover of the religion-based Muslim nationalism of pre-independent India. The Taliban and the Al Qaeda have now made it part of worldwide militant Islamism. From the Gandhian perspective, what is being threatened is the inclusive character of India. His spirit of minority accommodation was reflected in his support for separate electorates for Muslims in pre-partition India. That spirit is now reflected in Article 370 of the Indian Constitution that grants Kashmir special status in the Indian Union.

"CASTE HAS TO GO"[4]

Violence originating in politicized religion is not the only type of violence that independent India has to deal with. It has also to deal with violence originating in the practice of Untouchability and caste differences. No oppressive institution has lasted longer in human history than has the institution of Untouchability. The poet-saints of the sixteenth century fought against it, as did the social reformers of the nineteenth century. Independent India has outlawed it, and even criminalized it. Gandhi in the twentieth century in his own way fought against it.

Yet on this issue, he has come under heavy criticism in independent India. This criticism comes mostly from dalit intellectuals and politicians, who take their cue from the philosophy of B. R. Ambedkar, their illustrious leader. To understand the basis of the criticism, it is necessary to understand its social context, and to bear in mind the enormity of the sufferings that dalits had to endure over the centuries. Memories of the past weigh heavily on the present. Everything Hindu is suspect in dalit eyes, and Gandhi is no exception.

Gandhi's opposition to caste and Untouchability was deeply personal and remorseful. It started in 1898 in South Africa. Fear of ritual pollution being the psychological root of caste prejudice, he wanted his family to overcome it by a simple domestic practice: members of the family would clean the chamber pot of their paying houseguest, who in this instance, happened to be a Christian of Untouchable descent. Mrs Gandhi simply refused to cooperate, and the ensuing fight nearly wrecked their marriage. Two decades later, in 1915, a similar incident occurred, this time in his ashram in India. He admitted a family of Untouchables to the ashram. Mrs Gandhi, along with Maganlal Gandhi, his cousin and deputy at the ashram, threatened to quit. Although ultimately the dispute was resolved amicably, it showed, once again, how difficult it was to overcome caste prejudice at the personal level even in the Gandhi household and ashram.

Battle against caste and Untouchability became part of Gandhi's satyagraha movement. He played a leadership role in the Vaikom satyagraha (1924–5) in support of the dalits in Kerala. His strategy evolved between 1920 and 1940. Its basic elements were that by getting rid of caste and Untouchability, he hoped to purify Hinduism as a religion and reconstruct Hindu society as a social order. He firmly believed that the Untouchables were an integral part of Hindu society. In the hope of increasing their sense of self-respect, in 1932 he coined a new name for them, Harijans (children of God), following this up in 1933 by founding a service organization called Harijan Service Association. His study of the Hindu scriptures led him to the conclusion that the evils associated with caste and Untouchability had no divine sanction,[5] that they were of human origin, and that they were therefore capable of being remedied through human action. In the same vein, he saw no special sanctity attached to even the number four in the fourfold system of varna (the scriptural name for caste). He had no objection to even reducing the scriptural four into one: "if we wish to observe *Varnashrama dharma*, we should all belong to one caste, i.e., of Harijans".[6] "Finally, there will be only one caste...".[7]

The way to bring about a new one-caste Hindu society (or what comes to the same, a casteless Hindu society) was through a prudential mixture of social reform, mixed marriages, consensus among Hindu factions, legislation, and, above all, public opinion. "The present caste system is the very antithesis of *Varnashrama*. The sooner public opinion abolishes it the better".[8]

The contemporary dalit criticism of Gandhi draws heavily on Ambedkar. In the background are Ambedkar's important works – *Annihilation of Caste* (1936),[9] *Who Were the Shudras?* (1946), *The Untouchables* (1948),[10] *What Congress and Gandhi Have Done to the Untouchables* (1945),[11] and *The Buddha and His Dhamma* (1957).[12] The dalit perception was that Gandhi's interest in dalits was only a part of his greater interest in preserving Hinduism as a religion and the Hindu society as a social order. His defence of the scriptural varna and attack on historical caste, they found, smacked of scholastic juggling with words. Caste could not go, they held, unless varna went with it. The choice of the name Harijans, in their view, was paternalistic to say the least; it therefore had to be dropped in favour of the new name, dalit (the oppressed), chosen by themselves. Even if Hindu society were to get rid of caste, the dalits would not want to be a part of it for the simple reason that they now felt that they had a quiddity of their own. Besides, there was no way even a reformed Hindu could understand the depth of the humiliation that they had to suffer and still suffer. Non-dalits, however well motivated, could not emancipate them. They had to emancipate themselves. Gandhi therefore was not needed.

Additionally, dalits in independent India felt that they would need the protection of the law and the Constitution. This was made relatively easy by the appointment of Ambedkar as the Chairman of the Commission that drafted the Constitution, and as the first Minister of Law in independent India's first cabinet. (That Gandhi had played a role behind the scene to get Amedkar appointed to these posts did not seem to increase the dalits' appreciation of him.) Dalits also demanded (and obtained) special statutory privileges in areas of education and employment, even if this meant setting aside rules of fair competition based on merit and competence. Affirmative action was regarded as fair compensation for past sufferings. To cap it all, the dalits felt that their emancipation would never be complete unless they captured political power through the electoral process. To this end, they began to form their own dalit-dominated political parties, such as the Bahujan Samaj Party.

Perhaps the most significant emancipatory step that the dalits took was mass conversion to Buddhism, now called Engaged Buddhism.[13] Here, too, Ambedkar's political philosophy played a decisive role. His thinking was that the protection of the law and the Constitution, affirmative action, and political parties would not be sufficient to complete the process of dalit liberation. Religion also would be needed. Resort to mass conversion for political and social ends is not uncommon in independent India. But Ambedkar's endorsement of it has surprised many – given his very positive attitude towards the values of the French Enlightenment. His reasoning here seems to have been that the goal of overcoming the effects of a prejudice as deep as caste prejudice would require more than just secular means. The "secular system", Ambedkar writes, "cannot last very long unless it has got the sanction of the religion, however remote it may be".[14] He believed that Engaged Buddhism alone had the spiritual power that secular sources lacked. "The greatest thing that the Buddha has done is to tell the world that the world cannot be reformed except by the reformation of the mind of the man, and the mind of the world... The Buddha has energized your conscience itself that is acting as a sentinel in order to keep you on your path. There is no trouble, when the mind is converted, the thing is permanent". Again, "religion, if it is to be a moral force for the regeneration of society, you must constantly din into the ears of the people".[15]

How the values of the Buddhist Enlightenment would sit with the values of the French Enlightenment is the question that Ambedkar, and, for that matter, the dalit intellectuals, have not addressed. Apart from this, there is the point that what is good for the goose is good for the gander. What if Muslims and Christians were to advocate mass conversion as a solution to the caste problem? Indeed, Abul Hasan Ali Nadwi (1913–99), independent India's foremost Muslim thinker, is on record as saying that Gandhi's approach to Untouchability was bound to fail because it lacked the quality of a prophetic religion. "[A]s his approach was different from that of the prophets, he could not produce that fundamental change in the minds of his people which is essential to the success of a moral movement... We can, thus, say that the methodology of the prophets is the only sure and successful way of bringing about a radical change for the better in the religious and social affairs of humanity at large".[16]

Whatever the merits or demerits of mass conversion, it has added a sectarian dimension to the fight against caste. It has put dalit Buddhists on a collision course with militant Hindu groups that have emerged in response to them. They are now engaged in what is being called "caste wars". Hindu groups have formed loose militias, called senas, to advance their interests. Thus there are now Bhumi Sena, Kuer Sena, Lorik Sena, Shoshit Sena, Brahmharshi Sena, Ran Vir Sena, and Shiv Sena, to mention a few. This development has forced dalits to form dalit senas of their own.[17]

Similarly, the entrenchment of affirmative action into law has had unintended consequences. It has given caste consciousness a new lease on life. Those who oppose it, as well as those who benefit from it, see caste as an axis of power in independent India. Besides, where dalit political parties are in power, there is the potential of the oppressed of the past becoming the oppressor of the present. Such a turn of the wheel of Indian politics was perhaps unforeseen by Ambedkar.

Gandhi did not approve of mass conversion as a solution to the caste problem. Although he wanted the reform of Hindu society, that was not the ultimate goal of his political philosophy. Its ultimate goal was the creation of a caste-free India, where the Indian identity would become the shared common identity of everyone – dalits and non-dalits alike. Under no circumstance did he want to define Indian identity in terms of religion, any religion, including Engaged Buddhism. The means he proposed were secular, relying as he did on the humanism of human rights, internal reform of Hinduism, consensus, legislation, and public opinion.

Attempts to find solutions to the caste problem in independent India draw inspiration from both Gandhi and Ambedkar. Both are contributing, in their own way, towards the creation of a caste-free India.

THE MODERN INDIAN POLITICAL CANON

Political independence has generated serious intellectual interest in a number of fields. The field of Indian history, especially Indian intellectual history, is one of them. The urge to go back to the sources of one's history and tradition is natural and purgative. Romila Thapar's *Early India: From the Origins to AD 1300* (2002), P. V. Kane's monumental *History of Dharmasastra* (1930–62), and R. P. Kangale's three-part *The Kautiliya Arthasastra* (1969) are but a few examples of the many outstanding works of the post-independence period.

Interest in modern Indian political philosophy has also increased with the coming of independence. Indians want more than just political freedom. They want the ability to think about India with the aid of an Indian intellectual framework, and to create something original in the area of collective self-understanding. In other words, they want to have a modern *Indian* political philosophy.

Here, Indian political thinkers have hit a snag. For more than a century, for historical reasons, they had become dependent on Western intellectual frameworks of one kind or another, introduced into India in the nineteenth century by the colonial state. Later, Indians themselves embraced varieties of nationalism, liberalism, utilitarianism, and Marxism. Independence does not seem to wean them off their dependency on Western intellectual frameworks. This is especially true of Indian

Marxists, who, as far as the intellectual history of world Marxism goes, are not particularly original in their thinking. The post-colonial dependency of Indian political philosophers on Western frameworks gives their intellectual output a derivative character. What independent India has is 'political philosophy in India', not 'Indian political philosophy'. To have Indian political philosophy, one needs an Indian intellectual framework, which these intellectuals lack. This explains why they go on producing book after book on 'political philosophy in India'.[18]

Here, Gandhi has something very valuable to offer. Although not a philosopher in any formal sense, a philosophy definitely underlies his thought and actions. In this respect, he is not unlike Machiavelli in the West. A Florentine civil servant, he wanted to produce a political philosophy that would survive him. In Gandhi's case, he, too, wanted to leave a political philosophy that would survive him. He wanted to add to India's intellectual heritage by reinterpreting it and by adding to it what he thought he should take from the West. "My swaraj is to keep intact the genius of our civilization", he had written. "I want to write many new things but they must be all written on the Indian slate. I would gladly borrow from the West when I can return the amount with decent interest".[19] He felt that it was his duty "to augment the legacy of the ancestors and to change it into current coin and make it acceptable to the present age", without drowning himself, as he put it, in the ancestors' well.[20] He was persuaded that Indian civilization was "sound at the foundation", and that it was unwise to change what "we [had] tested and found true on the anvil of experience".[21]

The upshot is that he was able to update the old canon and contribute towards the formation of the modern Indian political canon.[22] It is virtually impossible today to discuss Indian politics without the help of concepts such as satyagraha, sarvodaya, constructive programme, trusteeship, Harijans, anasakti yoga – all concepts invented by him. Add to this, concepts such as swaraj, ahimsa (nonviolence), satya (Truth), *aparigraha* (freedom from excess), swadeshi, all found elsewhere in Indian thought but radically transformed by him, such that they have become genuine Gandhian concepts. All these are now part of the Indian political canon.

However, he contributed more than just a new set of political vocabulary. More importantly, he created an Indian intellectual framework within which the vocabulary is set. It is based on the traditional theory of the four great canonical aims of life (the *purusharthas*), now radically reinterpreted by him. The four aims are dharma (ethics), artha (political and economic power), kama (pleasure), and moksha (spiritual liberation). However, since the rise of the ascetic tradition in Indian culture going back to the days of the Buddha, these were made to work at cross purposes. Thus, if you were to pursue spiritual liberation, you could not at the same time pursue political and economic power as well. The discordance between the four aims, it has been pointed out, was seriously responsible for the political and economic stagnation of India.

Gandhi, among others, contributed to the reversal of the ascetic trend and the initiation of a new trend that promotes a working harmony between the pursuit of spiritual well-being and that of economic and political well-being. His writings are replete with pleas for such a trend. His entire life, as the famous Introduction and Conclusion (called 'Farewell') of his *Autobiography* state, has this initiation as its unifying aim. The grand vision underlying *Hind Swaraj* is the reconciliation of political swaraj with spiritual swaraj. His interpretation of the Bhagavad Gita claims that this is its real message for modern India. His Introduction to that work deserves close attention: "The common belief is that dharma and artha are mutually antagonistic to each other. 'In worldly activities such as trade and commerce, dharma has no place. Let dharma operate in the field of dharma, and artha in that of artha' – we hear many secular people say. In my opinion, the author of the *Gita* has dispelled this delusion. He has drawn no line of demarcation between moksha and worldly pursuits".[23]

The creation of the modern Indian political canon required the elimination of what was obsolete in tradition, the addition of what was missing in it, and the retention of what was valid and viable. Thus he deleted from tradition its preference for monarchy as the ideal form of government and caste as the desired form of social organizations. Retained from tradition were the need for a plurality of valid knowledge systems (science, philosophy, religious knowledge, etc.), the need for civic virtues such as nonviolence, Truth, and avoidance of excess, and of course the new intellectual framework. Added to the framework were civic nationalism, constitutionalism, fundamental human rights, work ethic, gender equality, a just political economy, the secular state – all taken from the West – and equal respect for every religion. While several other modern Indian political thinkers – such as Tagore, Nehru, and Ambedkar – have also contributed to the formation of the new Indian canon, they are not as comprehensive as he has been. He stands out.

The way Gandhi integrated ideas taken from the West within his Indian framework is exemplary for modern Indian intellectuals. It was marked by intellectual honesty and humility, and the absence of chauvinism. At one level, intellectuals everywhere belong to the same republic of ideas. However, when it comes to political philosophy, as distinct from political science, and social sciences generally, a distinction has to be drawn. Political philosophy cannot completely abstract itself from the transcendent source of the culture from which it emerges and to which it responds. That is why we have had a plurality of political philosophies – Greek, Modern Western, Indian, Islamic, Japanese, Chinese, and so forth. There is, in other words, no such thing as a universal political philosophy. This is not to deny the existence of universally valid political ideas. Such ideas do exist, and each political canon – if it is a sound canon – incorporates them in its own way. Gandhi, as we saw, integrated a number of universally valid political ideas into his framework. The outcome is that there is now a distinct mode of modern Indian political philosophy.

Gandhi was generous in acknowledging his debt he owed to the West. His intellectual formation would have been incomplete without the contributions from Victorian jurisprudence, Ruskin, Thoreau, Emerson, Tolstoy, and Mazzini, among others. But he took from them their ideas not their intellectual framework. What he took from them he reset within his own framework, thus avoiding eclecticism. Adam Smith was no exception. His comments on him in the context of the economics of khadi are worthy of full citation since one rarely if ever hears about them:

> I am always reminded of one thing which the well-known British economist Adam Smith has said in his famous treatise *The Wealth of Nations*. In it he has described some economic laws as universal and absolute. Then he has described certain situations which may be an obstacle to the operation of these laws. These disturbing factors are the human nature, the human temperament or altruism inherent in it. Now, the economics of khadi is just the opposite of it. Benevolence, which is inherent in human nature, is the very foundation of the economics of khadi. What Adam Smith has described as pure economic activity based merely on the calculations of profit and loss is a selfish attitude and it is an obstacle to the development of khadi; and it is the function of a champion of khadi to counteract this tendency.[24]

Gandhi's point is that Adam Smith should be adapted to Indian realities, even if this requires some theoretical innovation. A profit-driven economy by itself cannot meet India's needs adequately. India would need *additionally* an economy driven by benevolence. This insight underlies sarvodaya, his economic philosophy.

As far as the modern Indian political canon is concerned, Gandhi gives Indian political philosophers an opportunity to make a choice. Either they can go on doing what they had been doing for nearly a century, that is to say, doing 'political philosophy in India', or they can begin to do original 'Indian political thought'. If they take the second option, they have to stop treating him as a cult figure or a mere political strategist[25] and begin to treat him critically as a serious philosophic thinker. In this context, it is good to recall Sir V. S. Naipaul's comments. Speaking of *Hind Swaraj*, he says that Indians love to talk about this book but not to read it. "The book would not be read in India not even by scholars (and still hasn't been), but its name would often be taken as a milestone in the independence struggle, and it would be cherished as a holy object".[26] What is true of *Hind Swaraj* is also true of his other essential writings. Indian intellectuals as a rule do not study Gandhi as seriously as they do, for example, Marx or Mao. It is not clear why this is so – why this fascination for the 'foreign' and the lack of confidence in the indigenous. A leftover of colonial intellectual dependency?

If Gandhi has a message for Indian political thinkers of today, it is this: be original, without being chauvinistic, anachronistic, or irrelevant; and do not be imitative. You do not have to be Gandhians. Only, you have to get used to working within a framework that is simultaneously Indian and modern, one that can integrate whatever ideas you need to take from outside the Indian canon.

ECONOMIC DEVELOPMENT

Gandhi's vision of economic development was holistic, as was discussed in Chapter 7. It had to occur within the context, not of a materialistic vision of life, but one that allowed room for spiritual development as well. Second, it had to be adapted to the conditions specific to India, especially those affecting the poor and women, long suppressed by male domination. Third, it had to include concern for health, hygiene, and civic sanitation. Finally, and this may come as a surprise to many, it had to meet the aesthetic needs of people for a sense of order and beauty.

Independent India has only very partially realized Gandhi's vision of economic development. Its attention has been scattered in different directions, some rejecting Gandhi altogether, others picking this or that from him, and no one paying attention to the whole picture. Indian Marxists from the very beginning branded the Gandhian approach as a soft bourgeois approach – class interest wrapped in medieval piety. While Marxist factions from the 1970s onward have for tactical reasons chosen to operate within the bounds of the Indian Constitution, the Maoists have chosen to stay on the path of violent class war. In their view, Marxists in West Bengal and Kerala, who think that class war can be won without a violent revolution, are bogus Marxists. Currying favour with the poorest of India's poor, the Maoists hope to fill the vacuum left by a major failure of Indian economic development (the failure to eliminate chronic poverty). In several Indian states – for example, Jharkhand, Chhattisgarh, Andhra Pradesh, Bihar, and West Bengal – they are now engaged in guerrilla war, their declared object being to overthrow the Indian state by 2050.[27] They really believe in the apocalyptic transformation of India through violent revolution. Taking Marx at face value, they hold on to the notion that Marxism is not philosophy but science – the only universal science of society.

Gandhians (and ex-Marxists too) demur. They make the counterclaim that it is Marxism that is 'the illusion of the epoch'. Vinoba Bhave and Jayprakash Narayan – 'gentle anarchists' as some have called them[28] – focused their energy on Gandhi's *Constructive Programme*. They believed that *Constructive Programme*, carried out in isolation from the state, could radically transform India. The land-gift movement (Bhoodan and Gramdan) was probably the most well known of their undertakings: the landlords were to relinquish their extra land voluntarily, for the benefit of the poor. The program did not survive Bhave and Narayan. Narayan later branched into what he called, somewhat quixotically, 'total revolution'. According to this, villages would engage in direct government without relying on the state. This, too, fizzled out shortly after it was inaugurated in a few villages in Bihar.

Gandhi's writings on women are voluminous.[29] Their gist, as found in *Constructive Programme*, is this: 'custom and law' for centuries had kept Indian women 'somewhat' as slaves of men. A 'revolution' or 'radical alternative' is needed so that they can enjoy gender equality in all fields of life. In pre-independent India, he personally opened for them the door to the field of politics. However, in independent India, the door to the economic field remains more or less shut – not for want of modern law but because of the force of ancient custom. Where this is particularly true, for example, is the area of compulsory dowry. This was prohibited by a series of laws in 1961, 1984, and 1986, but they were poorly enforced, if at all. As in the case of the legal abolition of Untouchability (1955), conservative social pressures and custom have undermined the effectiveness of modern legislation. This reflects the broader issue of gender inequality. Amartya Sen has analyzed this matter in two masterly essays.[30] He has identified seven different faces of gender inequality in India, the most frightening being female infanticide and feticide, leading to a catastrophic tally of 'missing' women annually. The decennial census is a clear window into the reality of India's gender imbalance.

On a positive note, there are successful women's organizations that seek to open the door wider. Perhaps the best known of these is 'Self-Employed Women's Association' (SEWA), started in Gujarat in 1972 by Ela Bhatt (1933–). Inspired by Gandhi, it is a women's cooperative, organized by and for poor women, mostly from dalit ranks, but also from the Muslim minority community. Its success has drawn the attention not only of other parts of India but also of the international community.[31]

Part of Gandhi survives in independent India in the form of resistance politics – politics organized by nonviolent organizations to address specific political issues. The most famous of these is perhaps the Narmada Dam Andolan of the 1980s, organized to help the poor that were very adversely affected by the construction of a dam on river Narmada in Western India. Gandhians who led this movement, such as Baba Amte (1914–2008) and Medha Patkar (1954–), have become well known not only in India but also internationally. The same is true of the Chipko Andolan, a resistance movement started in the 1970s, to protest against the forest policy of the Uttar Pradesh government. Here, too, women, such as Vandana Shiva (1952–) and Arundhathy Roy, the writer, have played, and still play, a major role in mobilizing public interest in the environment.

Where independent India has come short is in the area of building an environmentally clean and aesthetically pleasing India. As Gandhi wrote in 1909 in a famous letter to Henry Polak, "Bombay, Calcutta, and the other chief cities of India are the real plague spots" and Benares and other places of pilgrimage "an abomination".[32] For him, health, sanitation, and beautification of the human habitat were integral parts of economic development. Although he was partial to the village, he wanted the cities, too, to be liveable. That is why we find two great works on art – Tolstoy's *What Is Art?* and Ruskin's *Political Economy of Art* – recommended for special study in Appendix I of *Hind Swaraj*. That was in 1909. In 1916, he took the trouble of getting *What is Art?* translated into Gujarati. As early as 1924, he had started the tradition of holding art exhibitions at the venue of the annual meeting of the Indian National Congress. He wrote many letters giving instructions on how to beautify villages, encourage folk music and folk art. In 1941, he added sections on 'Village Sanitation' and 'Education in Health and Hygiene' to *Constructive Programme*.

Yet no Gandhian organization has taken up the cause of village sanitation and city planning as a part of economic development. Village sanitation escaped the attention of even Vinoba Bhave; it had no place in Jayprakash Narayan's 'total revolution'. As Ved Mehta has rightly pointed out, Gandhi's ideas of sanitation were important tools in his fight against Untouchability. Yet he "died without making the slightest dent in the Hindu attitude towards excreta and sanitation".[33]

Urban planning in independent India leaves a lot to be desired. As Sunil Khilnani's excellent survey indicates, Indian towns and cities are caught between the pressures of rapid economic growth and the human desire for a pleasant living environment.[34] Observers are struck by the bewildering growth of urban slums in modern India. It is as if no one in India, not even Gandhians, has taken seriously *The Political Economy of Art*. The best that admirers of Gandhi in Gujarat could do was to build Gandhinagar, the new capital of Gujarat: Khilnani calls it "a cruel concrete homage to Gandhi".[35] Outsiders such as Paul Theroux, the writer, find in Delhi "a crisis of old-fangledness". He has called modern Bangalore "a monster": "the place had not evolved; it had been crudely transformed – less city planning than the urban equivalent of a botched cosmetic surgery".[36]

A noteworthy positive development in the area of architecture is the work of the British born Indian architect, Laurie Baker MBE (1917–2007), a missionary, often referred to as 'Gandhi's architect'. In 1970, he established in Kerala the Center of Science and Technology for Rural Development (COSTFORD). Its focus is on low-cost housing using local talents and materials – one of the success stories of Gandhi – inspired work in the area of rural reconstruction.[37]

The official path to economic development that independent India has taken is not exactly Gandhian. This is not news – except for the fact that it was taken under the direction of Prime Minister Nehru, Gandhi's heir. Nehru and his successors to the present day want economic development through rapid industrialization under state planning, with private enterprise playing a subsidiary role. Rural development was to follow in the wake of industrialization. Gandhi by contrast wanted economic development to begin at the village level, with least state interference, and industrialization, if of the right kind, was to come as supplementary to it.

Gandhi had his own idea of the Indian village. For Nehru, Ambedkar, and others, the village was a place to flee from; for him, it was a place to be redeemed. For the redemption to occur, however, the Indian elite had to become villagers in spirit, and, if possible, should have the actual experience of having lived in villages, sharing their sorrows and misery, tensions and conflicts, not to validate them but to lessen or even eliminate them, by personal example and persuasion. Gandhi set an example by living in Sevagram, his village ashram, from 1933 onwards.

Gandhi had understood that the well-off Indians (dalits as well as non-dalits) had an astonishing lack of empathy with the poor – caste differences reinforcing it. The mental distance between the rich and the poor remains great even today, making the removal of chronic poverty all the more difficult. The economic policies of successive governments in independent India have done little to shorten the distance. (Rahul Gandhi, Nehru's great-grandson, seems to be an exception, in that he wants to bridge the gap between the rich and the poor by siding with the latter.)

While Nehru disagreed with Gandhi on specific economic policies, he agreed with his public philosophy. *The intellectual relationship between the two has great normative value for every Indian today.* The differences between them were principled, friendly, and open.[38] They concerned mostly the means, not the end, which was to create an inclusive, free, equal, nonviolent, and prosperous India. Towards the end of his life, he became more and more introspective, and began to search for the meaning of his career as Prime Minister. As Sarvepalli Gopal writes, he spent "one or two hours every week" with Radhakrishnan, the philosopher-president of India, discussing not only affairs of state but also *listening to him* talking on philosophical subjects.[39]

In a long interview granted in 1960 to the journalist R. K. Karanjia, Nehru reflected on the impact that Gandhi had on him. Because of this, he was seeking to implement "the policies and philosophy taught to us by Gandhiji . . . His thoughts and approaches and solutions helped us to cover the chasm between the Industrial Revolution and the Nuclear Era".[40]

Nehru reached the conclusion that "apart from material development" that was imperative, human beings were "hungry for something deeper in terms of moral and spiritual development, without which all the material advance may not be worthwhile".[41] His goal was to create *"a fully integrated human being* – that is, with what might be called the spiritual and ethical counterpart of the purely material machinery of planning and development being brought into the making of man".[42] *"What the world is groping for today seems to be a new dimension in human existence, a new balance. Only a fully integrated man with spiritual depth and moral strength will be able to meet the challenges of the new times*. Material advance without spiritual balance can be disastrous".[43] These Nehruvian reflections are intelligible only in the context of the Gandhian philosophy that human development requires the integration of the material, the ethical, the aesthetic, and the spiritual.

Nehru shows how one may disagree with Gandhi on specific policies without disagreeing with his public philosophy. Today, most Indians – barring right-wing Hindus, Marxists, and Maoists – find themselves more or less in Nehru's situation. They believe that they can have both industrialization *and* Gandhi's public philosophy. He survives in India in and through their "abiding sense of hope".[44]

Notes

1 *The Collected Works of Mahatma Gandhi* (New Delhi, India: Publications Division of the Government of India, Navajivan, 1958–1994, 100 vols), vol. 18, p. 430. (Henceforth, *CWMG*.) For the text of the 1920 constitution of the Indian National Congress framed by Gandhi, see *CWMG*, vol. 19, pp. 190–8.

2 Ramachandra Guha, *India After Gandhi* (New York: Harper Collins, 2007), p. 751.

3 *CWMG*, vol. 60, p. 448.

4 *Ibid.*, vol. 62, pp. 121–2.

5 *Ibid.*, vol. 63, pp. 153–4.

6 *Ibid.*, vol. 82, p. 86.

7 *Ibid.*, vol. 86, p. 389.

8 *Ibid.*, vol. 62, p. 121.

9 B. R. Ambedkar, *Annihilation of Caste* (Delhi, India: Critical Quest, [1936] 2007).

10 Both bound in one volume, *Dr Babasaheb Ambedkar: Writings and Speeches*, vol. 7 (Mumbai, India: Government of Maharashtra, 1990).

11 In Ambedkar, *Dr Babasaheb Ambedkar: Writings and Speeches*, vol. 9.

12 *Ibid.*, vol. 11.

13 In 1956, Ambedkar led an estimated five hundred thousand of his followers to Buddhism.

14 Ambedkar, *Dr Babasaheb Ambedkar: Writings and Speeches*, vol. 17, part 3, p. 515.

15 *Ibid.*, pp. 555–6.

16 Nadwi, *Islam and the World* (Lucknow, India: Academy of Islamic Research and Publications, [1950] 1982), p. 49.

17 For more on this, see Susan Bayly, *The New Cambridge History of India*, IV: 3 (Cambridge, England: Cambridge University Press, 1999), pp. 342–64.

18 For the most recent survey of 'political thought in India', see V. R. Mehta and Thomas Pantham (eds.), *Political Ideas in Modern India: Thematic Explorations* (Delhi, India: Sage, 2007).

19 Gandhi, *Young India*, 26 May 1924, p. 210.

20 *CWMG*, vol. 51, p. 259.

21 A. Parel (ed.), *Gandhi: Hind Swaraj and Other Writings* (Cambridge, England: Cambridge University Press, 2009), p. 64.

22 See A. J. Parel, 'Gandhi and the Emergence of the Modern Indian Political Canon', *The Review of Politics*, vol. 70 (2008), pp. 40–63; and 'From Political Thought in India to Indian Political Thought', in Takashi Shogimen and Cary J. Nederman (eds.), *Western Political Thought in Dialogue With Asia* (Lanham, MD: Lexington Books, 2009), pp. 187–209.

23 *CWMG*, vol. 41, p. 98. I have followed the original Gujarati text here.

24 *CWMG*, vol. 59, pp. 205–6. See also *CWMG*, vol. 58, pp. 353–4, where a parallel statement is made about Adam Smith.

25 Among those who treat Gandhi as a strategist is the influential historian Bipan Chandra. See his *Indian National Movement: The Long-Term Dynamics* (New Delhi, India: Har-Anand, 2008).

26 V. S. Naipaul, *A Writer's People: Ways of Looking and Feeling* (New York: Knopf, 2008), pp. 166–7.

27 *Times of India*, 5 March 2010 (Internet version).

28 See Geoffrey Ostergaard and Melville Currell, *The Gentle Anarchists: A Study of the Leaders of the Sarvodaya Movement for Non-Violent Revolution in India* (Oxford, England: Clarendon Press, 1971).

29 See Pushpa Joshi (ed.), *Gandhi on Women* (Ahmedabad, India: Navajivan, 1988).

30 Amartya Sen, 'More Than 100 Million Women Are Missing', *New York Review of Books*, 37.20, December 20, 1990, and 'Many Faces of Gender Inequality', *Frontline* (Chennai), 18.22, Oct. 27–Nov. 09, 2001.

31 See Ela R. Bhatt, *We Are Poor But So Many: The Story of Self-Employed Women in India* (New York: Oxford University Press, 2003).

32 Gandhi to Henry Polak, 14 October 1909, *CWMG*, vol. 9, pp. 477–82.

33 Ved Mehta, *Mahatma Gandhi and His Apostles* (New York: Penguin Books, 1977), p. 250.

34 Sunil Khilnani, *The Idea of India* (London: Hamish Hamilton, 1997), pp. 107–49.

35 *Ibid.*, p. 135.

36 Cited in *Times Literary Supplement*, 14 November 2008, p. 10.

37 See Gautam Bhatia, *Laurie Baker: Life, Work, Writings* (New Delhi, India: Penguin, 1994).

38 See their 1945 exchange of letters in A. J. Parel (ed.), *Gandhi: Hind Swaraj and Other Writings* (Cambridge, England: Cambridge University Press, 2009), pp. 143–9.

39 S. Gopal, *Jawaharlal Nehru: A Biography*, 3 vols. (Delhi, India: Oxford University Press, 1984), vol. 3, p. 267.

40 R. K. Karanjia, *The Mind of Mr Nehru As Revealed in a Series of Intimate Talks* with a Foreword by Radhakrishnan (London: George Allen and Unwin, 1960), p. 23.

41 *Ibid.*, p. 32.

42 *Ibid.*, p. 34. Italics Nehru's.

43 *Ibid.*, p. 103. Italics Nehru's.

44 Judith M. Brown, *Gandhi. Prisoner of Hope* (New Haven, CT: Yale University Press, 1989), p. 4.

12 Gandhi's global legacy

DAVID HARDIMAN

Gandhi has been understood in many ways since his death in 1948, and although his reputation has fluctuated, regard for him and his ideas has in general increased over time. He is revered by many as a spiritual leader and saintly figure. He is seen by others as a great pacifist. He is admired for his method of militant nonviolent resistance – satyagraha – and many have sought to apply it in struggles for civil and democratic rights. He has been held up as a champion of national liberation who has provided a potent means for resisting colonial rule. Others have appreciated his critique of the industrial mode of production and his call for a self-sustaining economy and egalitarian society. In this chapter, we shall see how Gandhi has proved an inspirational force for many, but also a controversial figure whose legacy has often been disputed.

Gandhi has been revered by many as a saintly figure who worked for peace and harmony in the world. This image is often found in depictions of him in the West. His statue in London, in Tavistock Square, thus shows him in a cross-legged meditative pose with eyes downcast. The impression is reinforced by flowers and incense sticks, which are often placed by his admirers at the foot of the statue. He is depicted in a similar way in a mural in St Mary's Church in Oxford. In India, by contrast, he is normally depicted in statues as striding forth, staff in hand, about to battle the British in one of his satyagrahas. Many, particularly in the West, regard Gandhi as a kind of patron saint of pacifism. His reputation in this respect is, however, open to question. It has been pointed out that he in fact supported the British military in the Boer War and in World War I, and believed that it was better to defend national honour through the use of armed force than to act in a cowardly manner. This was hardly an endorsement of the pacifist position.[1]

Gandhi's most important legacy, however, has proved to be his technique of nonviolent civil resistance, though his term for such protest – satyagraha – has not proved popular outside India. His creation of a new

word in English, that of 'nonviolence' – which he took from the Sanskrit ahimsa – has, rather, become the standard term to describe such
a practice. This element of his life-work has been endorsed particularly strongly in the United States, perhaps reflecting the fact that there
was there a longstanding countercultural tradition that embraced nonviolence and civil disobedience, as seen in the Quakers and in figures
such as Henry David Thoreau.[2] His most important initial champion
in this respect was an American lawyer active in the labour movement,
named Richard Gregg (1885–1974). Impressed by Gandhi's campaigns
against the British, he went to India to study the Gandhian movement
at first hand, and became converted to the principle of nonviolence. He
published books on the subject in the 1920s and 1930s, the most important of which was *The Power of Nonviolence* (1935).[3] In this, he noted
that many were sceptical of Gandhi's nonviolence, holding that it was a
weak force to apply against a powerful opponent. In fact, Gregg argued,
it was a highly effective method, as it threw the enemy off balance
morally. In this way, it acted "as a sort of moral jiu-jiutsu".[4] Gregg thus
stressed the practical over and above the spiritual value of this form of
resistance. Although the book did not attract a wide readership at the
time, it was to prove in time to be a very influential work, as it set
out the terms and conditions for the Gandhi-inspired militant nonviolence that became such a major force in U.S. politics in the 1950s and
1960s.[5]

Gandhi was admired amongst African Americans in the United
States from the 1920s onwards. His work was publicized by Marcus
Garvey and W. E. B. Du Bois among others. In 1936, soon after the
publication of Gregg's book on nonviolent resistance, Howard Thurman (1900–81) – a distinguished Baptist minister, theologian, and aca-
demic who was from the American South – led a delegation of prominent African American Christians to India to meet Gandhi. Gandhi also
inspired Bayard Rustin (1910–87), who was from an African American
Quaker family of Pennsylvania. He and the trade unionist A. Philip Ran-
dolph established the Congress of Racial Equality (CORE) in Chicago in
1942. CORE staged nonviolent protests that challenged racist employment practices in Chicago. Rustin himself refused to serve in the army
during World War II, and was jailed for three years as a conscientious
objector. After his release, he took up the cause of Indian independence,
picketing the British embassy in Washington, and being arrested on a
number of occasions. In 1947, he and other CORE activists travelled on
buses through the South to test a Supreme Court ruling that African
American passengers could sit wherever they wanted to in buses. Rustin

was beaten up and jailed for six months under local segregation laws, a sentence that he accepted in a true Gandhian spirit. After his release, he took up an invitation to visit India as a guest of the Congress party.[6]

While Rustin was carrying on his protests, Martin Luther King (1929–68) was studying at Morehouse College, Connecticut, Crozer Seminary, Pennsylvania, and the School of Theology of Boston University. He was the son of a Baptist minister of Atlanta, Georgia, who was active in fighting for the rights of the African Americans of that city.[7] While studying at Crozer Seminary, Martin Luther King attended a lecture on Gandhi by Mordecai Johnson, who had just returned from a visit to India. Johnson argued that Gandhian nonviolent protest could be used in the battle for African American rights. King stated later that the "message was so profound and electrifying that I left the meeting and bought a half-dozen books on Gandhi's life and works".[8] He was encouraged in this research by one of his teachers, George Davis, who was a pacifist and admirer of Gandhi.[9] King was particularly impressed by the way in which Gandhi had channelled his anger at injustice into a constructive and creative nonviolent engagement. He realized that such a resistance provided a deeply Christian weapon that could provide a strong base for the mass mobilization of African Americans. Gandhi, in his opinion, ". . . was probably the first person in history to lift the love ethic of Jesus above mere interaction between individuals to a powerful effective social force on a large scale".[10]

King was also influenced strongly by Howard Thurman, who had led the delegation to meet Gandhi in 1936. Thurman was a professor at the School of Theology of Boston University when King was studying there for his doctorate between 1951 and 1954. In 1949, he had published his most important book, *Jesus and the Disinherited*, which – inspired in part by Gandhi – sought for a Christian means for combating oppression. Thurman argued that Jesus, who was from a poor Jewish family, had devoted his life to fight for his people. He stood for the self-pride and assertion of the colonized under the tyranny of Rome. Jesus understood, however, that the Roman Empire could not be fought head-on and that the battle had to be of the spirit. Christianity was thus forged "as a technique of survival of the oppressed . . . Wherever his spirit appears, the oppressed gather fresh courage; for he has announced the good news that fear, hypocrisy, and hatred, the three hounds of hell that track the trail of the disinherited, need have no dominion over them".[11] Thurman argued that the anger generated by injustice must be transformed into a constructive force. Later, King used to carry this book with him for inspiration during his campaigns, which began in 1955 with the

Montgomery bus boycott. He was instructed in nonviolent methods by Bayard Rustin, who went to Montgomery to work as an adviser in the campaign. This was the start of a long and fruitful comradeship between two great proponents of nonviolence. Rustin prevailed on King to dispense with armed guards and to embrace nonviolence as a key element of the struggle. King asserted that they were putting democracy into practice in a truly Christian way, and insisted that they should bear no enmity towards their opponents and that they should observe complete nonviolence. Rustin also helped forge strong links with African American radicals of the northern cities who raised funds to support the Montgomery campaign. After a year of resistance, the Supreme Court came down on the side of the protestors, with bus segregation being ruled illegal. King declared that "Christ furnished the spirit and motivation, while Gandhi furnished the method".[12] This struggle, coming less than a decade after Gandhi's assassination, provided a remarkable vindication of the Gandhian method.

King and Rustin established the Southern Christian Leadership Conference (SCLC) in 1957 to carry on this work. This led to a series of nonviolent protests in cities throughout the South against segregation in schools, on buses and at eating places, and for the right to vote. King himself was arrested and jailed on numerous occasions. In his application of nonviolent resistance, King was far more confrontational than Gandhi. He actively sought out situations in which he could deploy his techniques of protest, so that his life consisted of a series of engagements in rapid succession, with some being carried on simultaneously. He was on the front line himself, heading marches, giving inspirational speeches, courting jail, and negotiating with the authorities. Gandhi himself rarely led mass campaigns, and later in life preferred to fight alone rather than risk mass protest that could go awry. King, by contrast, constantly exposed himself to the huge risks involved in such experiments in mass nonviolent action. His most significant innovation in the method of nonviolent resistance was the concept of 'creative tension'.[13] He spelt this out very lucidly in his famous speech from Birmingham City Jail:

> I had hoped that the white moderate would understand that the present tension of the South is merely a necessary phase of the transition from an obnoxious negative peace, where the Negro passively accepted his unjust plight, to a substance-filled positive peace, where all men will respect the dignity and worth of human personality. We merely bring to the surface the hidden

tension that is already alive. We bring it out in the open where it can be seen and dealt with. Like a boil that can never be cured as long as it is covered up but must be opened with all its pus-flowing ugliness to the natural medicines of the air and light, injustice must likewise be exposed, with all of the tension its exposing creates, to the light of human conscience and the air of national opinion before it can be cured.[14]

To forge such a state of 'creative tension', King learnt to carry out care-ful research on a situation before he evolved a strategy suited for that particular place and historic moment. If the conditions were not right, he was wary about launching a struggle.

The period 1964–5 was a turning point for the civil rights movement. The year of 1963 had been one of triumph, with victory in Birmingham, Alabama, followed by the great march on Washington, where King deliv-ered his powerful 'I have a dream' speech. In 1964, President Johnson backed civil rights legislation that made it illegal to practice segregation in any public place in the United States. But in the same year, Newark, Harlem, Chicago, Philadelphia, and Jersey City exploded in race riots. King was jeered at when he went to Harlem at the invitation of the mayor of New York to try to cool tensions.[15] Harlem was the stronghold of Malcolm X, who in that year denounced what he characterized as the 'Christian-Gandhian groups'.[16] Malcolm X, with his violent language, had managed to capture the imagination of young African Americans of the northern cities. After his assassination in 1965, young radicals such as Stokely Carmichael began to preach 'Black Power', advocat-ing a violent seizure of power by a movement from which all whites would be excluded. Rather than being deplored, violence was celebrated as a cleansing force.[17] All over the world, radicals were celebrating the cathartic power of revolutionary violence and terror, and Black Power was just one example of this tendency.

Although King's assassination in 1968 brought an end to the period of the great campaigns for African American civil rights, the movement had transformed the political scene in the United States. Gandhian tech-niques of resistance had been shown to work in an American context, in a way that legitimized them for a generation of Americans. It had forged a whole vocabulary of protest, with songs such as 'Freedom Now!' and 'We Shall Overcome' becoming the new anthems of dissent. In his last two years, King himself became a leading figure in one such protest, that against the war in Vietnam. Besides massive marches and street demonstrations, there were public burnings of draft cards. Such protest was then extended into campaigns for women's rights, gay and lesbian rights, and the environmental movement. As Greg Moses has noted: " . . . it is commonplace to announce that King's death marked the end of an era, but in the broader life of the mind a logic of nonviolence was just beginning to make its way into the world".[18]

The lessons learned from all this were consolidated theoretically by the political scientist and nonviolent activist Gene Sharp, who published his major three-volume study *The Politics of Nonviolent Action* in 1973.[19] Sharp sought to show the many ways in which Gandhian nonviolence worked in a practical manner, and by so doing encourage its use as a viable, and indeed preferable, method of resistance. The emphasis was on developing nonviolence in a strategic way, just as military manuals had over time developed and improved methods of warfare. Strategy and efficacy was valued over and above moral or spiritual imperatives. Nonviolence was projected as a tactic rather than, as Gandhi had advocated, a whole way of life.[20] Subsequent political analysts inspired by Sharp, such as Peter Ackerman and Christopher Kruegler, have discussed a range of twentieth-century nonviolent movements in terms of their structural strengths and weaknesses, with failures, such as that of the Chinese students in Tiananmen Square in 1989, being explained primarily in terms of their tactical mistakes rather than by the ruthlessness of state repression.[21] Sharp himself founded the Albert Einstein Institution to study and promote nonviolent action. It has provided advice and training to nonviolent protestors, with some notable successes, as in the Otpor movement that overthrew Slobodan Milosevic in Serbia in 2000. By inculcating an optimism around such techniques, Sharp and his followers are able to give the oppressed the confidence and courage to rebel nonviolently. Success has not, however, been guaranteed, as seen in the continuing failure of the powerful pro-democracy movement in Burma, led by the Nobel Prize winner Aung San Suu Kyi, and advised at certain junctures by Sharp.

Gandhi's struggle against British rule in India provided an inspiration for African nationalists in the 1940s and 1950s. The Fifth Pan-African Congress, which met in Manchester in 1945, endorsed Gandhian passive resistance as the preferred method for resistance to colonialism in Africa.[22] Kwame Nkrumah launched his campaign of Positive Action in what was then the Gold Coast in 1950. In a pamphlet entitled *What I Mean by Positive Action*, he called for intensified nonviolent struggle, which would include strikes, boycotts, and non-cooperation. He referred to Gandhi's movement in India as an example of the successful use of these methods. Jawaharlal Nehru, observing this campaign, placed pressure on the British by letting it be known that if they suppressed the movement through force, India would immediately leave the Commonwealth. The protest proved remarkably successful, with the British handing over the internal government of the colony to Nkrumah's Convention People's Party in 1951 (full independence came in 1957). Nkrumah became labelled at that time as the 'Gandhi of Africa'.[23] Although Nkrumah took a leading role in organizing the All-African People's Conference of 1958, which advocated nonviolent opposition to colonial rule throughout Africa, he himself became increasingly authoritarian in subsequent years. He claimed that his faith in nonviolence was destroyed by the violence in the Congo, and particularly the brutal murder of Patrice Lumumba in 1961. During the 1960s, he became a strident advocate for armed revolution, even publishing a *Handbook for Revolutionary Warfare* in 1967, after he had been ousted from power in Ghana in a coup of 1966.[24]

The Zambian nationalist Kenneth Kaunda was particularly noted for his commitment to Gandhian nonviolence. He founded the United National Independence Party in 1960, which managed to win power in 1964 through a disciplined nonviolent campaign. However, despite the personal advice of the leading Indian Gandhian, Jayprakash Narayan, he refused to emulate Gandhi by renouncing power – instead becoming the first president of independent Zambia. He took up the post well aware that he would at times have to sanction violence.[25] In his book *The Riddle of Violence*, he argued that "violence and nonviolence, far from being absolute alternatives, are complementary in practice. As a tactic, the effectiveness of nonviolence is enhanced when it stands out in sharp relief against a backdrop of imminent or actual violence. It has been said that nonviolence needs violence in the same way that stars need the night sky to show them off".[26] Following this, once in power Kaunda provided strong support for the African National Congress in South Africa, which included its armed wing, allowing Zambia to be used as a base for its activities. Kaunda was not the only African leader to back away from nonviolence once in power. In Tanzania, Julius Nyerere emphasized that they had deployed nonviolent resistance during the independence movement, as it provided by far the most efficacious method in the circumstances. He stated, however, that he was no Gandhian, as he had applied nonviolence only tactically and did not believe in it as a principle. He stated: "My opposition to violence is the unnecessary use of violence. As to the violence of oppression, we are dealing with states and states wield power. So sometimes you have to use violence against the violence of the state".[27]

The anti-apartheid movement in South Africa evolved in a similar way at this time. After Gandhi had left South Africa in 1915, he placed his second son, Manilal, in charge of his work there. Manilal (1896–1956) ran the Phoenix Settlement, published *Indian Opinion*, and kept up the struggle for the rights of Indians. In 1946, he played a leading role in a major campaign of protest against new legislation that discriminated against those of Indian origin: this built directly on the legacy of Gandhi's own resistance to the white regime decades earlier. The satyagraha continued for two years, with mass rallies and the occupation of urban plots reserved by law for whites-only occupation. Indians of all classes were involved – men and women alike – and around two thousand were jailed.[28] Although confined to the Indian community, many black Africans were deeply impressed by the power of the protest. As Nelson Mandela later wrote:

> It instilled a spirit of defiance and radicalism among the people, broke the fear of prison, and boosted the popularity and influence of the NIC [Natal Indian Congress] and TIC [Transvaal Indian Congress]. They reminded us that the freedom struggle was not merely a question of making speeches, holding meetings, passing resolutions and sending deputations, but of meticulous organisation, militant mass action and, above all, the willingness to suffer and sacrifice. The Indians' campaign harkened back to the 1913 passive resistance in which Mahatma Gandhi led a tumultuous procession of Indians crossing illegally from Natal to the Transvaal. That was history; this campaign was taking place before my own eyes.[29]

Blacks Africans felt a novel sense of solidarity with a community hitherto regarded by them as being little better than lackeys of the whites.[30]

In 1949, the African National Congress committed itself to nonviolence in its struggle against apartheid. Manilal Gandhi wanted them to state that nonviolence was a moral principle to be observed at all costs, but the majority of the ANC leaders saw it as a tactical matter, arguing that in a situation of an overwhelming control of force by the white regime, violent resistance would have been futile. This became the official ANC line, despite Manilal's vigorous objections.[31] In 1952, the ANC launched a campaign against the pass laws in which blacks violated the law by entering white areas. Protests continued in the 1950s and 1960s under the leadership of Albert Luthuli (1899–1967), who was strongly committed to nonviolence as a principle, and who was awarded the Nobel Prize in Peace in 1960.[32]

Long before this, however, many of the ANC leaders had begun to question the strategy of nonviolence. New laws were being passed that criminalized even the mildest displays of dissidence. Protestors could now be detained indefinitely without trial. As Mandela stated:

> I began to suspect that both legal and extra-constitutional protests would soon be impossible. In India, Gandhi had been dealing with a foreign power that ultimately was more realistic and far-sighted. That was not the case with the Afrikaners in South Africa. Non-violent passive resistance is effective as long as your opposition adheres to the same rules as you do. But if peaceful protest is met with violence, its efficacy is at an end. For me, non-violence was not a moral principle but a strategy; there is no moral goodness in using an ineffective weapon.[33]

The matter came to a head after the Sharpeville massacre of 1960, in which sixty-nine nonviolent protestors were shot and killed by the police in cold blood. The ANC leaders retaliated by burning their passes in public, which led to a declaration of martial law and their being thrown in jail. Many of these leaders felt that nonviolence had had its day. After their release, there was a heated debate within the ANC, with Luthuli standing out for nonviolence. Eventually, the Gandhians were forced to bow to the majority line – that there should be underground violent resistance. The military wing of the ANC was, however, to be separate, and under the leadership of Mandela, Walter Sisulu, and Joe Slovo.[34]

These movements were all were played out against the background of the Cold War, with the United States and Soviet Russia standing in armed confrontation, demanding that new nation-states commit themselves to one side or the other – capitalist or communist. Both sides were vying to bring new areas under their control, which at times entailed a colonial or quasi-colonial occupation. This clearly violated the principle of *swaraj* (self-rule) that Gandhi and Indian nationalists had fought for since the early 1920s. In response, Jawaharlal Nehru played a leading role in establishing the 'Non-Aligned Movement' of countries that were either newly liberated or about to be liberated from colonial rule. At the Bandung conference in Indonesia in 1955, delegates from twenty-nine states of Asia and Africa came together on the basis of their commitment to an anti-imperialist programme. The Bandung Declaration demanded national sovereignty, respect for human rights, and equality among nations and peoples. The new nations claimed a right not to have to choose between either the American or Soviet blocs, and be drawn into conflicts that were not of their concern. This gave rise to the idea of the 'Third World'. There was a strong Gandhian element to this. This was seen in the refusal to be aligned with either capitalism or communism, and also in the moral dimension, that such confrontations based on a display of armed might were reprehensible and hardly a model for a future world of free nation-states. It was believed that the non-aligned states could implement development programmes independently for themselves, allowing a rapid economic 'take-off' that would quickly see them 'catching-up' with the First World. Although the stress on industrialization was hardly Gandhian, in some cases an approach was adopted that was more in tune with his beliefs – that of 'intermediate technology'. This involved programmes to implement appropriate forms of technology that, while cheap to construct and maintain, enhanced the productivity of workers considerably. There were other 'intermediate' methods, such as 'barefoot doctors' in China and elsewhere. Gandhi directly inspired the chief theorist of such methods, E. F. Schumacher.[35] Eight conferences of Non-Aligned Countries were held between 1961 and 1986. It provided a model for the new nations that emerged in the 1960s and early 1970s. Thereafter, with the failure of many of the programmes of independent economic and social development, the political degeneration of many new nations, the end of the Cold War, the seeming failure of the socialist model, and the resurgence of capitalism, this particular initiative lost its way.

Marxists had for the most part always disparaged Gandhi's thinking and practice, seeing what he strove for as mere 'passive revolution'.[36] During the 1960s and 1970s, many other radicals, dissidents, and socialists throughout the world came to accept such arguments, believing that the Gandhian way could never bring about genuinely revolutionary social and political change. They pointed to the ruthless deployment of state power in South Africa, neo-colonial warmongering in the other parts of Africa, in Vietnam, Latin America, and the Caribbean, and the successful armed resistance of the Vietcong, Cuban, and Algerian revolutionaries, all of which appeared to provide compelling proof that power – in the words of Mao Zedong – grew from the barrel of a gun. Encouraged by these armed victories, a romantic notion of the power of revolutionary violence took ahold. This was epitomized in the cult of Che Guevara. It was argued that, in the last instance, all states would defend themselves with a ruthless display of violence. Therefore, however much the state may be put on the defensive by mass strikes and other forms of civil resistance, the movement would at some stage have to escalate to the stage of armed struggle. Some who followed this line of thought formed underground revolutionary terrorist groups such as the Angry Brigade and the Red Army Faction, while in Northern Ireland, the IRA revived itself through such a programme.[37] Even India had its own revolutionaries of this sort, the Naxalites. They considered Gandhi as the foremost class enemy, and one of their iconoclastic acts was to smash his public statues.

Most of these attempted revolutions were for the most part repressed or neutralized so that they became an irritant rather than a threat to state power. In fact, many states thrived on such terrorism, as it allowed them to justify increased police powers and the suspension of civil liberties. This was increasingly realized by the late 1970s and early 1980s, and it was at this juncture that Richard Attenborough produced his influential film on Gandhi. As Markovits has pointed out, before this there was no significant portrayal of Gandhi on film.[38] The film focused on Gandhi the secular martyr, beginning with his funeral procession in Delhi and then focusing on certain key moments in the making of the Mahatma, from his arrival in southern Africa onwards. Although there was an unstated comparison with the life of Christ – something designed to resonate with a Western Christian audience – Gandhi's spiritual side was downplayed. Indeed, as Jawaharlal Nehru had insisted to Attenborough when the film was being planned: "Whatever you do, do not deify him – that is what we have done in India – and he was too great a *man* to be deified".[39] Accordingly, his morality was not expressed in explicitly religious terms, so much as in his ethic of resistance to injustice and oppression. The message was that nonviolent resistance is both deeply moral and highly effective. The film was made with the active support of the Indian government, and many leading Gandhian activists and scholars provided advice and guidance.

When it appeared in 1982, the film was highly acclaimed, winning eight Oscars. It helped to bring Gandhi's message to a whole new global audience, and it inspired many to use his methods to resist oppression in their own countries. For example, its showing in cinemas in Chile in 1983 provided important inspiration for the anti-Pinochet movement.[40] Similarly, Benigno Aquino was inspired by the film to resist the Marcos dictatorship in the Philippines more actively through militant nonviolence. His assassination in 1983, as he returned to his country to lead such a movement, set in train mass protests that led to the eventual downfall of the dictator in 1986.[41] The 1980s proved to be a remarkable decade for nonviolent protest movements, with, besides those in Chile and the Philippines, the Solidarity movement in Poland, the Intifada in Palestine, the pro-democracy movements in Burma and China, and the 'velvet revolutions' against Soviet power in Eastern Europe. The Burmese leader, Aung San Suu Kyi, had previously lived in India, where she had studied Gandhi's ideas, and she drew directly on his theory and practice in her protest.[42] The Chinese students who occupied Tiananmen Square in 1989 stated that they were influenced in their actions by Gandhi's example.[43]

In South Africa, nonviolence found a new lease of life at this time in the movement spearheaded by the United Democratic Front (UDF), formed in 1983. This led a series of strikes, demonstrations, and business and civic boycotts. It was backed by a range of churches within South Africa, providing a strong moral appeal, as well as a commitment to nonviolence. Moral guidance and leadership was provided by two ministers, Desmond Tutu and Alan Boesak, both of whom openly expressed their admiration for Gandhi.[44]

When violence broke out during protests in the townships, both Tutu and Boesak intervened personally to protect people from crowd violence. Tutu stated that the methods of the struggle had to be consistent with its ends so that it could withstand the 'harsh scrutiny of history'. Militant young leaders emerged within the townships who understood the strategic importance of nonviolence, such as Mkhuseli Jack in Port Elizabeth. They managed to reclaim control of the movement from those committed to violent methods, bringing a new discipline to the movement, and creating an alternative functioning civic force in the townships. There were boycotts of white businesses that hit the whites hard in their pockets. The growing success of such movements from 1985 onwards put whites throughout South Africa on the defensive, and played a major role in the eventual downfall of the apartheid state.[45]

Although Nelson Mandela had turned his back on nonviolence after Sharpeville, he made a point of valorizing Gandhi and his methods after his release from prison in 1990. He realized that further violence would merely stoke racial hatreds and jeopardize the future of South Africa, and that the climate now demanded peace and reconciliation. As he stated in his autobiography: "Animosity between Afrikaner and Englishman was still sharp fifty years after the Anglo-Boer war; what would race relations be like between black and white if we provoked a civil war?"[46] Mandela insisted on celebrating Gandhi as an authentic South African hero, and defended strongly the decision to erect a statue of Gandhi in Government Square in Johannesburg, which was now renamed Gandhi Square. This was condemned by some on the grounds that Gandhi had made racist statements about Africans when in South Africa.[47] Nonetheless, backed by Mandela and the ANC, the statue was unveiled in 2003. It depicted a younger Gandhi in the lawyer's robes he wore while practising in the city.

Gandhi has been regarded as an inspirational figure by many other activists. One such activist was César Chávez (1927–93), the leader of the Mexican, Filipino, and African American migrant farm labourers in California. As a child, Chávez witnessed at first hand how white American employers discriminated against Spanish-speaking labourers in a racist manner, pitilessly exploiting their lack of power. He began reading about Gandhi while working as a young migrant worker, and he soon became convinced that Gandhian nonviolent techniques could be utilized to fight for the rights of his fellow workers. He became a union leader in the 1950s, deploying the weapons of marches, boycotts, strikes, and civil disobedience to publicize the plight of the workers and win for them higher wages and better conditions of employment. He established a new union that became consolidated in 1965 as the United Farm Workers (UFW). The employers retaliated by bringing in strongmen to break up the protests and importing scab labour. Following Gandhi, Chávez insisted that the workers react to this provocation in an entirely nonviolent way so as to stress the moral superiority of their stand. He and many of his followers were jailed on numerous occasions. Chávez always quoted Gandhi frequently in support of his activism.[48] To this day, Chávez is considered an inspirational figure within the Mexican-American community in the United States.[49]

Gandhian methods were deployed also in the campaign against nuclear armaments. Gandhi had been an outspoken critic of nuclear weapons after the American atomic bombing of Japan in 1945. He condemned 'the supreme tragedy of the bomb', stating that it revealed most starkly that: "War knows no law except that of might".[50] Also that: 'I regard the employment of the atom bomb for the wholesale destruction of men, women and children as the most diabolical use of science'.[51] He refused to accept the argument that possession of nuclear weapons acts as a deterrent against war, on the grounds that there can be no lasting, durable, or moral peace through such means. The Campaign for Nuclear Disarmament (CND) formed a Direct Action Committee against Nuclear War in 1957 that made use of Gandhi's techniques of struggle in its annual Aldermaston March and campaigns of civil disobedience. Anti-nuclear activists also sought to disrupt nuclear testing through direct action. For example, in 1957, Harold Steele, a Quaker, sailed into the British nuclear testing ground at Christmas Island in the Pacific.[52]

In France, Lanza Del Vasto, who had lived with Gandhi in his ashram in India during the 1930s, founded a number of Gandhi-inspired 'Communities of the Ark' during the 1950s. Members adopted a Gandhian way of life, striving for self-sufficiency, and were involved in protests. In 1957, Del Vasto fasted for twenty days to end the torture of Algerians by the French military. In the following year, he started a separate organization, the Action Civique Non-Violent, dedicated to nonviolent political action. This body waged a campaign in 1959–61 for the right of citizens to refuse to serve in the army, and against the internment camps set up for Algerians in France who were suspected of supporting the liberation war in Algeria. After some of the protestors were arrested, an indefinite fast was launched by Louis Lecoin. The French government backed down, ruling that citizens had a right to refuse military service on grounds of conscience. This was recognized in law in 1963. The organization also campaigned against nuclear weapons, carrying out the first-ever occupation of a nuclear power facility in 1958.[53] José Bové, later famous as a leading anti-globalization activist, gained his initial experience in this movement.[54] When tried in 2000 for demolishing a McDonald's restaurant in the south of France, he told the court: "Gandhi dismantled a British installation in the cause of peaceful resistance to British rule in India. Our action was non-violent resistance by citizens... against American provocation".[55]

From the 1970s, the anti-nuclear and ecology movements worked hand in hand against the military-industrial complex. By its very name, Greenpeace exemplifies the unity between these two tendencies. Eco-warriors have deployed nonviolent civil resistance by breaking into places where nuclear weapons are kept, or sailing into nuclear testing sites. In 1972, a French naval patrol ship at the Mururoa Atoll nuclear testing site rammed one such vessel, which served to galvanize opposition to the tests throughout the South Pacific.[56] Despite this, they continued. In 1985, French secret agents planted a bomb on the Greenpeace flagship, the Rainbow Warrior, killing one crewmember. The resulting outcry led to the French government having to admit its culpability, two of its agents being convicted of manslaughter and jailed.

Other Gandhian-style activists were drawn into the environmental movement over time. César Chávez took up this issue as early as the 1960s. Rachel Carson's book *Silent Spring* had just been published, setting out the implications of the use of toxic pesticides in commercial agriculture all over the world.[57] Chávez knew that the pesticides were used in massive quantities in Californian agriculture, particularly in the growing of grapes that would be consumed by middle-class Americans.

His UFW launched a campaign to picket farms as a means to publicize this practice, which was poisoning workers, as well as consumers. He urged that consumers throughout the United States boycott Californian grapes. To make his point, Chávez deployed the Gandhian method of fasting. For example, in 1968, he went without food for twenty-five days to keep the pesticide issue in the public gaze. In this way, he won considerable support from middle-class well-wishers in the United States.

In Europe, one of the most prominent environmental leaders to be inspired by Gandhi was Petra Kelly (1947–92) of the German Green party (Die Grünen). Born in Bavaria, her family moved to the United States in 1960, where she became inspired by the civil rights and anti-Vietnam war movements. Returning to Europe in 1972, she became actively involved in the anti-nuclear movement, and in 1980 was a co-founder and first leader of the German Green Party, which brought together a wide variety of ecological action groups. In 1983, she and twenty-six other Greens were elected to the Bundestag. She served there until the 1990 elections, when the Greens suffered an electoral reverse. While a member of the Bundestag, she led a series of nonviolent protests against nuclear installations and military bases. These included protests in East Berlin and Moscow.[58]

Kelly drew her inspiration directly from the Gandhian tradition of nonviolent moral activism. One of her earliest political heroes was Martin Luther King. She studied political science at university in Washington, where she was introduced to Thoreau and his theory of civil disobedience. She was impressed by the way that King had acknowledged Gandhi and Thoreau as inspirational examples. According to her biographer, "Petra's gods were Gandhi and Martin Luther King. Her bibles were Thoreau and Gene Sharp".[59] She became strongly committed to a thoroughgoing nonviolence in pursuit of a politics informed by Truth.[60] Her nonviolence, like that of Gandhi, was not passive but active, and it entailed "seeking opportunities for dialogue or taking actions which would liberate people from the violent system (of thinking) which prevented them from seeing the power and rightness of nonviolence".[61]

Kelly claimed that her ecological values flowed from Gandhi:

In one particular area of our political work we have been greatly inspired by Mahatma Gandhi. That is in our belief that a lifestyle and method of production which rely on an endless supply of raw materials and which use those raw materials lavishly, also furnish the motive for the violent appropriation of raw materials from other countries. In contrast, a responsible use of raw materials, as part of an ecologically-oriented lifestyle and economy, reduces the risk that policies of violence will be pursued in our name. The pursuit of ecologically responsible policies within a society provides preconditions for a reduction of tensions and increases our ability to achieve peace in the world.[62]

Gandhi had warned of the consequences of wasteful exploitation by the forces of colonial capitalism, and he also endorsed organic agriculture, which was being pioneered at that time in India by Albert Howard. However, as Ramachandra Guha has pointed out, there is little in his published writings on the relations between humans and nature, or any sustained programme for a more ecologically friendly future.[63]

Gandhi has become such an iconic world figure that it would be possible to trace his influence in many more areas of life, and on many more rebels, protestors, and alternative thinkers than are mentioned here. Much more space would be required, also, to analyse how historians and political scientists have written about and analysed Gandhi in changing ways over the decades. All we can say here is that their attitudes have often been shaped by the wider political events and developments that we have discussed.

To conclude, in these and many other ways, Gandhi has provided an inspiration for succeeding generations. He has been invoked to legitimize demands for justice, mass movements, and political programmes – even in cases where the relevance of his life and thought is by no means obvious. In this way, as an iconic figure, he has proved very durable – reflecting no doubt the multifaceted nature of his personality, the wide range of issues that he struggled with, and his voluminous writings that can be deployed for many different purposes. Over and above this, however, there is a widespread recognition that he applied a strong moral integrity in his struggles against many forms of human oppression, in which he not only put his life on the line, but died for his ideals. In this, people throughout the world have found in Gandhi an inspiration and guide in their many battles, providing courage for them to assert their power and claim a better future.

Notes

1 C. Markovits, *The Un-Gandhian Gandhi: The Life and Afterlife of the Mahatma* (New Delhi, India: Permanent Black, 2003), p. 154.
2 For a study of this tradition, see S. Lynd and A. Lynd (eds.), *Nonviolence in America: A Documentary History* (Maryknoll, NY: Orbis Books, 1995).

3 R. B. Gregg, *The Psychology and Strategy of Gandhi's Non-Violent Resistance* (Triplicane, India: S. Ganesan, 1929); *Gandhiji's Satyagraha or Non-Violent Resistance* (Triplicane, India: S. Ganesan, 1930); *The Power of Non-Violence* (London: Routledge, 1935).

4 R. B. Gregg, *The Power of Non-Violence*, 2nd rev. edn. (London: James Clarke, 1960), p. 44.

5 J. K. Kosek, 'Richard Gregg, Mohandas Gandhi, and the Strategy of Nonviolence', *The Journal of American History*, 91 (2005) 1318–48.

6 T. Branch, *Parting the Waters: Martin Luther King and the Civil Rights Movement 1954–63* (New York: Simon and Schuster, 1988), pp. 171–2.

7 S. B. Oates, *Let the Trumpet Sound: A Life of Martin Luther King, Jr.* (Edinburgh, Scotland: Payback Press, 1998), pp. 7–8.

8 *Ibid.*, pp. 32–3.

9 Branch, *Parting the Waters*, p. 74.

10 Oates, *Let the Trumpet Sound*, p. 32.

11 H. Thurman, *Jesus and the Disinherited* (Richmond, IN: Friends United Press, 1981), p. 29, quoted in G. Moses, *Revolution of Conscience: Martin Luther King, Jr., and the Philosophy of Nonviolence* (New York: The Guilford Press, 1997), p. 182.

12 D. Dalton, *Mahatma Gandhi: Nonviolent Power in Action* (New York: Columbia University Press, 1993), pp. 178–82. The quote is from M. L. King, *Stride Toward Freedom: The Montgomery Story* (New York: Harper & Row, 1958), p. 67.

13 Oates, *Let the Trumpet Sound*, p. 339.

14 'Letter From Birmingham City Jail', in J. A. Washington (ed.), *A Testament of Hope: The Essential Writings of Martin Luther King Jr.* (New York: Harper Collins, 1991), p. 295.

15 Oates, *Let the Trumpet Sound*, p. 306.

16 Malcolm X, *By Any Means Necessary* (New York: Pathfinder Press, 1992), pp. 8–9.

17 Moses, *Revolution of Conscience*, p. 191.

18 *Ibid.*, p. 202.

19 G. Sharp, *The Politics of Nonviolent Action*, 3 vols. (Boston: Porter Sargent, 1973).

20 For a lucid summary of Sharp's approach, see K. Schock, *Unarmed Insurrections: People Power Movements in Nondemocracies* (Minneapolis: University of Minnesota Press, 2005), pp. 36–46.

21 P. Ackerman and C. Kruegler, *Strategic Nonviolent Conflict: The Dynamics of People Power in the Twentieth Century* (Westport, CT, Praeger, 1994), pp. 342–3. For a critique of such an understanding, see S. D. Huxley, *Constitutionalist Insurgency in Finland: Finnish "Passive Resistance" against Russification as a Case of Nonmilitary Struggle in the European Resistance Tradition* (Helsinki, Finland: Societas Historica Finlandiae, 1990), pp. 261–6.

22 B. Sutherland and M. Meyer, *Guns and Gandhi in Africa: Pan African Insights on Nonviolence, Armed Struggle and Liberation in Africa* (Trenton, NJ: Africa World Press, 2000), p. 25.

23 *Ibid.*, pp. 30–1.

24 *Ibid.*, pp. 35, 47–8.
25 *Ibid.*, pp. 62–4, 95–113.
26 K. Kaunda, *The Riddle of Violence* (San Francisco: Harper & Row, 1980), quoted in Sutherland and Meyer, *Guns and Gandhi in Africa*, p. 98.
27 *Ibid.*, pp. 83–4.
28 Uma Dhupelia Mesthrie, *Gandhi's Prisoner? The Life of Gandhi's Son Manilal* (Cape Town, South Africa: Kwela Books, 2004), pp. 308–15, 323–6.
29 N. Mandela, *Long Walk to Freedom: The Autobiography of Nelson Mandela* (London: Little, Brown and Company, 1994), p. 98.
30 *Ibid.*, pp. 97–8, 119.
31 *Ibid.*, p. 119.
32 A. Luthuli, *Let My People Go: An Autobiography* (London: Collins, 1962).
33 Mandela, *Long Walk to Freedom*, pp. 146–7.
34 *Ibid.*, p. 261.
35 E. F. Schumacher, *Small Is Beautiful: A Study of Economics as if People Mattered* (London: Abacus, 1975).
36 Huxley, *Constitutionalist Insurgency in Finland*, pp. 24, 54–6.
37 M. Randle, *Civil Resistance* (London: Fontana, 1994), pp. 57–8.
38 Markovits, *The Un-Gandhian Gandhi*, pp. 27–8.
39 R. Attenborough, *In Search of Gandhi* (London: Bodley Head, 1982), p. 111. Attenborough described his own involvement in the project as an act of moral and political commitment, and indeed devotion.
40 Ackerman and Duvall, *A Force More Powerful*, p. 291.
41 *Ibid.*, p. 375.
42 Schock, *Unarmed Insurrections*, p. 97.
43 Han Minzhu (ed.), *Cries for Democracy: Writings and Speeches from the 1989 Chinese Democracy Movement* (Princeton University Press, 1990), p. 378.
44 Randle, *Civil Resistance*, pp. 73–4.
45 Ackerman and DuVall, *A Force More Powerful*, pp. 347–64.
46 Mandela, *Long Walk to Freedom*, p. 272.
47 Rory Carroll, 'Gandhi branded a racist as Johannesburg honours freedom fighter', *The Guardian*, 17 October 2003.
48 R. Burns, *César Chávez: A Biography* (Westport, CT: Greenwood Press, 2005); J. C. Hammerback and R. J. Jensen, *The Rhetorical Career of César Chávez* (College Station: TX: A & M University Press, 2006).
49 See, e.g., Tricia Cortex, 'Memory of Pioneer Cesar Chavez Kept Alive', *Laredo Morning Times*, 4 April 2006.
50 'Atom Bomb and Ahimsa', 1 July 1946, *Harijan*, 7 July 1946, *CWMG*, vol. 84, p. 394.
51 'Talk with an English Journalist', before 24 September 1946, *CWMG*, vol. 85, p. 371.
52 Randle, *Civil Resistance*, p. 55.
53 L. del Vasto, *Return to the Source* (London: Jean Sedgewick, Rider, 1971), pp. 9–13; Mark Shepard, *The Community of the Ark* (Arcata, CA: Simple Productions, 1990).

54 Markovits, *Un-Gandhian Gandhi*, p. 68.

55 Charles Bremmer, 'José Bové: Big Mac Protestor a "French Gandhi"', *The Times*, 1 July 2000.

56 Michael Randle, *Civil Resistance*, p. 83.

57 R. Carson, *Silent Spring* (Boston: Houghton Mifflin, 1962).

58 'About the Author' in P. Kelly, *Nonviolence Speaks to Power*, ed. G. D. Paige and S. Gilliart (Hawaii: Centre for Global Nonviolence Planning Project, 1992), pp. 161–6.

59 S. Parkin, *The Life and Death of Petra Kelly* (London: Pandora, 1994), p. 106.

60 P. Kelly, 'Gandhi and the Green Party', *Gandhi Marg*, July–Sept. 1989, pp. 192–202.

61 Parkin, *Life and Death of Petra Kelly*, p. 108.

62 Kelly, *Nonviolence Speaks to Power*, p. 33.

63 R. Guha, 'Mahatma Gandhi and the Environmental Movement in India', in A. Kalland and G. Persoon (eds.), *Environmental Movements in Asia* (Richmond, England: Curzon, 1998), pp. 67–71.

Conclusion

JUDITH M. BROWN AND ANTHONY PAREL

The reader of this volume will have encountered many Gandhis. They have ranged chronologically from the boy growing up in conservative, Western India, under British imperial rule; to the diffident student in London and failed lawyer in Bombay; to the self-taught activist, public figure, and lawyer in South Africa; and finally to the influential leader of the Indian nationalist movement who was also, uniquely and surprisingly, the founder of several ashram communities, which he considered to be his best work and where he tried to work out the core elements of his spiritual vision of the good human life in the pursuit of Truth. The reader will also have encountered different aspects of Gandhi's life and thinking, including his developing ideas on the nature of politics, the state and the nature of the Indian nation, his wrestling with a range of acute human problems as they were manifested in Indian society, and his attempts to envisage an economic foundation for moral human lives and societies. Undergirding all of these aspects of his life and thought was his particular understanding of the nature of true religion, and his passionate quest for Truth as the underlying principle of all life, as another name for a divine force that addressed him personally and prompted his actions.

Furthermore, it is evident that during and after Gandhi's life, people appropriated him and his image, thereby creating further 'Gandhis'. Many groups and individuals have understood him in the framework of their pre-existing ideas, used him to forward their own agendas, or found him an inspiration for change in situations he never encountered himself. We know, for example, that while he was alive, and particularly during the years he was a major leader in India and increasingly known as a Mahatma, peasant groups understood him as a miracle worker, as a semi-divine saviour, but also used his image as a means of coercion and local discipline using moral assumptions already present in their worlds. His resulting charisma was a two-edged sword. It attracted many thousands who had previously had little connection with or interest in national politics. But it also meant that many who were apparently his 'followers' were in practice outside his control; and their actions caused him shame and grief. Indeed, in his final years, he often said that his compatriots had never understood let alone practised true satyagraha. After his death, different groups in India continued to appropriate his name and legacy to forward very different agendas, ranging from campaigns for reform of landholding and curbing the dominance of the rural rich, to the project of building a new nation. Jawaharlal Nehru, for example, as independent India's first Prime Minister, often invoked Gandhi's name as he tried to mould the way Indians interacted with each other in the new political situation. On an international stage, Gandhi was also appropriated by many who saw his ideas and practice of nonviolence as a crucial resource for dealing with conflicts of many kinds.

It is therefore not surprising that Gandhi and his life should still – more than half a century since his death – be an object of scholarly research and discussion, as well as popular interest.

This *Companion* offers to readers perhaps unfamiliar with Gandhi and his life a starting point for informed understanding of Gandhi in his historical context. In the first part of the book, several chapters have dealt primarily with the development of his life, and have examined his emergence as a figure of international significance within the context of the British Empire, in South Africa and India. They have also shown how he was forced to consider the nature of Indian national identity in the context both of pluralism and imperial rule, and how he felt compelled in middle age to enter the arena of all-India nationalist politics. It is clear that, from his time in South Africa, his deepening inner convictions and spiritual development forced him to grapple in the context of public action with the issue of ends and means, and to practise and refine modes of nonviolent resistance to many different sorts of injustices and wrongs, including, eventually, British imperial rule in India itself. In the middle of a busy life, he also thought profoundly about many fundamental human problems and about complex dilemmas within Indian society in particular. So the second part of this *Companion* has dealt with his key thinking on such issues, which developed in the context of his life and work in its particular South African and Indian contexts. He emerges as a serious but self-taught thinker; someone who wrote and spoke prolifically about many political, economic, social, and religious issues. However, his thinking was never divorced from his life of action. Thinking was generated often by practical social and political problems, or by the religious dilemmas he encountered or that people brought to him. Action was in turn informed by his thinking and believing. It is this interplay between an inner spiritual and intellectual life and the outer world of politics and social work that makes Gandhi such a dynamic and interesting figure.

How then are we to understand his contributions to the history of India itself, as well as to a wider world? These questions run through the second and third parts of this *Companion*. In terms of India itself, it is clear that his leadership of the Indian nationalist movement powerfully influenced its nature, particular the way it adopted nonviolent modes of resistance to imperial rule. There were many reasons why this movement rarely adopted violent means, but among them was certainly Gandhi's influence and the way he strove consciously to provide his contemporaries with a viable alternative to terrorism and other forms of violence. Many of his contemporaries, including Jawaharlal Nehru, found in satyagraha an effective and civilized mode of dealing with imperial rule, even though they were honest in admitting that they did not believe it to be a political and spiritual necessity as did Gandhi. Gandhi accepted this limited commitment among his associates and apparent followers with realism if regret. He did not live, however, to see the fate of many of his deepest hopes for India in terms of its polity, economy, and society. Clearly, in the decades since independence, the Indian state has developed in ways far removed from his vision of the good state, and despite the development of village panchayats as a bottom tier of political life, these are the result of top-down policy rather than the organic growth of self-governing local communities. India's economy is far from being as he would have wished, as its leaders have consciously taken the country down the route of industrialization and assumed that increasing consumption by a minority was a 'good', often at the expense of dealing with the devastating poverty of so many. Moreover, despite legislative attempts at social reform, many of those whose lives he attempted to change, such as women and Untouchables, still are far from equal participant citizens. However, as a writer and a thinker, he made two very notable contributions. He helped create the modern Indian political canon, which integrates what is taken from the West within an Indian intellectual framework. Second, drawing on the time-honoured Indian theory of the four canonical aims of life, he demonstrated how the pursuit of the secular and the spiritual could be harmonized in actual practice. Moreover, the range of issues with which he was concerned, and on which he wrote, helped to change the nature and content of Indian public discourse. After Gandhi, no Indian could speak of such matters as the treatment and role of women, the nature of caste, or the problem of Untouchability, or even of religion, in the same way as in the past.

In his own lifetime, he was both an Indian and an international figure within the British Empire. He worked to improve the position of Indians in South Africa by laying hold of their status as subjects of the imperial monarch; and then after his return from India eventually moved away from this position and claimed for Indians the right to national self-determination. Even though his sights were set on India, he nonetheless challenged the civilization that the British exported through their empire, as well as contested imperial rule itself. He therefore became a global figure, as well as the leader of Indian nationalism, and it is no surprise that he became such a significant figure in the global challenges to imperialism that developed after his death. He himself believed that he had a message for the world at large, though his duty was to offer it to and practise it in India first. In his lifetime, he was most significant in India itself, but perhaps ironically after his death, his insistence on spiritual values and his practice of nonviolence has made his influence even more of a global phenomenon than an Indian one. He still challenges people who study him, just as in his lifetime he challenged those who encountered him, to look at their own fundamental values, and how these should be worked out in daily life and in the world of human society and politics.

Guide to further reading

See also the notes in individual chapters.

Primary sources

Gandhi, M. K. *An Autobiography or The Story of My Experiments with Truth*, first pub. in 1927; available in several editions.

Parel, A. J. (ed.). *Gandhi: Hind Swaraj and Other Writings*. Cambridge, England: Cambridge University Press, 2009.

The Collected Works of Mahatma Gandhi 100 vols. New Delhi, India: Publications Division of the Government of India, Navajivan, 1958–94. (Gandhi's writings are arranged here chronologically and contain many substantial items, some of which are published individually as well. They include *An Autobiography*, *Hind Swaraj*, and *Constructive Programme: Its Meaning and Place*.)

Iyer, R. N. (ed.). *The Moral and Political Writings of Mahatma Gandhi* 3 vols. Oxford, England: Oxford University Press, 1986–7.

Brown, Judith M. (ed.). *Mahatma Gandhi. The Essential Writings* New Edition. Oxford and New York: Oxford University Press, 2008. (This has a substantial introduction and a select bibliography, which includes writing on Gandhi by his contemporaries. It also contains key sections of some of his major works.)

Secondary sources

Studies in Gandhi's life

Arnold, D. *Gandhi*. Profiles in Power, Harlow: Pearson Education, 2001.

Brown, Judith M. *Gandhi. Prisoner of Hope*. New Haven and London: Yale University Press, 1989.

Dalton, D. *Mahatma Gandhi. Nonviolent Power in Action*. New York: Columbia University Press, 1993.

Erikson, E. H. *Gandhi's Truth. On the Origins of Militant Nonviolence*. London: Faber & Faber, 1970.

Huttenback, R. H. *Gandhi in South Africa. British Imperialism and the Indian Question, 1860–1914*. Ithaca, NY, and London: Cornell University Press, 1971.

Markovits, C. *The Un-Gandhian Gandhi: The Life and Afterlife of the Mahatma*. Delhi, India: Permanent Black, 2003.

Parekh, B. *Gandhi*. Past Masters Series, Oxford and New York: Oxford University Press, 1997.

Swan, M. *Gandhi. The South African Experience*. Johannesburg, South Africa: Ravan Press, 1985.

Weber, T. *Gandhi as Disciple and Mentor*. Cambridge, England: Cambridge University Press, 2004.

Gandhi's thought

Alter, J. S. *Gandhi's Body: Sex, Diet and the Politics of Nationalism*. Philadelphia, PA: University of Philadelphia Press, 2000.

Bondurant, J. V. *Conquest of Violence. The Gandhian Philosophy of Conflict*. Revised Edition. Berkeley and Los Angeles: University of California Press, 1969.

Chatterjee, M. *Gandhi's Religious Thought*. London and Basingstoke: MacMillan, 1983.

Dasgupta, A. K. *Gandhi's Economic Thought*. London and New York: Routledge, 1996.

Fox, R. G. *Gandhian Utopia: Experiments with Culture*. Boston: Beacon Press, 1989.

Hardiman, D. *Gandhi in His Time and Ours. The Global Legacy of His Ideas*. London: Hurst, 2003.

Iyer, R. N. *The Moral and Political Thought of Mahatma Gandhi*. New York: Oxford University Press, 1973.

Parekh, B. *Gandhi's Political Philosophy. A Critical Examination*. London and Basingstoke: MacMillan, 1989.

Parekh, B. *Colonialism, Tradition and Reform. An Analysis of Gandhi's Political Discourse*. Revised Edition. New Delhi, Thousand Oaks, and London: Sage, 1999.

Parel, A. J. *Gandhi's Philosophy and the Quest for Harmony*. Cambridge, England: Cambridge University Press, 2006.

Terchek, R. J. *Gandhi: Struggling for Autonomy*. Lanham, MD: Rowman and Littlefield, 1998.

Essays and collections of essays

Brown, Judith M., and Prozesky, M. (eds.). *Gandhi and South Africa. Principles and Politics*. Pietermaritzburg, South Africa: University of Natal Press, 1996.

Brown, Judith M. 'Gandhi and Civil Resistance in India, 1917–47: Key Issues'. Chapter 3 of A. Roberts and T. Garton Ash (eds.), *Civil Resistance and Power Politics. The Experience of Non-violent Action from Gandhi to the Present*. Oxford and New York: Oxford University Press, 2009. (This volume is a very substantial collection of essays on nonviolent protest movements in the second half of the twentieth century.)

Hick, J., and Hempel, L. C. (eds.). *Gandhi's Significance for Today. The Elusive Legacy*. Basingstoke and London: MacMillan, 1989.

Nanda, B. R. *Gandhi and His Critics*. Delhi, India: Oxford University Press, 1985.

Parel, A. J. (ed.). *Gandhi, Freedom and Self-Rule*. Lanham, MD, Boulder, CO, New York, and Oxford: Lexington Books, 2000.

Rudolph, L. I., and Rudolph, S. H. 'The Traditional Roots of Charisma: Gandhi', Part 2 of their *The Modernity of Tradition*. Chicago and London: University of Chicago Press, 1967.

Index